Judith Tebbutt was born in 1954 in Ulverston, Cumbria. She has four brothers and a sister, and her mother and siblings still live in Ulverston. Judith met her husband David in 1979 while they were both living in Zambia. They married in 1985 and had their son Ollie in 1986. Judith trained as a mental health social worker, qualifying in 1999, and worked in a community drug and alcohol team before being employed in a medium-secure psychiatric hospital, where she was the senior social worker in the women's service. Judith continues to live in the same house that she shared with David for twenty years.

A Long Walk Home

*One woman's story of kidnap,
hostage, loss – and survival*

JUDITH TEBBUTT

with Richard T. Kelly

faber and faber

First published in the UK in 2013
by Faber and Faber Ltd
Bloomsbury House
74–77 Great Russell Street
London WC1B 3DA

This export paperback edition first published in 2013

Typeset by Agnesi Text
Printed in England by CPI Group (UK) Ltd, Croydon, CR0 4YY

A CIP record for this book
is available from the British Library

ISBN 978–0–571–30304–5

Lines from 'Apple Blossom' by Louis MacNeice (*Collected Poems*,
Faber and Faber, 2007) are quoted by kind permission of
David Higham Associates on behalf of the Estate of Louis MacNeice.

FSC
www.fsc.org
MIX
Paper from
responsible sources
FSC® C101712

2 4 6 8 10 9 7 5 3 1

For David
Our life together was too short but so very happy

A NOTE ON NAMES

The names of my first husband and of clients I knew as a social worker have been changed.

The pirates are identified by the labels – the nicknames – I mentally gave them as I encountered each individual. Eventually I discovered the names of some of them. Those who go by more than one name are:

Abdullah – Marvin
Ali – the Navigator
Daoud – the Negotiator
Gerwaine – Hungry Man
Ibrahim – the Fifth Man
Jamal – Kufiya Man
Kaalim – Vain Man
Mohammed – Smiley Boy

The Big Man is also, depending on my mood, described as the Fat Controller.

PREFACE

This book is the story of how, over a period of one hundred and ninety-two days, I was torn away from the life I knew and loved, and dragged down to the depths of despair; of how I endured enforced isolation and near-starvation at the hands of Somali pirates, and of how I made a choice to survive by any and all means that I could muster.

It's commonly said that 'we all have a book inside us' – a story to tell. But I have to confess that I am a reluctant storyteller. I know the reader will understand how dearly I wish that the events described in these pages had never happened.

However, my decision to write my story was born out of wanting to pass on an account of what I experienced to any future grandchildren I might have. I want them to know and understand that anybody, in the face of grim adversity, can rise to the challenge and overcome it. I should know, for I was one of those people – though the wisdom was dearly acquired, and the personal cost considerable. But by the same token I would also wish for them to know what an intrepid, brave and heroic grandfather they would have had, and also what a mentally strong and resolute man is their father.

The first real choice I had to make with regard to this book was whereabouts I would begin to write it. For various compelling reasons I didn't want to do that writing at home, since home had been the sanctuary of my married life, the place where my husband and I could shut out the world and simply enjoy each other's company. I didn't wish to contaminate the place that had so long been our haven with the bitter memories of my captivity.

And so, sixteen weeks after my release, during a stay with my sister and her family, I woke up in my niece's bed and began to write. Six months earlier, I had been languishing, lost to the world, somewhere in the arid depths of Somalia, held under armed guard by pirates in a squalid room nine feet long. I was sitting on a flea-infested mattress in the oppressive heat of my gloomy cell, semi-starved, fraught with nervous anticipation. I had been told, yet again, that I was going to be released 'soon'. Did my captors actually mean it this time? I was told so many lies from day to day that I could have quite easily lost faith in any idea of 'the truth'. And yet, behind it all, what kept me going was that I had a hope to cling to, an affirming flame in the dark, precious and inextinguishable.

But I am getting ahead of myself. My story really begins before the calamity that came along and cast me into that dungeon in the desert. It begins with the life I had, the one I knew and loved, and with the reasons why it was so dear to me.

I

Love is, among other things, to wish for the happiness of the person whom you love, to delight in seeing that happiness in that person. And I hadn't seen my husband quite so blissfully happy for some time – so deeply contented with where he was and what we were doing together. It was 3 September 2011, and we were on safari in the Masai Mara, Kenya.

Ordinarily David was one of those people who needed a few days' grace to relax properly into a holiday. But this time round his mood was really buoyant from the moment we boarded the plane at Heathrow. He had insisted on wearing his full safari outfit to travel – head-to-toe khakis and bush hat – so any passer-by in the airport could have guessed what part of the world we were headed to. Our son Ollie liked to rib David about sartorial matters generally, and his bush hat in particular, but another thing I'd always loved about my husband was that he didn't care too much what other people thought about his personal preferences. He was very comfortable in his own skin.

Now we had reached our Kenyan destination, Serian Nkorombo Camp, which the brochure had billed as a 'luxury tented encampment'. I have never been overly keen on tents, but the versions offered at Serian – five of them in all, nestled close to the river and to each other – were huge and comfy, with hard floors and bucket showers. Our journey had left me feeling shattered but David, as always, set to unpacking immediately while I sprawled across the bed. He was methodical in the place-ment of his socks, shorts, T-shirts et al. in their appointed place. And I loved watching him go about this. In no time he had showered, prepped his camera, and donned khaki shorts – or, to be precise, he had unzipped the detachable lower part of his khaki trousers. Finally he turned to me.

'I'm just going to have a look around outside, OK?'

'Fine,' I replied. 'My turn to unpack . . .'

He stepped out, and once I had done my own settling in I too went out to see what there was to see. I found David sitting, cradling his camera, by the banks of the fast-flowing Mara River. All was peaceful but for the sound of the rushing waters. There was golden light in the sky. He was watching the wildlife, richly in evidence. Some baboons on the far bank were grooming one other. Further downriver, where the waters were calmer, hippos bathed in the sun, yawning and groaning, some play-fighting with each other. Here and there I could make out the ridged backs of crocodiles. David, drinking it all in, wore a great smile on his face. This was so clearly everything he had hoped for.

Though we had shared more than a few wonderful holidays, I sensed that for David this one could be the pinnacle. But then we were in Africa, and Africa had played a huge and crucial role in our lives – in our coming together as a couple in the first place. We had been blessed by the place, it was our luck.

And David was so much at home in these ostensibly rather wild surroundings. He didn't mind roughing it, had always liked camping and the outdoors. As a boy he joined the Sea Cadets in Haverhill, even though there was no sea. Whereas my instinct for the outdoors had never stretched much further than my garden. When he was twenty-three, in the December of 1976, David had chosen to leave England for two years and work in Zambia. I had gone there four months earlier, only twenty-one myself, following my then husband and his new job, dutifully and rather unhappily. But it was in Zambia that David and I met, whereupon everything changed for us both.

David was a venturesome soul. Not to say that he wasn't equally happy at home with me, and his guitar and his beloved music and books, perfectly at ease not seeing anyone. But the experience of travel took him out of something and into what was – for him if not most others – a kind of comfort zone. Our very first holiday as a young couple was to Tunis, where I balked a little at the sight of open sewers and dead dogs in the street, but David regarded the local conditions as 'part of the experience' and took the view that there were always other and better things to see. Our next holiday was on a Swedish campsite beset by a horrendous rainstorm for seventeen hours solid. Our tent became an island in a newly formed duck pond. But I got used to a bit of adversity, and if David was always able to put up with more than I could then at least my powers of resilience improved from sharing these experiences with him. And of course, after thirty-three years together, in which we had both worked hard at our respective careers, we were able to treat ourselves to a bit more comfort than we'd been able to afford in the days of starting out together. This tent in Serian Nkorombo Camp was certainly a world away from – and a good deal drier than – the waterlogged dome in which we'd huddled at the site outside Gothenburg.

'What do you make of it then?' I asked David as we took in the sights and sounds of the Mara.

He smiled at me. 'I think we made the right decision . . .'

*

On our first night at Serian we realised we would be the only guests in the camp overnight. All I wanted to do was have a bite to eat and go to bed. David, though, was feeling sociable. He'd always had a facility for mixing with all sorts of people, making conversation even in unpromising situations. We met the Serian Camp manager, who told us he was writing a book about Africa, and so he and David instantly established common interests – books and Africa – and conversed at length. David told him of the previous safari we'd taken in 2006 where we'd ventured into the South Luangwa Valley – for David a sentimental journey, since during his time in Zambia he'd gamely led a group of fellow employees on an Outward Bound course at the Luangwa Game Reserve. (They were driven to and dropped at Point A in the bush and told to find their way back to Point B. Somehow, using crude maps and navigating by the stars, David managed it.) On that safari we had flown in and out of Lusaka Airport, just as we had both done separately back in 1976, and to my eyes the place had hardly changed in thirty years. The 2006 trip had been a purposeful revisiting, an opportunity for us to share some-thing of how we met with our son Ollie, who travelled with us and celebrated his twentieth birthday in Malawi.

David was content to stay up chatting with the manager, about Africa and all it had meant to him. His interest had first been kindled as a schoolboy when he read H. Rider Haggard's *King Solomon's Mines*. Of course the clichés of 'the dark continent', 'untouched by civilisation', have long been available to over-imaginative Westerners. But David was no armchair expert; he decided to discover Africa for himself. As he would tell it, he went out to Zambia in 1976 as a boy and two years later returned a man – his own man, out from the influence of his parents. And of course he came back with me – which he was wont to describe, with a grin, as 'a bonus'. But that time had been formative for him in many ways: he always spoke to people about Zambia with real fondness. And he was always on the lookout for opportunities to revisit Africa.

I was tired and decided to turn in first, and a solicitous camp attendant guided me back to our tent with a lantern. Nkorombo was a beautiful camp, well lit, security guards much in evidence and helpful. Remote as the place was, I felt perfectly safe – and excited about how this week would unfold.

*

We had been keen travellers throughout our married life, and our choice of holiday destination was usually initiated by David. In 2010 he suggested to me, with his familiar look of enthusiasm, 'Let's do a safari next year . . .' Our experience in 2006 had been wonderful, the itinerary planned with the help of a specialist travel company called Safari Consultants, and we knew we would use them again. So I was happy to approve David's proposal for 2011.

I especially fancied the idea of seeing gorillas in Uganda. David, though, had a longstanding passion to explore the Masai Mara. We compromised – as we always did. Marriages, after all, are made out of compromise to a big extent. Living with another person changes you: you cease to be a free agent, you renounce a little of what was your personality, but you gain something much more considerable. I know I wouldn't be the person I am, or anywhere near, without David.

This time our compromise was that we would do 'the passion thing' for David: the Masai Mara it would be. The gesture in my direction was that we design not too exhausting a schedule – no constant hopping of planes between far-flung stop-offs, as we had committed ourselves to in 2006 (one of our three internal flights on that occasion being on a six-seater aircraft that gave us all a mid-air scare when it briefly developed a frozen pro-peller). This time we would be on safari for one week, and in the second week we would enjoy a beach holiday – home comforts and pure unadulterated do-nothing R&R. My beach suggestion was Zanzibar, where one of my brothers had got married and given me a great account of the place. David put the idea to Safari Consultants, but they advised us that Zanzibar would entail most of a day's travelling. Might we consider the Kenyan coast? There was a place called Kiwayu Safari Village where intrepid travellers could truly 'get away from it all'.

David and I looked at the Kiwayu website, watched the pro-motional video, read some glowing customer reviews. Previous guests had included Mick Jagger and Tracey Emin. For all that, I still fancied Zanzibar. But David was persuaded by Kiwayu. The northernmost island of the Lamu Archipelago off Kenya's northern coast, Kiwayu sat thirty or forty kilometres south of the border with Somalia. Neither David nor I thought anything of this proximity at the time. If we had, I don't believe it would have altered our decision.

By the time September 2011 came round we were both in great need of the holiday, and were looking forward to it avidly. We thoroughly intended to have a proper break, to relax and 'come together again'. Like so many couples we had hectic work lives and had fallen somewhat into the habit of passing one another like ships during the week. Weekends were all too easily lost to the mundane chores of keeping the household running, and we were lucky if we shared Sunday evening together in peace. David's work as Finance Director at the publishing firm of Faber and Faber was never less than demanding. The nature of my job – as a social worker in a medium-secure psychiatric hospital – dictated often long and stressful days.

It was in David's nature to fret before we went away – to fret, in fact, over most aspects of life. A compulsive checker, he would routinely wake me up to ask if I'd switched off the oven or locked the front door. So whenever we travelled it was accepted that he would oversee all logistics and arrangements, and hold our passports and money in the wallet he'd bought especially for that purpose. Come the morning of our departure I'd tumble out of bed to find him dressed and smelling of aftershave before I'd brushed my teeth. And once we got to where we were going, he would continue to try to 'organise'. It wasn't from a lack of faith in me so much as a need to be in charge of things. He had always been the loveliest kind of control freak.

As such I was surprised, but pleased, when David decided this time to leave his mobile phone at home. It was unprecedented. Previously he had always kept that umbilical link to the office in case they really needed to contact him. But now he was cutting the cord, truly adamant about getting away from it all. We agreed we would take my mobile in case of emergency, so Ollie could contact us or we him. Ollie was in Glasgow, having lately started a new job that he was enjoying, but we expected he would be down south while we were away, visiting his girlfriend Saz (short for 'Sarah').

His abandoned mobile phone aside, David was customarily rigorous in every other respect of his preparation. He informed me that he had taken out Air Ambulance insurance, in case of any emergency that would require African 'flying doctors' to come and airlift us from the scene. We were able to have a laugh about that, David with his schoolboyish giggle that belied his sober demeanour. Ollie joshed David too ('For heaven's sake, Dad . . .') but David was simply obeying his usual instincts.

'It's best to be safe,' he told us both.

A fortnight before we were due to fly, David and I were sitting on the sofa on Sunday evening, sharing what was left of the weekend, watching *Countryfile* on the BBC. David looked at me meaningfully.

'Jude – if anything happens, you'll be OK.'

I wasn't sure what he was talking about, and could only wonder at where that thought had come from.

'David, what do you mean, "If anything happens . . . ?"'

'I mean, the holiday, Africa, you know? If anything were to happen – I just want you to know you'll be OK. If I died now I'd be happy because I know you and Ollie are going to be looked after. And I know you'd get through it, you wouldn't be frightened –'

'David' – I cut him off as lightly as I could, knowing that his heart was, as ever, in the right place – 'I don't really want this conversation. Nothing's "going to happen" . . .'

He took my point, we left it at that. The following week Ollie came to visit and we were in the kitchen, chit-chatting – I was washing up – when I heard David tell Ollie, 'Now, Ollie, if anything should happen to Mum and me on holiday then –'

Ollie groaned good-naturedly. 'Oh no, here we go again . . .'

'No, listen. If anything should happen, our will is in the safe. And you know the code, don't you?'

'Yes, Dad . . .' Ollie was skating over it, to a degree, knowing as I did that this was just one more example of the care David always took over things – and us – but one that it was probably better not to keep in the forefront of our minds. And I didn't think about it again, at least not before we embarked on our journey to Kenya.

*

After two nights in our luxury tent at Serian Nkorombo Camp we moved the short drive away to Serian's 'fixed camp' on 5 September. These lovely new surroundings were still very much close to nature. David was delighted by three pipistrelle bats he found roosting in the ceiling of our room, and he hushed me as he gently moved close to snap photos of the sleeping creatures.

Each morning we made ready to head out on safari by 6 a.m., fortified by hot porridge and tea. It could be notably cold in the morning, sometimes raining, but whatever the weather we would clamber up into the back of the high-wheeled truck we had to ourselves – with our guide Steve, and driver John – and wrapped ourselves in snug Masai blankets. I pulled the brim of my hat down to my eyebrows, stuck up the hood of my thermal jacket, donned thermal gloves and altogether resembled a pensioner fit to be wheeled down Blackpool Promenade on a brisk November morning. David conceded to the blankets, but underneath he remained every inch the dauntless outdoorsman in khaki shirt and shorts.

Though as a native of Cumbria I've always rated the Lake District unmatchable in the global league table of physical beauty, I had to admit that the Masai Mara was stunning – with its mountains and rivers, rolling plains dotted with herds of giraffe, elephants making their ponderous way, their young ones in tow. But the chief lure for the sightseer at this time of year was to witness the seasonal migration across the Mara of great herds of wildebeest in search of fresh grazing pasture. David had always wanted to see this spectacle, and if early September wasn't optimum time we kept our hopes up none the less.

One morning Steve got word through the guides' relay system that a pair of rhinos had been sighted, and John drove us to the spot at speed. Of course the same word had reached camps all over the reserve, and we arrived to find six or seven trucks surrounding a copse wherein the rhinos, quite understandably, had turned shy and effectively invisible. David and I looked at one another and knew that neither of us felt good about joining this particular circus: it wasn't what we'd come for. So we went quickly on our way, which turned out to be another 'right decision'.

Soon we were parked up close to a neglected section of the river that Steve knew to be popular for smaller herds of wildebeest seeking a crossing. He had an instinct we should sit tight, and we did, for two and a half hours. For a long time we were watching a sedentary herd of a few hundred zebra from a distance. Then two or three zebra detached themselves and scrambled down a hillside to the riverbed, seemingly curious. One zebra very cautiously started to cross the rock-strewn river – and David and I gulped to see crocodiles, curious themselves, moving smoothly downstream, coolly predatory. But the plucky zebra made it over and up the bank to near our truck, then let out a braying sound that alerted its grazing fellows back over on the other side. 'It's happening,' whispered Steve.

Slowly, the zebras got to their feet and made themselves into a winding line, a procession that threaded down to the riverbank and picked its way across. Herds of wildebeest, which had been only dark dots in the distance, got the idea and followed suit. And in short order hundreds of animals were splashing across the Mara, and David and I sat rapt, feeling privileged to witness it from yards away. The din made by the horned wildebeest was phenomenal: restive and snorting, they banged their hoofs on the dirt, then tumbled down the embankment, clattered over rocks and threshed through the water. We were silent, transfixed, not moving a muscle before this extraordinary display of unstoppable nature. And as far as we could see, the basking crocodiles had no success in trying to spoil it.

Another of our treasurable moments came as a result of David's hawk-eye vision. We were out in the truck en route to investigate a sighting of a cheetah and her cub on a hillside. And we were travelling at speed, the clear plastic windows of our soft-top truck rolled down against the rain, when I heard David suddenly say to our driver, 'John, can you stop and back up a bit?' John obliged and David pointed something out to our guide.

'Steve. Over there. Is that a serval . . . ?'

And it was. This incredibly rare, tawny, black-spotted wild cat, hardly bigger than a domestic feline, was nestled flat down in the long grass. Unaccustomed to exposure, it peered up at us in great surprise. David gently raised his camera and squeezed off a few shots. Even Steve had never seen a live serval before, yet David had made the spot. He was thrilled, and I was thrilled for him.

The cheetah we then found was hardly less of a treat. In horizontal pouring rain at 7 a.m., flaps down on the truck, feeling alone in the world, we watched as she came out of the undergrowth, creeping low on the ground, then sat up, proud and erect, surveying all around her, establishing that all was completely safe. Then she turned her head, issued a squeak – and we heard an answering squeak, and from the undergrowth came a tiny spiky-haired cheetah cub that ran to sit by its mum. We observed them in complete silence for an hour. David was captivated. For a while I just watched him, the grin on his face, how fully 'in the moment' he was.

Back in our room that night David was a contented man. As he rested on the bed I started to write out a postcard to Ollie, listing all the animals we had encountered over the week. 'What else did we see?' I asked David when I got stuck. He filled in things I'd forgotten, but clearly the card would have to be a work-in-progress. I tucked it away, to be completed and mailed later.

*

On our last day in the Masai Mara we decided to embark on what was billed as a 'moderately taxing' full-day walking safari up the Siria escarpment to Suguroi Hill Tree House, passing through herds of giraffe and elephants and coming precariously close to lion and water buffalo. For starters, though, we had to get to the other side of the fast-flowing river, which meant crossing a rope bridge suspended above the ravine. But David had always suffered from vertigo, so badly that he could hardly stand on a chair. I could see that, for once, he was nervous, so I volunteered to go first, terrified myself but not wanting to show it, hoping to make it look easy. 'Don't look down!' I called out as cheerily as I could. Slowly but surely David made it over. I couldn't have been more proud of him.

Across the river lay another of the Serian encampments, and we were met and escorted to its reception area – a big and sumptuous living room with heavy wooden furnishings. The concrete floor was being keenly polished by a young employee who skated over the surface with cloths tied around his feet, and David introduced himself to the 'skate'. This sight – and the aroma of polish – made for a powerfully fond aide-memoire. David looked to me, I to him, and we smiled and hugged. Neither of us could have missed the reminder of the curious time we'd once spent, both apart and together, in Chililabombwe, Zambia.

It was a strange post-colonial world he and I had stepped into back in 1976. Previously all I knew of Africa was what I had glimpsed, aged eleven, in the pages of an encyclopaedia donated to my family by our local vicar (who took a commendable interest in the struggling families of his parish). But both David (a qualified accountant) and my then-husband Peter (a trained electrician) had been hired by Zambia Consolidated Copper Mines, a newly nationalised enterprise which was nonetheless bringing in overseas specialists to ease the transition to state ownership. In this environment the only native Zambians you interacted with were those who were employed around your house and garden: in other words, a typical expatriate community, with its bowls club, polo club, squash, tennis and rugby clubs. As a bachelor David had no qualms about having his domestic work done for him. Moreover at work he demonstrated his competence so effectively that he was promoted from accountancy duties to a position as administrator of Chililabombwe Hospital: a line of work in which he had no experience. But he set about it with his customary vigour.

My domestic situation and status in Zambia were rather more complicated than David's. Peter and I had met and married young, 'the done thing', each knowing little of who the other really was. Too late we found out we really had nothing in common and no means of making the other happy. And nothing could change that, not even our radical relocation from grey and rain-misty Ulverston to the heat and colour and aroma of Africa. Though I had approached the move with much trepidation, I was quickly fascinated by this exotic place of hibiscus and frangipani, where turquoise-headed lizards darted down from the trees in your garden, and tall women in vividly coloured robes and elaborately tied headscarves swayed elegantly down the road, often bearing babies on their backs. But while the experience of being under a bigger sky certainly broadened my perception of the world, it did nothing to improve the hamstrung state of my and Peter's marriage.

While I rattled around in a four-bedroomed house with a big garden, Peter worked long shifts, and we tended to socialise separately. We were effectively living apart under the same roof, and the notion that I was going to spend the rest of my life with him seemed to me an utterly forlorn and threadbare one. But then in my vulnerable position, five thousand miles from home, I really couldn't say what the future would hold – until I met David.

It was at a squash club one day in Chililabombwe, as I was waiting around courtside to support the home team, when I saw a man striding toward me – handsome, fit and tanned. He asked me if I could help him find his opponent, who, I happened to know, was already on court warming up. As this man walked away he looked back at me and we smiled at one another. In my head I heard a voice. 'He's the one . . .' And I didn't know him from Adam.

No sooner had I met David than he kept cropping up in company. It quickly got to the stage I was looking for him, hoping to see him. We were always in a group situation, to my chagrin, but for me he exuded a stunning magnetism. I had strong feelings for him of a kind I hadn't recognised before, and I didn't know what to do with them. It came as a great surprise. 'Why do I feel sick every time I see him? Why am I hoping to bump into him when I go to the postbox?' But then, never having been in love before, I couldn't say what I had lacked. If he came and sat next to me I would feel terrific excitement – but, more than that, the most remarkable feeling of completeness, as if for him and me to be sitting side by side in life was exactly what fate had intended. I knew it was wrong – I was still married. I didn't know anything about him. And we had exchanged nothing but chit-chat.

One night we ran into one another at the local arts theatre: we sat together for the show, then he walked me home. I was wearing some unsuitably high-heeled shoes that had been sent to me from England, and at one point I tripped up, but David took my arm and so saved me from falling off the pavement into a storm drain. Inwardly I was thrilled by the touch of his hand on my arm: there was a strength there, and also what I believed to be a caring. I felt something open inside me – the unhappiness of my marriage couldn't be hidden. I told David of my predicament and how I planned to leave Zambia in a few months. Gently David told me he was aware my marriage wasn't a happy one. A while ago I had 'caught his eye': he had begun to ask other people about me, been as curious about me as I had been about him. What he told me just filled me with joy. I was sure he was the man I wanted to spend the rest of my life with – that with him I would be happy. Incredibly, I still didn't know his last name. But now we had made a breakthrough.

For the next two or three months David and I spent time together in a very chaste and necessarily secretive sort of romance. He drove me to places he loved, the bush, a big lake and its environs, which were home to crocodiles, egrets, hippos and blue monkeys. We took walks, confided our hopes in one another. And somehow we came to a decision – we didn't know how but we wanted to be together. The only problem was that I was leaving Zambia, six months before his contract expired.

In the end I left my husband having packed a single suitcase. At 4 o'clock one morning a sympathetic friend drove me to the airport, where I got on a flight to Malindi and thence home to England. For six months David and I corresponded between

Zambia and Cumbria, making plans for the life we would share. We both enthused about seeing the world and the adventures we might have. For sure we knew we wanted to make a home together, but we also shared a yen for far shores and fresh experiences: together, without doubt, we would be travellers. People might have thought we were crazy, deluded – but in ourselves and in each other we had unshakeable faith.

So in all it was a long way we had come, David and I, from our respective and disparate upbringings, from Zambia and across thirty-three years spent together, to where we now stood in September 2011, taking in the fantastic views from the top of the Siria escarpment down over the plains of the Masai Mara, which stretched as far as one could see.

We were advised of a daring optional extra to the itinerary of this trek, namely that we could stay out overnight, sleeping in the Suguroi Hill Tree House without doors or windows, under 'moonbeams and starlight'. David, adventurous as ever, looked very tempted.

'You must be crazy,' I told him.

'Oh, I'm sure it would be safe.'

'From lions and cheetahs? How?'

'They post a guard just a ways off with a rifle.'

'Oh, great. Now are you quite sure you paid up that Air Ambulance insurance you told us about?'

In all I thought this was one gamble that wasn't worth taking, and David came round to my point of view. It was a simple compromise. On the way back to our camp, as we retraversed the rope bridge, he affected a 'no-hands' pose, grinning at me.

*

On the final morning at Serian, 10 September, we rose at our usual 6 a.m. Over breakfast we met Dr Ben U, a brain surgeon from Santa Monica, California, who had helped us out during the week with some medicine for upset stomachs. He snapped a photo of us. David had grown a little beard, adding to his air of contentment. Ben and his wife had been in Uganda looking at gorillas. David and I had decided that would be our next jaunt – that, or else the Ngorongoro Crater in Tanzania.

We said our farewells, got in the truck, took a meandering drive of a few hours to the airstrip. It was cold. As usual I affected a windcheater, hat, scarf and gloves, while David remained impervious in his shorts. To our delight John produced a couple of Masai blankets for us to take home, a gift I'd hoped to pick up at some local store. We could take them back to Bishop's Stortford, sit outside, light the chiminea and be cosy, as we loved to be outdoors on summer evenings.

At the airstrip Steve and John stayed with us until the plane came, by which time David and I had met up again with Ben and his wife, who were also leaving. We regaled them with stories of the animals we'd seen. In truth we were a shade rueful to be on our way. I had loved our week, though not as much as David – I'm not sure it was possible to exceed the evident pleasure he took in all aspects of it. He said we would be sure to return one day. The talk turned to our next stop, Kiwayu Safari Village. David was looking ahead keenly.

'What's the first thing you're going to do?' he asked me.

I couldn't honestly say. I had some mixed feelings about where we were going. Kiwayu wasn't our first choice; still in my mind I felt it ought really to have been Zanzibar. Now I wasn't sure what to expect, just on the basis of pictures viewed online. The safari had been a lively, busy itinerary. In Kiwayu? David would be refreshing his sailing skills and catching up with the stack of books he'd brought. I was less certain how I would occupy myself, beyond resting and reading. Perhaps snorkelling, swimming, walking – and of course spending much longed-for time alone with David.

We flew into Wilson, the smaller part of Kenyatta Airport, Nairobi, which was replete with the flavour of Africa – the heat and the colour, sounds and aromas. And I remembered my arrival at Lusaka Airport, Zambia, back in 1976, coming from a small and insular home town: how alien I had felt all of a sudden, wearing a rollneck sweater and cowboy boots in the intense heat, seeing black-skinned men and women for the first time in the flesh. In Africa you had to accustom yourself to a certain rhythm of life, different types of amenities and ways of doing things. I felt very fortunate to be here now, as did David. And slowly my sense of anticipation did build – I wanted to get to Kiwayu. Wherever I was with David I felt safe and happy, sure that he could sort out any problem. And he had imparted at least some of his sense of adventure to me.

*

David's and my relationship should never have happened, really, not by most rational analyses. How many people travel five thou-sand miles from home, meet and fall in love, then live together happily for thirty-three years? It must be a rarity. Things should have gone wrong: we were from quite different backgrounds, my family and David's very disparate. We had got together on a leap of faith, one could say. But we started to live together immedi-ately, and it just worked.

We had to wait for those six months while David worked out his contract in Zambia. David's employers would have been glad to hold onto him for another two-year stint, and I could have gone back there in tow as his girlfriend, but he was ready to call time on an experience he had really enjoyed and felt the benefit of. In those six months we were apart he lived in some style in a beautiful four-bedroomed house with swimming pool. But not everything was idyllic in Chililabombwe: David saw a harsh and brutal side of life too. He had a twenty-year-old houseboy, James, whom he liked and trusted, and who lived in quarters (*kaya*) connected to the main house. One morning David had awakened and been a little perturbed by an unusual silence about the place. He went to James's *kaya* and found the boy dead by decapitation. The appalling scene shook David badly, and he was further perturbed by the seeming insouciance of the police, who indicated that James's fate was no great surprise. David found out later through a friend of James that the boy had been killed because of some dispute arising between rival tribes. This horrendous episode didn't change David's essentially positive view of his African experience – he saw life more in the round, accepted that bad things could and did happen – but it did make a case for us starting our life together in Suffolk rather than Zambia.

When at last David flew back to the UK in December 1978 I got the overnight train down south to meet him, and from the moment he stepped into the arrivals hall at Heathrow, tanned and smiling, I knew the wait had been worth it. It had been 'meant to be'; we'd just had to go a long way around it. From there we never looked back.

We started our life together at his parents' house in Haverhill, me still awaiting the finalisation of divorce proceedings with Peter ('irreconcilable differences', readily agreed on both sides), which came in the post to my mum's house in 1979. Quick as we could we moved out, set up home together, took the best work that we could find. David's ambitions led him into publishing, and over the years he would advance steadily from one reputable company to the next. Meantime we moved from house to house as and when we had to, making a home and then trading up. We married, since we thought we ought to, in 1985. Ollie was born the following year.

I would find my own working vocation by a more roundabout means, but a big part of it was down to David's encouragement. Confidence had always been an issue for me. You can't really forget where you come from, and I don't want to, because it's an integral part of me. But I had grown up a sickly child in a working-class northern household, one that grafted hard for precious little reward. And, just like so many young people in that situation, I slowly became aware that no one had any very high expectations of my being able to make my way in the world. For all that, I always felt there was something inside me that wanted expression – that one should try to change the given, 'the done thing' for so many girls I knew, of factory work, marriage, childrearing and nary a thought to realising one's true potential. And it was David who pushed me, made me believe in myself: 'You can do this – at least give it a go. If it doesn't work, do something else. You've got it in you.'

We were two parts of the jigsaw that fitted together, made an entity. At times we had wondered aloud to each other, 'Do you think it's fate . . .?' For me my life with David was certainly a privilege. At the same time, in some fundamentally superstitious way, I sometimes thought to myself, 'Perhaps I don't deserve this. Bad things happen, this can't last, because it's just too good.' I was visited by just such a feeling a few weeks before we left for Kenya. But my life's experience, also my professional experience, had taught me not to listen to negative voices, and I put them aside and moved on.

*

At Nairobi David and I boarded a small ten-seater plane bound for Kiwayu. There was only a handful of other passengers. The two-hour journey passed off without incident, and as the plane started its descent we both were struck by the vivid turquoise of the sea, and the verdant forest with the Kiwayu resort skirting its edge. The lower we got, the more keenly I was looking out for a landing strip of some sort. The plane circled over an opening in the forest then came down to land – in a field, effectively. That felt a little odd. *This is remote*, I thought to myself. It was 4 p.m.

David and I were the only two passengers disembarking at Kiwayu. But as we gathered up our belongings a woman behind us said, 'You'll have a wonderful time in Kiwayu!' As we looked out of the window a flock of bright-plumaged bee-eaters was swooping in front of the stationary plane, miraculously managing to avoid the still rotating propeller blades. I marvelled at their vibrant colours and markings as well as their notable agility. This aerobatic display seemed almost to have been staged just for us, a welcome to the resort.

As we alighted from the plane another couple was waiting to board, and the woman remarked to us that she didn't want to leave: they'd had such a lovely holiday, David and I were certain to have a wonderful stay . . . And I did take this as reassurance. After all, the omens seemed to be in our favour.

2

As we left the plane David and I were greeted by two Kiwayu employees – or, at least, we took them as such, since they had already stashed our luggage in the back of a waiting beach buggy. Then, without saying a word, they drove us a short distance down a sandy lane to the reception area of the resort. A man came out to greet us, cheerfully informal in T-shirt, shorts and bare feet. He introduced himself as George Moorhead, the resort's owner-manager.

For all George's evident friendliness I had begun to feel a curious sense of isolation. There was simply *nobody else around*: hence none of the usual pleasant holiday-spot ambience – the sounds of children laughing and playing, of splashing water and hotel staff going about their business. Instead, the silence was very pronounced, a 'peace and quiet' that felt just a shade remote, even intimidating. I was well aware that Kiwayu advertised itself as a secluded getaway, but, still, the reality wasn't quite as I had imagined. I found myself put in mind of the *Marie Celeste*. The 'exclusivity' of the place seemed, at least for the moment, to have excluded any other signs of life.

George offered us a bite to eat and escorted us to a restaurant area. I was quite glad to see a waiter appear – another person! – and he brought some pasta and salad for David and tea and cake for me. The refreshments were very welcome, though I was still scrutinising our new surroundings. The restaurant seemed to be constructed from bamboo and thatch, its windows unglazed and hung with roller blinds. A cooling breeze blew through the space and I could hear the rhythmic roll of the sea, a sound I'd always loved. On this occasion, though, it wasn't calming me. I couldn't get over how open and exposed to the elements this resort was.

After we had eaten, David and I browsed a small gift shop, and I was eyeing potential take-home gifts for Ollie and his girlfriend Saz when George reappeared, offering to take us down the beach and show us our *banda*, the rondavel-style cottage where we would be staying.

'It's amazingly quiet here,' I remarked to him. 'Where's everybody else?'

He smiled. 'You're in luck, as it happens. You're the only two people here. We've got more guests coming in on Monday and Wednesday but as of tonight and tomorrow you've got the place all to yourselves . . .'

I'd suspected as much, but hadn't really wanted to hear it confirmed. Rather than a perk, it struck me as a slight cause for concern, that we should be so much alone in this rather lonely place.

David and I were still clad in our safari khakis but I took off my boots before we left the restaurant area and walked down onto the beach, which curved away ahead of us in a horseshoe shape. It was pleasantly warm, the sand was firm, and water lapped gently at our feet. George and David strode on a few paces in front of me, chatting the whole time. David was enquiring about the sailing, the local wind conditions, the possibility of taking a Laser dinghy out. I heard George mention that he'd be happy to arrange 'a romantic dinner' for us one night on the headland. But the headland seemed to me rather far away. And the longer we walked, the less comfortable I felt. I threw backward glances, the restaurant now seeming quite a ways away. I had begun to wonder how best to convey to David that I was uneasy – if he hadn't already intuited as much.

We reached a spot where the row of *bandas* stretched out before our eyes around the curve of the bay.

'Which one's ours?' I asked George.

'Just a bit further down. We've put you in Banda Zero . . .'

As we passed the other *banda*s I could see the privacy they offered, set back from the beach, secluded from prying eyes. But then there was no one around from whom one's privacy needed shielding. The cove was picture-postcard beautiful, but quite deserted apart from the three of us.

We came to the end of the line. 'This is yours,' said George. We struggled up a soft sand slope, and there George introduced a waiting employee who would be 'looking after us'. I was more concerned with looking about for a door to the *banda* – in fact, we entered through another doorway with nothing more than a blind rolled up over it.

Inside, blinds were also rolled above the unglazed windows. George guided us through a big, handsomely furnished space. In the living area were two slung hammocks, a bookcase, a huge chair, a dark wood chest strewn with books and magazines. The sleeping area offered a big bed with white linen sheets, bedside lamps, and a mosquito net neatly and protectively folded all around the bed frame. Then there was a dressing area with wardrobes and hanging for clothes, where our luggage sat waiting for us. And behind that was yet another lounge-type area with day beds and hammocks. Anyone would call it well appointed. I was less certain whether other guests would be more relaxed than me about sleeping in a room where one couldn't turn a key in any sort of a lock.

In the dressing area was a fixed mirror over his-and-hers sinks, and a small wooden box sat between the sink bowls. As I inspected this more closely, George piped up.

'If you've got any valuables, jewellery, watches? Just pop them in the box overnight. There are monkeys around, they'll take anything . . .'

At some other time that idea could have amused me. Now the thought of monkeys creeping in and picking through our belongings while we slept only riled my nerves a little more.

George left us to it. David looked at me, smiling, solicitous – he must have read my expression.

'What's the matter?'

'I'm not sure, David. I just feel a bit uneasy, being in a place that has no doors or windows . . .'

'Chill,' he said cheerily – the first time I'd heard him try out that particular expression. 'This'll be our Robinson Crusoe experience. It's going to be great, trust me.'

I wasn't convinced that playing castaways would give us the 'chill-out' holiday we'd planned for. But, as always, I had to love David's unflappable can-do attitude, and I really wanted to share in it with him.

We unpacked, showered, lounged around our new habitat awhile, had some fun trying to negotiate the his-and-hers hammocks. But even the shower stall managed to spook me slightly, since it was external to the *banda*, accessible through another doorway and down a slatted path, with nothing but dense foliage at either side.

Around 7 p.m. we dressed and left the *banda* in the fading light, retracing our route back down the beach to the restaurant. Dinner was simple, grilled fish and potatoes. Curiously, a man whom we assumed to be staff sat at an adjacent table, saying not a word, only looking at us, and in a not especially friendly fashion. Afterwards we decided to have a nightcap and wandered over to a bar area. In short order George Moorhead reappeared and pulled up a stool beside us. We sipped gin and tonics and he told us keenly about Kiwayu, how it was a family business originally set up by the father of his Italian wife. We learned about his schooling, his second marriage, how his wife and child had just been staying but had now returned to Nairobi ... David did most of the talking for our side, me chipping in here and there. Though George was good company I wondered if he had sensed my unease, and felt himself somehow obliged – 'part of the service' – to spend his evening with us in this fashion.

We had a second round of drinks, then, unusually for us, a third. I was more than ready for bed, but outside it was dark, and I was feeling a bit daunted by the thought of the trek back down the beach to the *banda*, though I assumed there would be security guards round and about. In time, though, there was really nothing for it but to say our goodnights and, leaving George at the bar, we headed out, armed with a wind-up torch to help us find our way.

Outside the moonlight danced on the sea's surface and aided the general visibility. All was still and peaceful. The tide was coursing in, wetting our feet as we walked. Flicking our torch beam hither and thither we spotted crabs, evidently disturbed by the light, emerging from the sand and scurrying away – quite a comical sight. We smiled at one another, and I took David's hand.

'So what do you fancy doing tomorrow?' he asked. I had no idea.

'Let's just relax. You can do your thing. I'll be happy just to have a swim, read my book ...'

'We're going to have a great time, I promise. Tomorrow I'll take the Laser out. George says the snorkelling is brilliant. We can take a walk into the village ...'

I knew David was genuinely in no way put off by the sparseness of our surroundings. I could also tell that he appreciated my anxiety, and was trying to overcompensate, to lift my spirits with the tonic of his own enthusiasm.

Up ahead we saw a light that could only be our *banda* and we clambered back up the sandy slope, pushed the door's roller blind aside and went in. Whoever had pulled down the door blind had also lit a lantern for us, turned down our bed's sheets and closed the mosquito net around it. David inspected the net quite closely: 'This is really good quality, I'm impressed . . .' My heart went out to him – always accentuating the positive. I was still thinking vaguely of monkeys – even about what day our flight home to the UK was.

I changed into pyjama bottoms and a vest top. David undressed to his underwear. We washed, brushed our teeth, and I availed myself of the wooden 'strongbox', where I carefully placed my jewellery, my hearing aids and the wristwatch I used to operate them. With my aids removed, the ambient sound of the world around me became just a shade muted.

Hearing difficulties run in my family, and I hadn't been able to escape my share of them. It was David who first brought me to the realisation that I was losing some hearing: 'Did you hear what I said, Jude?' Though my left ear functions fairly well, in my right I am effectively deaf, and since 2007 I'd been wearing aids – not at home, where the doorbell or the telephone or TV were perfectly audible, but always for out-of-doors activity.

David and I parted the mosquito net and climbed into bed, David switched off the light, and the room was profoundly dark. I was much too tired for any more misgivings. Now I just looked forward to sleep and its unravelling of all the day's cares. We drifted off together just as we always did – lightly holding each other's hand as we lay there.

*

A shout startled me out of sleep. It had to have been a shout, since I wasn't wearing my hearing aids – and it could only have been David. What I heard was: 'What the fuck is going on!?'

Groggily I looked over to David's side of the bed. The light was on – and in an instant it was as if I had been slapped awake. His sheets were empty and crumpled. Then I realised he was out of the bed, standing at the foot of it, inside the mosquito net. But someone else was there too – someone I couldn't see clearly.

What I could make out was that David was standing with his feet planted, arms outstretched above his shoulders, his left hand lower than the right – as though he were locked in a tussle with someone taller than him. He didn't notice me because he was looking rigidly up and ahead, wide-eyed, wholly focused – and clearly alarmed.

I felt a prod, as if from a stubby finger – but harder, metallic – and then I realised the sheets had been pulled off the bed. I looked left and made out two more figures standing within the net – two black men, one in a black jacket, the other in a white vest, both holding rifles. In the turmoil of the moment I thought they must be Kiwayu security guards: some emergency had arisen, they'd come to ensure we were safe. But then why was David shouting – and struggling?

In the next instant these two men seized me tightly by my upper arms, wrenched me out of bed and through the mosquito net, and began to haul me towards the doorway. I heard myself shout: 'What's happening!? What's happening!?' Yet the voice didn't seem to issue from my throat, constricted as it was by terror.

I looked back and saw David, still locked in his grapple with the shadowy assailant. Then I was tugged out of the doorway, and I felt sand and twigs under my bare feet as I was bustled sideways down the incline and onto the firmer sand of the beach.

The two men started running and dragging me along between them. I was screaming, trying to impede our progress by digging my heels into the sand. I had to get back to David – if he wasn't being hauled off too. But my resistance was useless: these men were just too strong for me.

I could feel the wind on my face, could see the moon above, nightmarishly full and bright – and heard the crash of the sea's waves, louder than my screams. Onward they dragged me, following the curve of the beach, towards the headland still off in the distance, jutting from the sea and silhouetted by moonlight. In the melee I thought one thing clearly: *Footprints – we're leaving footprints in the sand. When people come after me they'll know which way to go – David will know.*

The forced pace was so hectic that I was quickly out of breath. I fell over my own feet, only to feel one of the men seizing me by my hair and pulling me to my feet. I reached behind me, dug my nails into the offending hand, but then I felt a brutal jab – the butt of a rifle – in the small of my back, followed hard by two smarting slaps about my head. My knees buckled but I managed to keep upright.

We splashed in and out of the shallow tidewaters, soaking the legs of my pyjamas. Still I pleaded with them: 'What are you doing? Where are you taking me? Stop it, take me back, I won't say anything . . .' But they stayed grimly silent. The sheer force of their manhandling me ever further away from the *banda* was its own chilling response. I struggled to comprehend why I couldn't see any security guards, why it appeared that nobody else could see or hear what was happening to me.

Then I was being turned, sharply, into the sea. For a moment I feared I was to be drowned, my head thrust under the waves . . . Instead I realised that something was coming over the water towards us. Without my hearing aids I couldn't hear an engine – but in that horrible stillness I saw a fisherman's skiff gliding ever closer. I could make out the dusky figure of a man sitting at the stern by the engine – a navigator, his hand on a rudder. Then my kidnappers started pulling me through the knee-deep water towards this boat.

My mind screamed: *God, no, if they get me on that boat and take me away, where will we go? Who's ever going to find me?*

One of my kidnappers clambered aboard, the other forced me up against the boat's side – under my hands its texture was rough, like painted fibreglass. Then I was shoved upwards from behind and pulled in from above and I keeled forwards into the boat, tumbling and banging my temple. It was a small vessel, maybe six feet wide, ten to twelve feet long. The men gestured irately at me. I gathered that I was being ordered to sit myself on one of a number of big yellow plastic containers that littered the boat's floor. So I sat, and they flanked me at either side. The Navigator swung the boat around – and we sat for some moments, me breathless, scared, wondering what they were waiting for. Then two figures came splashing through the water towards us from the shore. One hurriedly lifted himself aboard, the other first took hold of the side of the boat and shoved it forwards before hauling himself in and taking a seat at the prow – as if he were the ship's captain, the leader of this particular gang. He was a tall, stocky man wearing a padded and hooded khaki jacket. I knew these two latecomers could only have come from Banda Zero. They must have left David behind – knocked him unconscious? – so that they could make their getaway.

The mood among the five African men was urgent, determined. In desperation I looked back, raking the beach with my eyes. Had no one on Kiwayu heard us? Wouldn't someone come and stop this? But the resort looked as good as deserted. The Leader barked something at his Navigator, who yanked the outboard motor's cord. The engine came to life with a high-pitched whine. Then the skiff lurched off and away, seemingly straight out to sea and the blackness of night.

It felt as though I were being catapulted, fired out of a gun – and I was almost too stunned by the violence that had been visited on me to apprehend my own terror fully. In the sky to my right the moon was huge and luminous, and it cast a wide ribbon of silver across the sea's surface – an image of romance, turned here into horror. I looked back and watched, helpless, as the shoreline – my lifeline – raced away from me.

3

If the skiff had looked weathered and old, its engine had to be new – certainly powerful – for it soon got up to a breakneck, hell-for-leather speed, faster than anything I'd ever known. It skimmed and bounced over the tops of the waves, but when it slammed into a swell then bucketloads of water were flung on board. In my hopelessly inadequate vest and pyjama bottoms I was soon soaked, and shaking with cold as well as fear. A small blanket was thrust upon me and I pulled it round my shoulders, but it barely sat there, and quickly it became sodden and useless.

The rate of knots at which we travelled was also serving to bash me up and down where I sat, precariously, half afraid I would be tipped overboard. Although my legs were wedged painfully between these yellow containers, I listed from side to side. One of the men grabbed the back of my vest top so as to steady me, and I got a grip on one heavy container's handle. But each time the boat smacked into a sloshing wave the impact was excruciating. Pain shot up my spine, and I couldn't stop myself crying out.

The five men, in their shorts and hooded jackets, were oblivious to my distress and these conditions – they looked hell bent on the fastest escape from Kiwayu. My initial entreaties to them had died in my throat. I kept looking behind me, scouring to see any sign of movement from the resort – but all I saw was the shoreline growing smaller, until it had disappeared from sight.

Stuck in a fast boat on the Indian Ocean with five edgy, aggressive criminals, I saw nothing I could do other than to try to keep my head amid the crisis. If this was a kidnap then I had to assume we were headed for some kind of bolt-hole or safe house, maybe further up the coast, where I would be held for money. I told myself that David wouldn't allow this outrage to go on for long. He would come to find me. He would strain every sinew, do whatever had to be done to get me freed.

Suddenly I could hear a spluttering noise emanating from the engine, which hitherto had seemed so super-charged, and then abruptly it cut out, and the boat was doing nothing more than bobbing, adrift, on the water. The gang exchanged some short, sharp words. One of them hastened to his feet – one of the two who had abducted me from the *banda*. He rummaged out a piece of tubing, unscrewed the cap of a yellow canister and appeared to suck some of its contents up into his mouth. Then he transferred the pipe into the engine, got his lips round it again, and I realised he was attempting the old trick of petrol-siphoning.

As this went on, the Navigator sitting behind me came to my shoulder. 'Would you like trousers?' he said.

For a muddled instant all that I could think was *He speaks English!* I peered more closely at him in the dark. He was tall, maybe six foot four, rail thin and gaunt, with a goatee beard.

'Yes, thank you,' I replied. And he produced a pair of tracksuit bottoms, navy with white stripes – dry to the touch, so from where they'd come I knew not, but I pulled them on over my pyjama trousers, grateful not only for the courtesy but for this discovery that here was somebody with whom I could communicate – with whom *David* could communicate, whenever this gang let it be known what they wanted in return for me.

Moments later, another unexpected consideration: the man who had been siphoning fuel was now pressing his bulky black waterproof jacket on me. I put it on without hesitation, yanking the zipper right up to my chin to combat my shivers.

The Leader was trying to restart the boat by yanking the cord but he tried and failed, once, twice, thrice. I had a sense the gang was feeling confounded, nerves fraying a bit as their efforts proved fruitless. They kept changing places, hastily, and the motion of the boat unsettled me. Now bundled up in the heavy jacket and trousers, I took fright at the thought that if all this rocking were to pitch me overboard then I would sink straight to the seabed.

I was emboldened to speak up.

'Where are you taking me? What do you want?'

The man sitting at my right – who had been last onboard together with the Leader – looked at me and laughed in my face, showing me a protruding over-bite of very white teeth. He seemed very young, nineteen or twenty. Rubbing his index finger and thumb together he chanted, 'Money, money, money, money . . .' The Leader shot him a stern look and he clammed up. But I was satisfied at least to have my assumption confirmed: I had been kidnapped for ransom. So a process would have to follow, and with any luck the end of it would come quickly and painlessly. Until then I would just have to keep calm and focused.

The engine coughed back to life, and the skiff lurched off once more, again at a fair speed if not quite so scarily fast as before. The Leader resumed his place up on high at the prow. Once or twice he glanced my way. I had begun to think he must have been the man with whom I'd seen David struggling, since the other latecomer to the boat, young 'Money', was so physically slight by comparison. And among the five members of this gang it was his presence that I found the most unnerving.

*

On we went, in silence save for the boat's drone, for quite some time, until I felt the vessel begin to slow and saw a sandy spit of land come into view. Could this be the gang's bolt-hole? As we neared the shore Money and the Siphoning Man jumped from the boat and waded through knee-high water up onto the sand, then strode up the beach towards the cover of some foliage and disappeared from view. The Leader stared after them but we made no move, just sitting there in the dark gently bobbing up and down on the water. The fifth of my captors, one of the pair who had abducted me from the *banda*, gave off a hostile air if I glanced at him, and so I tried to focus on the English-speaking Navigator. I was desperate to get some idea of our whereabouts, and I suddenly recalled George Moorhead mentioning Lamu as somewhere to which David and I might like to take a boat trip from Kiwayu. I turned to the Navigator.

'Where are we? Is this Lamu . . . ?'

He shook his head. 'Somalia . . .'

That struck me, forcibly; and a horde of phrases leapt into my head, all of them unwelcome: 'war-torn Somalia . . .', 'ungoverned Somalia . . .', 'the failed state of Somalia . . .' I knew nothing of the place other than what I'd seen in news reports, but the news from Somalia was nearly always bleak. I cursed myself for not having cottoned on before now that this would be our destination – away from scenic, civil, tourist-friendly Kenya and towards Somalia, a place where the whole world knew the rule of law didn't apply.

I had to get a grip on my runaway thoughts or else, I knew, I would start to panic – and panic was an indulgence I couldn't afford. Again I tried to summon up positive thoughts of David: *He'll have come round by now – hang on to that. He'll have gone to get George. They'll have raised an alarm, got people out to look for me.*

Maybe the British Embassy knows that I'm missing by now. They'll have a plan, it'll be put straight into action . . .

Now the two men were wading back through the water, each lugging a yellow container identical to those already on board. With difficulty, assisted by the Leader, they hefted these items over the boat's side to land on the floor with a thud. I understood: we'd stopped here for no purpose other than to take on fuel.

The Leader muttered something over my head in the direction of the Navigator, who tapped my shoulder. 'You sleep now,' he said. They produced and unrolled a thin mattress, and lay it on top of the canisters. I was told to lie down – it was wet and ill-smelling – then they threw the sodden blanket over me, and then I felt another heavy layer go on top of that. In the blackness beneath these covers I stretched out. To be unable to see where we were going was a worry. But to be lying down at least relieved the raw pain I felt in my coccyx from having been bashed about all through the high-speed journey. I was physically spent – the fatigue of stress, fear and adrenalin crept over me – and in time I must have slept.

*

As I regained consciousness I could tell from my recumbent position that we were slowing down again. I sat up, hauled away my covers and faced the new dawn. The engine had been killed and the skiff was drifting toward the crescent-shaped cove of a mangrove swamp. The waters were flat and calm, the boat making the merest ripples that broke against the trunks of the mangroves. Those trees – with their twisted, contorted roots and looming branches that seemed to force their way out of the water – had a forbidding look to them, like some gate set up by nature to guard a lost world.

Looking about me in the light of daybreak I could finally make out with clarity the faces of my motley crew of captors. Immediately on seeing the man who had loaned me his jacket, I thought, *My god, he's the image of Marvin Gaye* . . . The likeness was so incongruous and striking, I knew in an instant that this was a man I could easily pick out in a line-up.

But other than the Navigator – who smiled at me – my captors paid me no mind, looking remote and focused as before. Throughout the journey they had barely exchanged a word with one another. Now was no different. The division of labour between them, though, seemed very clear and spoke volumes. The Navigator worked the boat's rudder; Money took hold of mangrove branches so as to pull the boat deeper into the swamp; 'Marvin' beckoned me to stand up and get out into the shallow water, where spiky protruding mangrove stumps scratched my feet, so he pulled off his big leather sandals and pressed them on me. Then the boat was tied up and 'the Fifth Man' took charge of unloading it. The Leader, who had been first off the vessel, stood by and watched, his face inscrutable. There was no friction within this gang: the Leader ran the show, the others followed his command.

The Navigator led me to a large shrub, where he took a machete and slashed away at its lower branches then told me to 'get inside' – by which I gathered I would have to manoeuvre myself under the hacked-out portion. This was a knotty task, as my borrowed jacket kept getting snared on thorns, and I had to watch where my hands went too. I gestured that I'd like to remove the jacket, at least doff its hood, since keeping warm was no longer a factor. But the Navigator was adamant: 'Your head, you must cover.' And I could see he would not tolerate dissent. Under this shrub the mangrove swamp was now at my back and

I was staring at arid countryside before me. The thorns and branches dictated that the only way for me to sit was in a crouch with my knees to my chin – intensely uncomfortable, as every bone in my body was aching. And yet just to be on dry land was preferable to me to being on that boat.

I watched the gang confer together in a circle, glancing occasionally at me. For a while I had been wringing my hands, a nervous habit of mine, and in doing so now I realised I was still wearing two diamond rings – one of them my mother-in-law's engagement ring. Suddenly their value in the eyes of these bandits became crystal clear to me, and I twisted the rings so the stones were palm side. I was gripped by the need to secrete them safely away. But I had no pockets, no obvious hiding place. Thinking fast, I beckoned the Navigator to the shrub and told him that I needed to go to the toilet. He relayed this to the Leader, who nodded agreement, and I was allowed to pick a spot at a distance but within sight, behind another smaller shrub. There I crouched and worked as fast as I could, 'worrying' the rings off my swollen fingers until they came free. Then I tied the rings onto the cord of my pyjama bottoms and tucked the cord away next to my skin – now sure that the prized possessions were safe from discovery, and pleased by my own quick thinking.

As I stood up I noticed a definite footpath in front of where the boat was moored, winding steeply through some under-growth and overhanging trees, a path clearly well trodden. I was curious. But now I was being beckoned back to my cage.

*

We remained in the mangroves for the day, in blistering heat. But for a few shards of shade from the shrub I was exposed to the direct sunlight, and I sat there, roasting, sweaty, itching from insect bites all over me. Hours passed, though I had lost any accurate sense of time. Marvin and the Navigator sat opposite me, the Leader and Money to one side. They lazed about, talked to each other, their urgency seemingly spent. At intervals a couple of them would head up the path in front of the boat, and return after a little while.

Perhaps because of all else that I'd had to contend with, hunger and thirst had been crowded out of my mind – until the Navigator came over and proffered me a beaker crudely fashioned from a plastic Evian bottle with its top cut off. In this was some cloudy-brown water. I took a wary sip, but I knew this was all wrong and had to make them see.

'If I drink this I will get sick. You know that? If I get sick you will have to take me to hospital. I have to drink bottled water.'

He nodded, took my point. 'OK. You get fresh water, tomorrow.'

Though I had made myself understood, that 'tomorrow' nonetheless made my heart sink. Everything in me hoped for the fastest possible resolution to my predicament. I was badly dismayed to think that their plans for me might be more complex.

Above all I was yearning for David – to see his face, hear his calm and caring voice, be held by him. Back in the UK it was Sunday. Ollie wouldn't be working. I imagined that by now David must have contacted him with the bad news, and also the wider family – his brother Paul, and on my side most likely my sister Carol, who could be trusted to relay it. I dreaded, though, to think how my ninety-year-old mother would react to this seismic shock.

With one violent stroke, the shared holiday that had been bringing David and me such happiness had been turned into the grimmest of nightmares, one from which I was desperate to awake. I longed for home. Wishful scenarios were running through my head of how David and I would speak of this ordeal in the future – rarely, for sure, in hushed tones, thanking our lucky stars. 'That time you were taken,' David would say. 'Thank god it was only days, not months, years,' I'd reply. And I had to believe that would be the case – that if I wasn't to be rescued today then it would have to be tomorrow.

I wasn't tired, but to my surprise my captors, one by one, stretched out on the ground and fell asleep – Money wrapping himself in a filthy pink sheet. Their rifles – AK47s, old, with frayed straps – stayed at their sides. I wasn't convinced this was how a seasoned band of kidnappers would go about their business. And yet they seemed to have accomplished something just by getting me onto the muddy banks of the mangrove: some kind of step had been attained, and now they were biding their time, conserving their energies. Clearly they were banking on my making no attempt to escape, and they were right, since quite simply I had nowhere to go.

For a brief period I dozed myself, my head on my knees. When I stirred I saw three men asleep minus the Leader. Then I felt a new desperation, to see that the tide that had brought us to the mangrove had disappeared. Now the view was only of mangrove stumps, roots of trees and wet sand. Any boat that happened to be patrolling the coast would never get near enough to see anything of us.

Money stirred awake in his sheet, like a pupa emerging from a cocoon. Since I was the only one conscious I had dared to remove the hood of the jacket, as my head had begun to throb from the effects of the heat. But now Money leapt up, shouting at me, eyes bulging. He grabbed his rifle and pointed it at my head. There was a derangement about him as he gesticulated wildly. As I shrank from him I gathered that he meant not to shoot me but for me to replace the hood over my head.

The Navigator was awake too now, and he hastened over to us, but only to take Money's side.

'You must keep on,' he said sternly. 'No hair showing!'

'Why?'

'It is our religion.'

I just hadn't made the connection, thinking my head cover was only part of their effort to keep me hidden rather than anything to do with piety or modesty. But now, shaken, I understood. Evidently these men were very observant Muslims. I had to wonder, were they 'radical' or 'extreme' about their faith? How did their beliefs incline them to treat women? The evidence so far was not encouraging. I wondered if it might do me any good to pretend I had some religion of my own. Would they be any more circumspect about shoving a gun in the face of a believer?

*

Darkness came down. I still hadn't eaten since I'd been snatched away from Kiwayu. The Navigator brought me some tea, again in the filthy plastic 'beaker' but I drank it as I was very thirsty. It was hot and sweet. He lingered, and crouched by me.

'They need your husband's mobile telephone number? They have to ring him. They want money – when they get money you go back.'

I was struck by his repetition of 'they', this man seeming to want to distinguish himself from his partners in crime.

'Just take me back now,' I ventured. 'Then we can sort out money.'

He shook his head. I wasn't surprised.

'I'm sorry,' I said. 'I can't remember my husband's number.'
This was the truth, frustrating as it was to me. At the same time
I knew very well that David's phone was sitting at home in
Bishop's Stortford, unattended, so any effort in this line would
be wasted.

'Tell them to ring Kiwayu Village – speak to the manager,
George Moorhead? He will get my husband on the phone, his
name is David. Then you can sort this out, he will get you
money.'

'OK, OK, yes,' the Navigator nodded. He loped off and relayed
this to the Leader. But in short order he was back and asking
me to try again to recall any family phone numbers. It was hopeless – I simply couldn't do it without my own phone in front of
me. The Navigator gave up, clearly disappointed. I was annoyed
that I couldn't perform this simple task so as to initiate the process that would mean my freedom. But I remained hopeful.

*It may take time, but this is resolvable – depending on how much
they want. Sixty, seventy thousand pounds, maybe? We can do that,
I know it, we've got that money.*

It was fully dark and the only light was from the moon when
Marvin came over and signalled for me to crawl out from under
the shrub. Just to stand was a welcome reprieve from the painful
crouch I'd been forced to adopt all day. He led me by the hand
to the boat. I was very hungry, very apprehensive of what was
going to happen now, and yet relieved somehow to be moving. The boat was fastidiously reloaded, canisters and all, in
complete silence. These men seemed barely to leave a tread on
the ground.

Once we were aboard, though, there was a hitch: the boat
wouldn't budge, and I realised – as they had – that the boat's pro-
peller blades must have got entangled in mangrove roots. Two

of them struggled to lift the propellers clear of the water, and a third hacked away at the tangle with a machete. It took some time, during which I felt once again that there was something oddly inept about this kidnap. Each time they fired up the engine it only whined in complaint and the boat remained obstinately stuck. I was hoping against hope that someone somewhere could hear this straining din. Finally the engine returned to its peak roar and once more I was ordered to lie down on the mattress, under the same clammy, ill-smelling covers.

*

Again we sailed all night, and for a time I slept, waking as if to déjà vu, for the boat was edging slowly into the reach of another mangrove swamp. The men executed their appointed roles: the boat was steered in, moored, unloaded. But this time I saw the Leader give some instruction to the Navigator, whereupon he shinned barefoot up a mangrove tree and began to hack down branches with the machete.

I was led, with an unhappy familiarity, to a large shrub, low-growing with thick branches. I knew what was coming but I didn't crawl under until prompted. This shrub, at least, enabled me to lie down under it, and so I got onto my back and rested one leg on a stray branch. From there I watched my captors cover the boat with a thick camouflage of the branches the Navigator had chopped down. Its bright turquoise hull was soon entirely buried under foliage – invisible, for sure, to any plane passing overhead. Inwardly I cursed them for having taken such care. Looking about me, I noticed one or two discarded cigarette packets and stubs ('Sportsman' brand), also some empty tins of tuna and water bottles scattered around. I could only deduce that this peculiar hideaway had been used before.

The men settled themselves a little way off from me, on a flat open space up an incline, and there they 'pitched camp'. They lit a fire, hung their rifles on branches, removed their wet clothes and either laid or hung them out to dry, and changed into clean clothes that they produced from black plastic bags. There was the sense of an organised unit, making ready for at least an overnight stay (though I realised the Fifth Man was nowhere to be seen, the unit seeming to have shrunk to a quartet). I also saw the Leader retrieve a mobile phone from another bag and make a call.

But then all the bivouacking came to a halt as the Leader and the Navigator began – methodically and in unison – to pray. With water from one of the yellow containers (was it consecrated?), they washed their hands and heads and inside their mouths and ears. Then, crouching, they balanced on one foot while scooping handfuls of water to cleanse the other – a gymnastic feat, executed with near synchronicity. I watched in fascination. For all that I knew my predicament, still my mind was taken out of it for the time that I observed this rigorous procedure. It seemed to me now that this was the likely reason why the men had vanished periodically the day before. They must have retired to some appropriate 'private' patch of ground where they could pray.

They stood, held out their palms upwards, then crossed their arms over their chests, all the while reciting words I couldn't make out or understand. Then they knelt, placed their hands on their knees, and prostrated themselves, foreheads and flats of their palms pressed to the ground. This I recognised as the customary Islamic gesture of submission to Allah.

The whole spectacle made me thoughtful. I had always been inclined to respect people's avowed religious beliefs as an obviously meaningful part of who they are. I was never persuaded, though, that 'being religious' made one a good person: showing respect and deference to a higher power seemed less important to me than showing kindness to one's fellow man and woman. And these men, I felt, were making a mockery of their faith. Having kidnapped a defenceless woman in order to sell her for money, they were now prostrating themselves before their god. Was it so that they might be forgiven the offence?

Their prayers complete, the men turned back to worldly business. They slung the bright orange tarpaulin from the boat between two trees and secured it, making some shade for themselves. The Leader got busy once again with his phone. They boiled water over the fire and brewed tea, all huddled under the shade of the tarpaulin. Suddenly I saw their mistake and grinned inwardly. After all these pains to conceal the turquoise skiff, if a plane passed overhead nothing could have been more conspicuous to it than that orange tarpaulin. Fresh hope arose in me: as long as they all sat blithely under a covering as bright as a Belisha beacon then somebody might spot us from above.

It was as if my thoughts had been broadcast out of the top of my head. Within moments Money and the Leader stomped from under the tarpaulin and cocked their heads to the skies, as if listening for something. A plane? If so, I couldn't see it, much less hear it. But in a trice the men had pulled down the tarpaulin, folded it and stashed it. Crestfallen, I clung at least to the notion that it had indeed been a plane they'd heard – a plane looking for me.

The Leader then strode away from the group down a path that led around a corner and disappeared. I watched him all the way until he vanished from view. Where did the path lead? I had to find out. I signalled for the Navigator, told him I needed the toilet. By now I had devised two sounds to express and distinguish the need: either a hiss or a grunt. I found that by a grunt I was permitted to walk a little further away from them than by a hiss. This time I selected a reasonably private shrub as near to the bend in the path as I could. But I couldn't see much of where it led. Escape was on my mind, but with it came the fear that if I tried and failed I might put myself in greater jeopardy. My ordeal had lasted two days – another forty-eight hours and it might be all over. When I got the inevitable signal to hurry up and move back nearer the camp I complied.

As the day wore on my captors once again spread themselves out on the ground to sleep, rifles by their sides. A fantasy entered my head in which I ran over, grabbed up one of their weapons without their waking, instantly figured out how to fire it, and strafed the lot of them with bullets – the Leader too, whenever he returned. As I was idling in my mind, knowing I was utterly incapable of any such thing, I began too to think about how much more perilous it might be for me to do this than not to.

*

The Leader returned after a few hours, toting some plastic carrier bags as though he had been shopping. Marvin came over to me with bottled water, which I drank gratefully, and some biscuits – labelled 'Encore', each the size of a pencil eraser, in long cellophane strips. They tasted dry and disgusting.

Come evening the gang boiled water in a metal container and cooked rice. I watched them eat. I remained unfed. One thing I took from all of this activity was that there had to be a village near by: the Leader must have sourced his provisions from somewhere, unless this place was a semi-permanent dumping ground.

Once darkness was complete they dragged the mattress off the boat and deigned to come down from their incline and join me. I came out of the shrub, they threw the mattress to the ground, I lay down and they lay either side of me, wrapping themselves head to toe in sheets that they secured at each end. There was something very unnerving about this procedure, as if they were preparing themselves for their own burials.

They seemed to fall asleep simultaneously and soundly. But for some time my eyes were wide open – I was alert and frightened of who or what might emerge from the bush. I had never before slept out for a night under the stars – unlike David. I shuddered to think that only a few nights ago on the Masai Mara – nights that now seemed terribly far away – the notion of passing a night in the Suguroi Hill Tree House had felt like the riskiest thing imaginable to me.

Still, a voice inside – rational and calculating – told me to keep calm, stay alert, exert whatever self-control I could summon. I would need to draw on inner resources to survive this, for however long it took. I was alone and I was scared, yes, but I had experienced times of loneliness, vulnerability – even peril – before. And then as now, the inner voice had told me: *OK, there's nobody else here. So you are just going to have to rely on yourself.*

4

There were times in our marriage when David would say – fondly, in jest – 'I just want to look after you, you're so tiny . . .' It's true that I'm on the diminutive side, and I never minded my husband pointing it out in affection. But I deeply disliked the idea of anyone else getting the idea that I was frail or delicate or helpless. This was a perception I'd had to struggle against all my life, and so it was doubly important to me that people understood I wasn't someone to be pushed around. Otherwise I would have been surrendering to the cards that were dealt me at birth.

I was born in December 1954, premature, tiny and underweight. Worse, I was diagnosed with a 'hole in the heart' between the right and left ventricles. As such I grew up a sickly child, endlessly susceptible to viruses and minor infections. This might have mattered less if my family had had the means to cosset me, but life was a lot harder for all of us growing up in Ulverston, Cumbria.

I was the fourth of six children and we were raised in a terraced council house in a typical northern street, a close-knit community where the neighbours vied a bit over who had the shiniest front step and happily took in next door's kids if they came home from school to an empty house. Sometimes that was me and my siblings, simply because our mum and dad had to work all hours. Consequently we had to bring ourselves up to some extent.

My dad Thomas was a big man who did odd jobs of casual manual labour, while my mum Gladys worked as a cleaner. Their example meant that in our family there could be no passengers, no refugees from the work ethic. Like thousands of other working-class families we just got on with it. But, for all that industry, we struggled. At my first school I was one of the kids who needed school milk and free dinners, and I was subjected to a fair bit of verbal bullying for wearing hand-me-downs that usually looked the worse for wear. My mum was well versed in the art of make-do-and-mend, but one day she went to the school to complain to teachers after I was ridiculed especially for wearing an old and threadbare duffel coat of my brother's.

My attendance record at school was patchy in any case, on account of my poor health and susceptibility to any illness that was going around. I missed so many days that the truancy inspector started turning up at our door. In truth I wanted to be at school very badly, for I was afraid that otherwise I'd start to lag behind the rest of the class. The anxiety knocked my self-confidence. For a long time afterwards I carried with me a nagging sense of being 'not quite up to scratch'. The issue of my health was bad enough to prompt our local doctor to lobby for us to be allotted a larger council property, with electricity and amid a better environment, so that at least we kids weren't all sleeping in one room. And that move did make a difference.

My siblings and I did have fun times, knocking around like a little tribe, climbing the fence of the local council depot to run up and down the aggregate sand heaps, or traipsing the two or three miles to Canal Foot estuary opposite Morecambe Bay, which we called 'the beach', though there was no sand there – a pretty gritty, muddy, smelly place, but great for playing at mudslides.

Generally, though, on these excursions I was the only girl. I hung around with my brothers a lot, but they were obliged to

JUDITH TEBBUTT

take me and at times, I'm sure, grew tired of me. As a result I was often on my own, but at such times I'd simply resolve just to find something to do. And for all that this was thrust upon me, I learned not to be afraid of solitude. I found that I really didn't mind my own company. And this encouraged in me a bit of resourcefulness, the important ability to count on myself.

I loved to climb trees, sit in my perch, listen to the wind and watch the world. My favourite spot was up a copper beech tree in the grounds of the local vicarage. In the first house where I lived, our backyard never got any sun, perpetually gloomy, always hung with a line of washing. But I perfected the skill of shinning up the fifteen-foot stone wall so that I could gaze out over the allotments behind us – at crops of tall sunflowers, people tending vegetable patches, chickens clucking behind chain-link fences. It did my spirits so much good just to climb free of the darkened yard up into the light, where the sun shone and I could observe all these good and useful signs of life – until such time as some neighbour or other would shout at me, 'Oi, you, get down off that bloody wall!'

*

The year I turned twelve, in 1966, was memorable to me for quite a few unfortunate reasons. I sat my 11-plus exams, desperate to get to into the local grammar school. But nobody reckoned I would pass, myself included. I failed, and took the depressing news to mean that perhaps I was meant to keep my horizons low in life. That summer before I was due to start at the local secondary modern I learned that I would have to travel to Pendlebury Hospital in Manchester for a coronary angiogram to assess the state of my heart condition. I hoped this would be a mere day trip – the kindly vicar, he of the local vicarage, gave me a

Tiffin chocolate bar for the journey and a get-well card. But instead I was driven the hundred miles to Manchester by my Uncle John, dropped off at reception and left alone on a children's ward for some weeks, without visitors.

The angiogram itself was a frightening and traumatising experience to me. I was taken into a room of nurses, my wrists and ankles strapped to four corners of a bed, and the catheter was inserted in my groin without local anaesthetic. Thereafter I languished at the hospital until my stitches could be removed, alone, without any communication from my family, until the day Uncle John turned up to take me home. The test results, when they were delivered, made clear that my heart was going to require surgery at some point. But the problem was put aside for the time being, and I certainly couldn't have faced much more upset at that time.

Secondary school did prove a solace to me in that I made a proper friend there, Janet, who lived on the road below ours and was someone with whom I could walk to school. We liked to go together through the churchyard of St Mary's and Holy Trinity, whereas lots of other children would sooner take the long way round on dark mornings when the gloom around the graves might have seemed disconcerting. But I found the ambience of this place somehow protective. I was fascinated to read the inscriptions on gravestones and to imagine the lives of people who had died before I was born. Of course there was also a very sharp poignancy in the stones of people – sometimes children, infants – who had died before their time. Conversely, though, it gave me a warm and consoling feeling wherever I saw that a husband and wife had been buried side by side – the sense that they had shared a lifetime together, and it had happened that one had died before the other, but now they were conjoined again.

I didn't know if Janet shared in all the sorts of feelings that St Mary's churchyard evoked in me, but for sure both of us would get very cross if we saw anybody playing around the tombstones. The notion of respecting the dead – of never, ever trespassing on a person's final resting place – occurred to me as a totally natural and instinctive piety.

*

Things did improve a little for our family in the latter part of the 1960s. My dad found regular work at the local shipyard, my brothers finished school and dutifully went out to work, even I worked Saturdays at Woolworth's (on the footwear and electrical counters) so I too could contribute to the upkeep. By my teens my health had improved to the extent that I could lead an ordinary life.

And yet as my school years drew to a close I grew more and more preoccupied by the feeling that life could offer more than what everyone around me was so well used to. My parents had had to toil so hard for such small tangible reward. It wasn't the life I would have wished for them, and emphatically not what I wanted for me or any family of my own I might have. But my prospects all seemed to tend in one dispiriting direction. I was desperate to figure out a way I might still improve myself – some kind of escape from the given.

After finishing school at sixteen I managed to fund myself (by working at a fish-and-chip shop) through a course at Lancaster College of Further Education, and there I picked up a few formal qualifications but, probably more importantly, a bit of precious confidence in my own initiative. But it couldn't keep me from the seemingly inevitable, and within a year I was working on the assembly line at Ashley's electrical components factory, dirty and mundane work relieved only by the fact that I ended up sitting next to my old schoolfriend Janet.

Fate took an ironic turn, though, for it was at Ashley's that I met Peter, who became my first husband. And by marrying him I became the first person in many generations of my family to leave Ulverston – albeit initially moving no further afield than a little two-up two-down in Barrow-in-Furness. The really radical removal, of course, was eighteen months later – to Zambia. And though I could never have anticipated it, Zambia gave me everything, because there I met David, who turned my life around entirely.

*

For all that David gave me, there were inevitably things in my life that he couldn't change or influence or even really help me with – things I had to deal with alone, as we all must – and foremost among these was the concern over my long-term health.

In my early twenties I was told by a doctor that if I didn't have heart surgery then by my fifties I would be chronically affected – constantly breathless, my mobility impaired. At that point I thought my fifties lay impossibly far away in the future. And for a few more years I put the matter aside, happy to be with David, relatively fit and active. But then I had to have a surgical procedure on my ear, and the hospital tests detected my heart murmur. I was told this would certainly affect my giving birth. So I discussed it with David and resolved to have the necessary surgery. I was booked into a former army hospital, an off-putting place of cramped rooms and long dark corridors, with nothing in the way of communal space. David dropped me off there but his work meant that he couldn't stay. And so after the nurse settled me in I was on my own again in a small room, sitting on the bed, intensely conscious of the weight of silence and solitude, very apprehensive over what was going to happen to me.

Probably we all like to think that in growing up we put childish things behind us and become functional adults, fully capable of facing any eventuality life might throw our way. But I believe most of us retain a shadow inside of the children we were; and sometimes in life situations arise that threaten to reduce us once again to the status of the child – unknowing, dependent, helpless. Alone in the hospital room I faced just such a situation.

You're here now. What do you do? You've got to be strong and you've got to get through this on your own.

There was no turning back. And I was in the hands of others – I could only wait to be acted upon. But what was in my power was to control my feelings and try to be brave. Life experience had taught me a little resilience, and I intended to use it.

5

I'd never known a more grim awakening than the one that began my third day in captivity, as I came to on a dirty mattress sandwiched between four male strangers, so heavily asleep as to appear lifeless. Their unwelcome physical proximity, on top of everything else they were inflicting on me, felt repulsive and violating. It was as if I were frozen to the ground, wanting to be anywhere else yet unable to move a muscle. How long would I have to lie there? Finally the pain in my back caused me to shift somewhat, and more or less instantly the Navigator stirred awake at my side. Then his cohorts, too, came alive – except for Money, who seemed to have the teenage skill of staying sound asleep in his pit.

The Navigator began to brew tea, which had the effect of rousing Money. Then Marvin took me by the wrist and urged me up the incline to where the gang had made camp on the previous day. Once I had struggled upwards, my feet slipping out of Marvin's own oversized sandals, I saw the Leader was already ensconced there. He didn't look at me and I averted my eyes from him. As ever his very presence made me anxious, for the simple reason that as far as I could tell my life was in his hands.

Still, I sat, as Marvin indicated I should. And I was glad to be free from the confines of the thorny shrubs, albeit worried about the sun blazing down directly overhead.

Presently I felt the unpleasant sensation of a nosebleed, which caused great consternation to my captors. The Leader signalled to Marvin to do something, anything: he produced a piece of cardboard and clumsily rubbed it around my face, scratching me in the process. Left to myself, not especially glad of the 'help', I wiped away some more blood with my hand; and in touching my face I became abruptly conscious of more than one other injury. I could feel a swelling over my right eye, and a scab forming on the cut I had sustained when I was first thrown into the skiff. I felt I should extend the examination – know the worst – and looking about I realised that many of the small insect bites to my body, some even in the webbing between my toes and fingers, were turning into blood blisters where I must have scratched at them. Spotted bloodstains on my vest top I knew had come not from my nosebleed but as a result of said scratching.

The nosebleed, at least, had coagulated by now but I had no means to wash myself and so I sat there in my dirty, bloody state, finding the heat even more than usually hateful. The Leader then issued some further instruction to Marvin, who proceeded to rig a sheet between the branches of two small trees to make a shade. I settled down there at their invitation, and I was glad of the respite from the beating sun, as well as the space and the change of scenery, such as it was.

We stayed there for, again, what seemed like hours. The Leader picked his now customary moment to get up and walk away out of sight. Marvin dozed off near to me, the Navigator and Money did likewise beneath a tree. I began to feel a cooling breeze, for which I was grateful, and I unzipped the black jacket far enough for the breeze to work its way around my body. Such was the improvement, I decided to risk incurring the usual wrath by untying the cord around the jacket's hood and pulling it down – all the time keeping a wary eye out for any stirring among my captors. There was none, and so I sat, mercifully bareheaded for the first time in days.

There was a limit to the consolation I felt. My body was wet with sweat, my hair plastered to my head. My face was caked in blood from the nosebleed and the cut above my eye. I was sure I was a wretched sight. And I had to begun to worry seriously about septicaemia, given the various cuts to my feet and the rash of bleeding bites around my body, now most exquisitely sore on the rubbed skin around the waistband of my trousers.

My mind began to wander. This time, should I – could I – attempt an escape? I started to shift my leg along the ground from left to right, making a rustling noise in order to gauge how deeply my captors were sleeping. Nobody stirred. From lying down I sat up, carefully zipped up the jacket and replaced the hood, then leaned my back against the tree trunk – and coughed sharply. Again, no reaction. They seemed to be sleeping soundly.

I got to my feet, stepped out from the shade and began to walk down the incline towards the winding path, which would lead, I was sure, to a village. My plan, swiftly formed, was to find and don a *burka* as soon as I reached the village, so that every part of me save for my eyes would be cloaked from view, and I could remain undetected while pondering my next move. I was quite sure, though, that this would involve my locating a car or truck with its keys conveniently left in the ignition – whereupon I would drive to the capital, Mogadishu. As I understood it there were UN camps there, places where I would be greeted, welcomed, given food and clean clothes. Tomorrow's headlines would read ENGLISH WOMAN MAKES DARING ESCAPE FROM KIDNAPPERS: FULL STORY, PAGE 5. By which time I would be reunited with my beloved husband and son . . .

'You eat!'

I jerked my head up sharply. Marvin stood over me, his frame occluding the sun and casting a long shadow. His hands were proffering to me the makeshift beaker of sweet tea and the packet of revolting Encore biscuits.

It was probably a fortunate thing that he had propelled me back to reality – to the fact that, far from hastening away from the scene, I hadn't even got to my feet. I accepted the unappetising offerings, much more concerned by how quickly and deceptively my imagination had raced away from me.

I spent the rest of the day brooding over my escape plan, realising the chance was lost and that, in any case, I had no idea where I would go, or whether the effort might not expose me to even greater danger. It was such a struggle to rationalise what was happening to me while I felt myself to be on the edge of existence, unsure what the next day or hour or minute would hold – whether, even, it could be my last. The grim feeling persisted that the only way out of this nightmare was one that would, in time, be dictated to me.

*

Around dusk my attentiveness had waned, for when Marvin and the Navigator began to dismantle the camp – packing things away, folding up tarpaulin, carting items down the incline to where the boat was moored – I realised that Money and the Leader were nowhere to be seen. Marvin approached me, pulled down the sheet that had hung over my head, and folded it up. The procedure was swift and silent and soon it had erased any sign that we had been there.

My stomach began to churn: something, clearly, was going to happen but I'd no idea what. The Navigator came up to me.

'We move.'

'Where are we going?'

He gave no reply other than 'Come now.'

My best guess had been that we would get back in the boat, so I was surprised when we began to walk in the opposite direction towards open grassland. I followed, stumbling and tripping over the uneven ground, the grass coarse against my bare feet. Marvin, again, gave me his sandals. He and the Navigator were laden with bulging black bags, blankets, and provisions.

As we trudged along I found my mind returning to the long walk David and I had taken for pleasure less than a week earlier, up the Siria escarpment. It was a memory so fresh and fond that I wished I could reach out and touch it, return to it, relive it. Instead I was trekking through darkness to a destination unknown, blindly following the footsteps of hostile and hateful strangers.

We walked for maybe half an hour until we approached a wooded area where, once again, I was pressed under a shrub. It was a big rambling growth, with a dome like a blackberry shrub, its trunk and thick roots twisted round each other, and the ground underneath was quite soft, so that by carefully positioning myself I could get comfortable. But I was left there, and couldn't see my captors. I recoiled to see a huge centipede, as thick as my middle finger, crawling down a branch towards me. The Navigator must have heard my gasp of surprise because he pushed through the shrubbery, gently removed the insect onto a stick and whisked it away.

Eventually I was brought the first food I'd had in two days. I couldn't tell how they'd prepared it, but it was dollops of rice, steaming hot, in the bottom half of a plastic Castrol GTX container. Marvin showed me a tin of tuna with an enquiring look on his face. When I nodded he dumped the contents out onto the rice and tossed the tin aside, like the rubbish I'd seen earlier.

I ate tiny bits with my fingers – the rice tasted awful, petroleum-flavoured, inevitably. But I knew that I had to eat, and to try not to be sick. They were eating too, forming rice into balls with their fingers and pushing these into their mouths. I tried to imitate the style, without success, and they laughed. Then the Navigator, wordlessly, took the machete, hacked a shard of yellow plastic from an oil container and fashioned a kind of spoon for me. It was a prisoner's meal, for sure, but I took some reassurance in knowing after all that it wasn't their plan to starve me.

*

I slept awhile. When I was shaken awake it was dark, the moon was out and I was beckoned from the shrub by torchlight. Marvin and the Navigator were loaded up once more with bags, and clearly we were on the move again. I was filled with foreboding. Marvin held on to the sleeve of my jacket and guided me through the bush, down a shallow dip, over a grassy plain and up the other side. The stars in the night sky were vividly bright: I could see the hazy glowing arc of the Milky Way, and pick out the seven stars of the Plough. I felt a pang in my heart to think that David, were he with me, could have named all the various constellations. He had learned to navigate by the stars as a Sea Cadet, the same knowledge that got him through his Outward Bound course in the Luangwa Valley, Zambia.

We walked on through long, dry grass, me struggling in the dark to make out what lay before us beyond the shapes of trees. Marvin was trying to hurry me, tugging me, but I struggled. I was conscious that we were moving down a slope, and then we made a definite turn and came over a headland – all this in utter silence, no one speaking a word.

Down below us I could see a horseshoe bay and houses, faintly lit, dotted around the shoreline. It was civilisation of a sort, and I wondered whether this was the place they had come to procure their food and water.

We got onto a pathway heading down, which led us past a house – a small single-storey structure with two little windows shedding yellowish light. The thought of people inside, so close to us now, was so strong that I had a sudden impulse to do something, to shout out for help. Marvin clearly read this, for he looked hard at me, made the cut-throat gesture with his index finger straight across his neck, then pressed the finger to his lips. The message was unmistakable, and menacing. I put my head down and pressed on. We continued on the track at a steady pace, onto softer sand and down to the shoreline. I began to feel my feet sinking into what felt like wet, spongy seaweed, the cuffs of my pyjama bottoms getting soggy again. The Navigator had moved on ahead and I couldn't see where he was going, the darkness just enveloped him. Then Marvin dropped sharply to a crouching position and pulled me with him, holding onto me tightly. We stayed like that, in silence, for fifteen long minutes.

Something in me was sick at heart to see the lights in the little houses dotted round the bay – the evidence of other lives, of ordinary people going about their daily business, oblivious to the stranger in their midst. I thought of families who perhaps had just put their children to bed, of women sewing or cooking, safe and assured in the ordinary world. And here was I in the dark outside, a hostage, crouched and shivering, waiting for god knows what.

I made out the shape of a boat slipping silently into view, and then three torch flashes in quick succession, blink–blink–blink. That was the awaited signal, for Marvin hauled me up and led me into the shallow water. I could see the Navigator ahead. Then Marvin beckoned me to climb onto his back and bore me in this way up to the skiff. It was clear to me now: Leader and Money must have sailed the boat around to this cove earlier in the day, then most likely waited under cover of darkness for Marvin and the Navigator to bring me here at an appointed hour.

I was manhandled back aboard. Money was manning the rudder, the Leader in his customary place at the prow. As ever I hated the sight of him, the silent keeper of whatever was the plan for me. Where were we going now? The engine was started and we lurched off and away out to sea.

6

For a time in the darkness it had seemed as though we were just ploughing the open waters of the ocean, with no land in sight anywhere – until I became aware of coastline, on my left and perhaps half a mile away in the distance. Gradually I could make out the lights of a large coastal town – bright, numerous, and uniform, like a string of street lamps running along a promenade. I turned to the Navigator (who had, of course, now handed navigating duties on to Money).

'Those lights, where is that?'

'Malindi,' he replied.

I knew that Malindi was on the Kenyan coast. But had we really turned round and headed back into Kenyan waters? I didn't know what to believe, but the idea was exciting. We passed by the town's lights and ploughed on. I was sitting up amid my captors, but only because I had flatly refused to remain hidden on the sodden mattress under the usual coverings, since the combination of the skiff's breakneck speed and the pervasive stink of petrol had left me nauseated and battered about on the floor of the boat. My protest had earned me a seat on a yellow container, but there was little relief from the boat's turbulent progress, and the pain and nausea persisted.

We travelled through the night. I wearied, my head began to droop, yet I was doggedly determined to hold on to some sense of where we were going.

As dawn light broke we were sailing at a gentler pace on a calmer sea, and the coastline in the distance had changed to one of pristine white-sand beaches, completely deserted. If this had been Kenya, I was almost sure we would have seen sun beds and swimmers.

The boat began to slow, and I saw ahead of us a bizarre sight: an oil tanker, run aground on a sandbank in shallow water, its hull rusted, its prow jutting out into the sea, evidently abandoned to its fate. It leaned slightly to the right, water lapping its sides. Money cut the engine and we drifted to a standstill, in line with the tanker. Again I had to consult the Navigator.

'Why are we stopping?'

He pointed a bony finger to the sky. 'Planes.'

He seemed anxious. I, of course, was inwardly encouraged.

'What sort of planes?'

'Al-Shabaab.'

His tone implied that 'al-Shabaab' was a thing to be feared and avoided, but I was none the wiser.

'How long are we going to be here?'

'Until night. Then, tomorrow? We take you to Mombasa. You meet David, in the Blue Room Hotel? You've heard of it?'

I shook my head, comprehending nothing, but lifted by a sudden tide of euphoria. It was just as I hoped. This horror was going to be over; the end was suddenly in sight. I was going to see David. He must have sorted everything out, just as I'd known he would.

I couldn't keep my imagination at bay, thinking now about this 'Blue Room Hotel', how I would be conveyed there, how the 'drop' or handover would be arranged. Whatever the logistics, I saw myself walking free, and I saw David coming towards me, arms wide, our reunion, the joy of that – strong enough, I knew, to erase everything I'd been put through.

*

The joyful prospect, though, couldn't counteract the physical effect on me of having sailed through the night, thirsty and unfed in filthy conditions. This had exacted a toll and, as we sat bobbing under the heat of the day I was gripped by seasickness. I had to retch repeatedly over the side of the boat. My captors looked on, scornful, displeased. There was nothing I could do: my stomach churned, my throat began to burn with the constant bringing up of bile.

As the morning wore on, in our stationary, unshaded position the sun's heat grew more fierce. I was still in my heavy jacket, two pairs of wet trousers adhered to my body, unbearably clammy and itchy. My head throbbing, my back aching, I didn't know how much more discomfort I could tolerate. The thought of David was the one solace.

My captors had resumed their sleep rota, but the Leader was alert and muttering into his mobile phone. I had a bottle of water from which I took small sips. They didn't seem to drink a drop, as if they had trained their bodies out of the need. I'd begun to feel some control over my innards once more when all of a sudden I was seized by the neck from behind, pushed down on top of the canisters and a tarpaulin thrown over me. Stunned, I tried to stand, only to fall against the side of the boat, head first, reopening the cut I had sustained on the first night. I felt blood trickle down my temple again. Then the tarpaulin was back over me.

I guessed they had heard a plane overhead. But their aggression towards me – as though I were an object, with a price on my head but disposable none the less – made me newly afraid. I tried to keep calm, swallow my indignation. I was on the brink of tears but I fought them. *Keep it together*, I urged myself. *Tomorrow night you could be with David. This will be over. You have to hang on until then.*

After a while I knew I just couldn't endure another bout of being covered on the floor of the boat – not the sickening motion nor the clammy heat nor the foul commingled smells. Slowly I pushed my head out from under the tarpaulin and retched over the side of the boat. Some of what I brought up spattered back in my face and down my clothes as a result of the boat's ceaseless bobbing. The indignity of it was total, and yet by now I was past caring. I just felt that physically things could not get any worse. And so I looked to the Navigator. 'Me sit now,' I croaked.

He and the Leader conferred, and with a nod of the head I was permitted to sit up again. I saw we had drifted a little from the tanker. Money slept in a foetal curl by the engine. Mercifully my stomach began to settle, and when the gang shared a big flat piece of unleavened bread between them and offered me a small chunk I accepted and ate it, knowing it was probably all I would get before we reached Mombasa.

Gradually I was aware of the sun sinking and the heat going out of the day. I started to let myself feel the thrilling prospect of release. The Leader had made phone calls constantly but now his phone rang. He had a quick conversation and at last we began to move again, albeit slowly. As it got darker the engine roared back to life and we set off, hugging the coastline. What followed, though, was a succession of intermittent stops, and at each of them the Leader would have an anxious phone conversation before we could resume. By the second such occasion I was fairly sure they were hunting for a specific place at which to bring the boat ashore, but were having great difficulty finding it. After each stop and phone call, our progress was slow, seemingly cautious, the gang scanning the shoreline with fretful eyes – obviously looking for a landmark or beacon of some sort. The procedure came to consume hours. *They're lost*, I thought. And the worst of it was that for the first time since my ordeal began, I had a measure of hopefulness over where we could be heading.

*

The 'beacon', when it presented itself, turned out to be the flashing headlamps of a four-wheel-drive car, parked up on a headland over a cove and facing full out to sea. Satisfied at last, my captors sailed us into the shallows of the cove and cut the engine. Money hopped from the boat and began to pull it by the prow towards shore. Marvin helped me out into warmish water. The moon was bright and up ahead I saw the driver-side door of the car open. A tall, slender, smartly dressed man climbed out. The Leader had splashed out of the skiff and strode directly up the shore towards this driver, who came down the incline onto the beach to greet him.

I was struggling to recover my land legs and needed to answer the call of nature. With niceties long since made redundant, I just squatted in the water to pee. The gang left me to it, and I was able to observe how they were greeted by the driver – warmly in the case of the Leader, stiffly in the case of Marvin, who then trooped back with a pair of yellow rubber flip-flops meant for me, HAPPY NEW YEAR printed on their insoles.

Marvin led me on an awkward scramble up the incline to the waiting car, a big beige Compact SUV. There I was pushed into the middle of the back seat, and for a moment I felt oddly un-comfortable to be dripping wet inside a dry vehicle that had sheepskin-covered seats. Still, I was sitting in relative luxury after hours spent perched atop a petrol canister.

I noticed an elderly man, tall and lean, in the passenger seat. He didn't give me so much as a glance. The dashboard, I saw, was covered in the same sheepskin as the car seats, and a clock set in the dash read 11:30. The driver climbed in: straight away I smelled aftershave, and the view from close quarters confirmed that he was well dressed, clean-shaven, like a young businessman in pressed trousers and open-necked short-sleeved shirt, the rectangle of a phone visible in his top pocket. Marvin got into the car at my right, the Leader at my left, both toting their AK47s, and the engine was started. I looked back out through the rear window to the cove, but the skiff had vanished from view; and since Money and the Navigator were no longer with us, I had to assume they were continuing their journey by water.

We drove off at high speed, over sand dunes that caused the vehicle to bounce madly up and down. I was jostled between my captors, thrown from side to side, at one point bashing my head on the roof.

'Can you bloody well *slow down?*' I shouted at the Driver.

He only laughed. However reckless his speed he seemed highly alert. But when the car jumped right over the crest of one dune and landed with a jarring thump I really believed we were going to have an accident. I was as frightened as I'd felt up to this point in my ordeal.

Finally we got off sand and now the headlights illuminated through the pitch darkness a path that appeared to be strewn with shrubs and boulders. The Driver made some sharp turns of the wheel so as to hurtle by them, throwing us all around a bit more in the process. I was holding on tenaciously to just one thought: Mombasa, meaning David. My whole being was clenched in the hope that where we were headed was this 'Blue Room Hotel' the Navigator had promised. Still it began to concern me that out of the car window I kept seeing the same things, shrubs, bushes, as if we were travelling haphazardly, without direction – or, worse, round in circles.

But nothing seemed to bother the Driver and the Leader, who bantered easily with one another between front and back seat. The car stereo was turned on to Arabic music, loud enough to sound blaring even to my ears. The Passenger flew into a kind of seated dance, his arms flailing around as he wailed along to the music. Once again, the menace of my situation was taking on an edge of derangement.

It came as a mild relief when I saw that the terrain had turned to a harder track stretching out with visible tyre marks ahead in the light of the SUV's high beams. After a while I was aware that Marvin and the Leader had nodded off to sleep. They had relaxed their grip on the guns, which now pressed hard into my legs, barrels pointing up. The Passenger pushed his seat back, clearly ready to sleep too. Crushed in the middle of the back, my feet astride the central ridge, legs aching, I knew that I wouldn't be getting any sleep for myself. And indeed I stayed awake through this horrible journey in near-total darkness.

*

The car's clock read 05:00 and, though the flat desert landscape all around us was darkened still, there was a coral-orange glow on the horizon that signalled the dawn. The Driver brought us to a halt, and my captors climbed out and commenced the ritual of their morning prayer as the sun struggled up. While they indulged their pieties, I got out of the car only to relieve my bladder. The terrain surrounding us had a stark, forbidding form of beauty. The air was cool and the view, for miles on all sides, was of a kind I had never seen.

But my hopes of being reunited with David in Mombasa had begun to feel thin, deluded, supplanted in my head by a slow-growing fear that some new and awful unknown was about to be visited on me. Whatever the Navigator had said, whatever his intentions, how could I depend on a promise passed down from what, clearly, was a band of unscrupulous money-hungry crooks? My welfare meant nothing to them other than to the degree that it affected my exchange value. I began to feel terribly small, insignificant, alone, as I'd never felt before – desperate to be redeemed from this.

When our journey recommenced, and we came out of desert into scrubland, part of me still looked out of the window in vain for any sign of coast or sea that would suggest Mombasa. But the only sights to see – intermittently, amid the far-reaching aridity of the landscape – were sights that spoke of the desert. At first I thought I was experiencing a mirage when, in the distance, I saw a camel train – a lone herder leading one tethered camel and, behind them, maybe fifty more. But it was real, and bizarrely breathtaking. Then, as if from nowhere, there came into view a house made out of branches and tarpaulin, rounded like a dome. A man stood outside, and he waved to us as we sped past. Later, no less surreal in my eyes, we drove by a set of dormitory-like buildings, concrete, long and single-storey with corrugated-iron roofs, surrounded by high chain-link fencing. Three children came up to the fence, and held on to it as they watched us speed off.

After that, the terrain became tough once again, until we latched onto a well-defined dirt track. I saw a huge black-and-white four-wheel-drive approaching from the other direction, and Marvin and the Leader exchanged looks, glancing too at their rifles. I let myself imagine this car would be my rescuer, who had been tracking us since we came on land, ready now to make an arrest . . . But when our car veered aside the other vehicle sped by.

It wasn't long before another car was heading our way – a beige Toyota Land Cruiser, no licence plate, two men in front – and this car pulled over, as did we. From out of the Land Cruiser came a corpulent and strikingly ugly man, poorly dressed, who lumbered towards us. A diminutive sidekick emerged from the passenger side and ran along at his heel.

Our Driver got out and went to shake the Fat Man's hand. In short order everyone but me was out and greeting one another with smiles and hardy handshakes. The Leader appeared especially relieved to me – cheerful, as if by this rendezvous he had accomplished something significant. I sat in the back seat, where I'd sat for six or seven hours, nonplussed, the confusion in my head much exacerbated by hunger, thirst and fatigue. I only wanted to know if these men would take me to David. Any other prospect was unthinkable.

Marvin came and beckoned me out of the car, his now usual role. My legs were jelly when I stood. Nothing was said. The Leader went to the back of the Fat Man's Toyota, Marvin shoved me in the same direction. The vehicle had little platform steps, and inside it was fragranced with the cloying smell of Parma violets. I was in the middle once again, flanked by Marvin and the Leader. And there was another man, big, wearing sunglasses, whom I somehow hadn't noticed until now – proof of my mental distraction, as he was clutching a huge machine-gun and had two ribbons of bullets across his chest.

Jesus Christ, this is serious, I thought. *Stay calm, if you can.*

Machine-Gun Man seemed to want as much distance from me as possible, but once the back doors were slammed we were all in a fearful crush, and that big gun was laid across our knees. The Fat Man took the wheel and we were off.

For these men what followed might have been a Sunday drive, chit-chat punctuated by laughter. I didn't look at anyone, feeling clueless and dismayed. But I had to know one thing, and I asked with no idea whether or not they would understand.

'Are we going to Mombasa . . . ?'

Marvin said something to the others and they all laughed. So, I had my answer. I think I had known in myself for a while that they responded to my sporadic queries with whatever they thought might shut me up and keep me usefully calm and compliant. But knowing this for sure now didn't help me with the brute truth that I had nothing else left I could rely on.

*

We drove on through country that became wooded, passing only one other car along the way. For a short while our route was obstructed by a pair of donkeys pulling carts piled high with firewood, until the Fat Man honked his horn. And we passed a lone round hut that seemed to have been constructed from branches and roofed by multi-coloured plastic bags. Such primitive conditions amid such a hostile environment filled me with cold foreboding.

In time a village came into view, on a plain surrounded by dunes and scrub brush. We entered, passing by a restaurant, a hairdresser's and a pharmacy on the way. The village was long – many houses, lots of donkeys, but also a surprising number of four-wheel-drive cars parked about too. The Toyota began to slow down and turned a corner. Before me loomed the big grey steel gates of some kind of compound, criss-crossing spikes on top, standing open onto a yard. We pressed on through this entrance, pulled up, and the gates of my new prison closed immediately behind us.

7

Within those metal gates the first sensations to strike me were of searing heat and hard light bouncing off the thick stone walls of the enclosed yard. As many as fifteen men were thronging around the Fat Man's car, all with shouldered rifles, all staring at me. I climbed out, dazed and scared. I had the sense these men had been expecting us – without knowing truly *what* to expect. And now they saw me, lurching from the Toyota, a slight woman in an oversized man's coat, looking filthy, bedraggled, bloodied. They appeared to be every bit as puzzled by their new captive as I was wary of them.

The ground under my feet in the yard was sandy. The compound walls were plastered all around with some rough render. The wall facing me had obviously had a window in it at some point but the gap had been crudely plugged with rocks. As I was escorted around the Toyota I saw in the right-hand corner of the yard a sort of terrace with a sloping roof of corrugated iron, four doorways indicating rooms all in a row. This terrace had a covered walkway and a low wall of breezeblocks in front of it. The Fat Man, the Leader and their associates headed directly for the room at the far right of the terrace. Marvin pulled me towards the opposite end, taking me up steps formed in the dirt by foot traffic, through the metal double-doors furthest to the left.

Within was a gloomy room, maybe fifteen feet square, with a high ceiling to which plastic sheets bearing an Arabic pattern in bright blue and yellow had been nailed up. Nailed drape curtains – creamy and golden in bands, held together where they joined by three plastic pegs, red, green and yellow – also masked the walls. There were no windows that I could see, and only a little natural light seeping in through breezeblocks set in the wall near the ceiling. On the floor was some coral-pink linoleum that didn't fit the space, stopping underneath the rudimentary base of a bed at one side. The bed was of a size suitable for a small child, made out of odd pieces of wood crudely hammered together. As I was peering about me Marvin left the room. For the first time in days I felt properly alone, free of constant scrutiny.

My mind reeled. I wasn't panicking but inside I felt a mob of emotions – fear, confusion, recrimination. The tale they had spun me of a reunion with David in Mombasa had, clearly, been an arrant lie. Given the arid landscape we'd driven through to reach this village I knew in my heart the most likely truth was what the Navigator had first told me on the boat: that we were in Somalia. My biggest worry was just how far inland I had been transported – and to where, exactly.

What could I possibly take now as a positive view on my plight? Evidently it was going to take longer that I had hoped to raise the money to free me – however much that was.

OK, I told myself, *you've been unharmed to this point – more or less. You can't do anything, can't go anywhere, can't speak to anybody. So keep your head, and see where this leads.*

I sat there for perhaps a quarter of an hour, pensive, realising only belatedly that I still had the hood of my borrowed jacket up. I was cursing myself for how completely I'd accepted their prohibition on this when Marvin reappeared in the doorway.

'You wash?' he asked.

'Yes, please,' I replied. 'Can I take this hood off?'

Inevitably he shook his head and indicated I follow him outside and down the covered walkway. A handful of men milled around, bristling with guns. We passed two rooms with closed doors, and a third with one of its two door panels open, then stopped at an outhouse-type structure with a curtain over its doorway. Marvin gestured for me to enter.

'No one come in,' he muttered, positioning himself to stand guard.

Inside was dark and cooler, thanks to the curtain. I saw before me a couple of piles of sandbags, a black bucket filled with water – cold to the touch – a stainless-steel cup, and a change of clothes. I had hoped, forlornly, for a shower. There was no soap, nor anything with which to dry myself, but I understood by now that beggars couldn't be choosers.

I undressed, gingerly, conscious once again of the livid extent of insect bites and scratches all round my body, even under my arms and breasts. Blood was smeared where I had scratched, and the abrasions were most painful at my waist where the waistband of the trousers had rubbed some of my skin raw. I rinsed myself down as best I could, though I felt stinging sensations where the wounds were deepest. It worried me, too, that the water might not be clean: another risk of infection. Still, the result was that I felt cleansed, to a degree, for the first time since I had been taken.

I rinsed my hair, too, then put on the clean clothes: an over-sized red-and-black floral dress that hung from my shoulders, a sarong, a pair of grey jersey shorts bearing a Mercedes Benz logo, and a headscarf – evidently the new means by which I was to save all these big men from the upsetting sight of my hair. The shorts, I saw, had a drawstring – and straight away I knew what to do with that. Carefully I transferred my wedding rings from where they had nestled on the string inside my utterly bedraggled pyjama bottoms, and I tied them up securely inside the shorts using a triple knot.

Outside again I saw a portable electrical generator parked between Room 4 of the terrace and this storeroom. Then Marvin pointed out the toilet block, next door to some more sandbags by the front gates. I peered inside at a hole in the ground, a narrow ledge round the walls crowded with shampoo bottles and cigarette packets, a crude beam with nails acting as a hanger. My presence stirred up a cloud of flies. Evidently I would be sharing this with twenty men. I could not suppress a shudder.

I was taken back to the room, past the shiftless men, and left to my own devices. I lowered myself to sit on the bed and felt it judder under my weight. Still, a bed was a bed, better than a floor – which, I could now see, had a whole assortment of little bugs marching across it. In truth, the room seemed better suited to insect life than human habitation – the unwelcome intruder, if anyone, was me. But by now I didn't feel so very averse to a few creepy-crawlies, as long as they weren't going to get too curious about me. After those days in the mangrove forest I'd grown reluctantly accustomed to the sensation of them crawling across my skin.

I could feel a sort of calm settle on me. But I was keen to collect my thoughts, use this time on my own to formulate a plan for how I was going to approach this new phase of my predicament.

I had to expect I would be held here until a ransom was paid for me. So I needed to gird myself, call on whatever resources I had to stay strong – mentally occupied, physically fit – until they released me. I would have to devise a structure, a 'routine' that could occupy my days, however many of them lay ahead.

This need was inherent in me: I had always been the sort of person who required order and structure in order to feel assured and on top of things. Here, I was painfully aware that I had not one iota of control over my circumstances. All of that had been stripped from me the minute I was wrenched away from Kiwayu, and the disempowerment was painful to me. So I felt I had to claw something back, reinstate a bit of self-autonomy some- how – even if only of a symbolic sort.

My routine would have to include exercise. David and I had always gone running and used the gym, both to stay fit and as a means of winding down. Was there a way for me, even in these cramped, dark, deprived conditions, to keep active? Mulling it over, I began to pace out the length and breadth of the room. And, curiously, just walking round the space of my confinement made me feel a little better, somehow.

It seemed to me I ought to have enough stamina to walk for about half an hour, every hour of the day. And with that, my decision was made: regular walks would be my main routine. I made a mental note to ask my captors for a watch. Any kind of routine had to run to a clock, and in any case I wanted to know the right time for as long as I was stuck here.

While I paced, I could hear men outside, talking, laughing. Eventually Marvin returned, bearing a small ladder, accompanied by a woman dressed in the full enveloping *jilbab* and *khimar*. She was short and round, and the aroma of cooking fat came with her. But her face, perfectly framed by the *khimar*, was pleasant and her demeanour friendly. She carried bed linen, a pillow and a mosquito net. Marvin scaled the ladder and tried to secure the net to a wooden baton by bashing a nail into place with a rock. It took him three attempts with three different-sized stones. The woman, meanwhile, made up the bed, chatting away in my direction all the while, as if I could understand her every word. For all that I was baffled, I found her affable presence welcome in the circumstances. Her *jilbab* was a nice grey-pink shade, shot through with silvery strands. 'Very pretty, what you're wearing,' I said to her, gesturing from head to toe. She appeared to appreciate the compliment.

Marvin then hefted in a cardboard box that was filled with a dozen small bottles of water. I spotted a label of origin: Bosaso.

'Bosaso, where is that?' I tried asking Marvin.

'Big town,' he muttered.

I was glad of the water, and quickly decided that the cardboard container could serve as a bedside table for me. I was also given a battery-powered lantern, which shed enough light round the room to see and, perhaps best of all, a purple bar of Lux soap.

Then they were gone and I was alone again. Surveying the habitat – with the mindset of someone resolved to 'get by' – I decided that if this was my prison for a while then it could have been a lot worse. It was rudimentary, airless, but not uncomfortable – relative luxury next to the thorny shrubs of the mangrove forest. If I had to serve some time in this place, I believed that I could do it.

My solitude was disturbed by one of the guards from the yard stepping into the room. But the man didn't say or do anything – he just loitered there for a bit, staring at me – then stepped out again. He was only the first of many who came in, apparently just to gawp at me, in the hours that followed. Some faces were friendly, others not. I wasn't intimidated, was careful to meet their gaze, even to force a smile – since I knew that, whatever I thought about them, it would be better if they formed a good opinion of me.

*

It had got dark outside when the woman in the *jilbab* returned, on her own. She came towards me, bearing in her hands something concealed by a red-and-white checked gingham cloth. At close quarters her face was open and wide, her skin beautifully unlined. I guessed she was maybe ten years younger than me. But I could also see that her hands were those of a woman who toils – the skin coarse, visibly worn by work.

She drew off the cloth to reveal a pair of samosas nestling in an aluminium bowl, exuding just-cooked warmth, smelling delicious. She put her finger to her lips and showed me a complicit smile – one woman to another, a gesture of surprising kindness. Was this an ally, someone I could trust? I accepted her gift gratefully, and after she hastened out of the room I devoured one of my two savoury treats, deciding to save the other for later.

From the bed I found myself studying those curtains around the walls. The pegs pinching them together had to be concealing something. The lantern picked out sequins sewn into the fabric that shimmered and glittered, making an incongruously pretty little light show. The silence was disturbed by a low ambient noise coming through the walls: my ears had detected it vaguely on a couple of occasions earlier. As I climbed under the bed sheet and nearer the wall, it became clearer still – one man's voice, a melodic wail, singing in sentences at variable pitches. I decided it had to be the *muezzin* of a mosque, sending out the call to prayer. His voice filled every corner of the room, despite my muted hearing. I was in a village, and if the local populace was half as devoted as the men who kidnapped me then I imagined they would be answering the call, wending their way to the mosque.

I was afraid to drop off to sleep, alone, in a place like this. I said to myself, mantra-like, 'This is temporary. It won't be too long. You're just going to have to get through it.' But I was so tired that I knew sleep would be a blessing. And eventually I succumbed.

*

I was woken before dawn by the return of the *muezzin*'s low persistent wailing, his lone muted voice like a mournful clarion. The smoky smell of burning wood was pervading the room from outside. Reluctantly I knew I needed the toilet and, creeping out, I was met by the surreal sight of more than a dozen men sleeping in their shroud-like blankets. Five were directly outside my door, others sprawled around the yard. In the grey early light they resembled casualties laid out in the grim aftermath of some battle or massacre.

Back in the room I dozed off again. When I stirred, sunlight was coming in from the gap in the ceiling and a young man, tall, maybe eighteen years old, was peering at me through the mosquito net.

'El-lohhh!' he said with the widest of smiles that showed off the whitest teeth, a perfect set of gnashers that would be the envy of a Beverly Hills dental clinic. He had brought me a thermos container, burgundy-coloured, with a screw top. Inside I found boiled potatoes, roughly diced.

My sheet was pulled up to my neck to preserve my modesty. He could see my hair but I thought, 'Really, what's the worst that could happen? He'll not be struck down dead.' The boy gave no indication of being bothered.

I nodded acknowledgement to the boy and he backed away and out. I had slept naked, and I knew I had to dress quickly and get my headscarf tied in place, or else risk incurring the wrath of the most pious among my kidnappers.

I pondered anew what should be the plan for my walking routine. Should I try to walk for an hour, say, then give myself an hour off? No, that was too arduous. Stepping about the room confirmed for me an impression I'd formed the day before, namely that there were lots of stones stuck underneath the linoleum, some of them quite big and sharp, making the floor uneven and awkward to negotiate. I resolved to clear a proper path, a 'flat track' for myself to walk around. Wherever I stepped on a stone I lifted up the lino and tried to wiggle it out.

My breakfast had been an austere dish but I soon saw that my captors would be on better rations. Through the door I noticed a woman enter the compound – tall, statuesque, beautiful, in *jilbab* and *khimar*, *de rigueur*. She brought food up to and under the breezeblock wall, flasks of tea, stainless-steel dishes with lids on, plates piled with unleavened breads. Three of the guards took charge of removing the lids from steaming hot food, and began to eat. Two of these men had been sleeping directly outside my door – one a heavy-set, heavily bearded man with bloodshot eyes who ate with particular gusto; another a rather loud, vain, self-admiring fellow with very white teeth and a goatee. The third, chunky and bearded, wore a Bedouin-style *kufiya* draped over his head. They seemed to form some sort of senior Triumvirate: Hungry Man, Vain Man, Kufiya Man.

I got the feeling that some of them knew each other from before, were friendly with each other, at ease. Certainly this Triumvirate and the Leader had a clannish look to them.

Gradually other guards, aware that the first meal of the day was served, joined the Triumvirate and scooped food from the steel dishes with their hands. They ate messily – but if I didn't think much of their table manners, I certainly envied their menu.

*

That night, after dark, I was visited by a delegation of sorts. It was led by Fat Man and his Sidekick from the car that had brought me here. The Leader and Vain Man were present but the principal figure in the party was a new face to me: a small, trim man, smartly dressed and neat in appearance, his goatee carefully tended, a whiff of cologne about him.

At his back some of the compound guards were trying to push their way into the room too. The men always took their shoes off on entering the room, as if it were a mosque. This was meaningful.

Then Fat Man thrust out a pudgy arm in the way of a barrier and glared at them, whereupon they got into a kind of line. I had thought of Fat Man as nothing more than a driver: now I realised he exercised some sort of control over the compound guards. He adopted a stance, leaning against the wall and looking over his right shoulder at me. He had a slight squint in his left eye, and big protruding teeth, his head somehow disproportionate to his girth, which was concealed by a big tent-shaped shirt.

The real authority, though, seemed to issue from the new man, who gestured and muttered something, whereupon two plastic picnic chairs, one green, one blue, were carried into the narrow room (albeit with some difficulty), followed by a table that bore the same yellow-blue Arabic motif as the cover on my ceiling. It was a very narrow space, so in order to carry in the plastic picnic chairs they had to open both doors to make leeway.

The new man beckoned me to sit facing him at the table, and then dropped a packet of white napkins and a toothbrush and toothpaste onto the table top. I accepted these provisions with a nod, instantly looking forward to brushing my teeth. The man, meanwhile, produced an exercise book and opened it.

'Do you know where you are?' he said, in clear English.

'Africa, somewhere. I was in Kenya . . .'

'Now you are in Somalia. West Africa.'

This detail confused me. 'Somalia's *East* Africa, isn't it?'

'East, West, pah …' He gestured as if to say it was neither here or there. 'Do you know who these men are behind me?'

'Well, no, of course I don't.'

'They are Somali pirates.' He seemed to study my face for a reaction. 'You are very lucky. Somali pirates, they don't kill people, don't torture people. They just want money. That's why they took you. When they get money you will go home.'

I nodded my understanding, silently glad of this clear stress on my remaining unharmed. The man took out a pen from his shirt pocket.

'Now, we need information from you. To contact your family, to get money.'

'Well, I can tell you, you won't get any money from my family, they haven't got money to give. But you can contact my husband, David.'

'What is his mobile phone number?'

'I've said this before – I can't remember his number. But it's pointless anyway, my husband hasn't got his phone with him. If you phone Kiwayu Safari Village you can speak to him. The only phone he's got is my phone. And no, I don't remember that number either.'

The man looked irritated. 'Why have you not got your phone?'

I felt an annoyance of my own. This fellow didn't seem quite as smart as his manner endeavoured to project. 'Because I was dragged out of my bed and onto a boat in the middle of the night by men with rifles. So I didn't have time to pick up my phone.'

He shook his head and sighed. 'OK. That is our problem.'

'Yeah, it *is* your problem.'

'How many people in your family?'

'There's my husband, and we have a son.'

'What is your son's phone number?'

Again I was blank. 'I – I'm really sorry, I can't remember that either.'

Scorn reappeared on the man's face. 'You can't remember your husband's number, your son's . . . ?' He tossed his pen at me in seeming disgust. 'You can't love your husband, or your son, if you can't even – '

I didn't let him finish, because outright fury had boiled up in me. 'Don't you tell me I don't love my husband. I've been with him thirty-three years – I love him. And I love my son. Loving someone has nothing to do with remembering a phone number.'

Livid, I snatched up the pen, minded to throw it back in his face. But I caught myself. *Be calm, be in control, keep above it all.* Slowly, then, I pushed the pen across the table to him. I could tell the other men in the room had been struck by my raised voice: they shuffled somewhat, exchanged glances, looking in particular to the Leader. But this man had really incensed me. I glared at him, unabashed.

'OK,' he said. 'But I have to contact *someone* – speak to them to tell them you are here, and will be here until money is paid. So I need to ask you questions.'

I nodded. In my own way I was as keen as him to move this process forward – the swifter the better. He asked me to confirm my name, how many brothers and sisters I had. I told him.

'And your parents, are they alive?'

'My mother's alive, but she is ninety years old. And I don't want you contacting her, because that will give her a heart attack. Understand? You can't do that. It's my husband who you need to contact.'

'Your husband's work, what does he do?'

I took a moment's thought before answering – worried that to tell them David was the 'Finance Director' of a respected publisher might pump up their estimation of what price to put on my head. Whatever I said needed to have the effect of deflating expectations.

'He helps to make books. Books, that you read?' I added since the man seemed first to frown.

'How big is your house?' he asked.

'We have what's called a semi-detached house? Which is like only half of a house?'

'How many cars do you have?'

'One car.'

'Just one. And just one child . . .' He shook his head. 'That's bad, that's very bad . . .'

Again his attitude stuck in my craw. 'What do you mean, "very bad"? I don't know what you think is normal, but some women can only have one child, and I am one of those women. And I'm really grateful. I was very lucky to have my boy.'

'Yeah, well, at least you had a boy, that was lucky, yes.'

I had begun to feel exasperated – stuck in this jerry-built holding cell somewhere in Somalia, while this self-important man shared his backward moral view of the world with me.

'How old your boy?'

'He's twenty-five.'

'He has a job?'

'Is that relevant? No, he hasn't got a job,' I lied.

'What about you? You work?'

Again I balked slightly, not wanting to paint them a rosy picture of a well-heeled three-salary household. Still, I did intend to let him know who I was.

'I work in a hospital.'

[87]

'Hospital?'

'Yes, a psychiatric hospital. I work with women who are very unwell.'

He grimaced. 'Women who have, uh . . . sick heeds?'

'Heads.' I shrugged and nodded. He seemed at first to recoil from this detail. He turned and muttered something to the others, which earned me another grim stare from Fat Man. But then, nonplussed, he wrote the detail down carefully in his book beneath all the other information. And with that, he seemed to be done.

'OK, you should get a good night's sleep. Tomorrow we do a video, then negotiation start. I help them get money for you.'

'Is that what you do? You're the negotiator?'

'That's right. Negotiator. I'm not a pirate. Tomorrow I come and we video you.'

'Where will you send that video?'

He sighed. I got the impression he didn't care for my asking questions. 'We send it so your family can see it.'

'Well, like I've said, don't send it to my mother. And there's something else you need to know. It's my mother's birthday in two weeks' time. We have a big celebration, all my family get together? I have to be there. I have to be out of here in two weeks' time.'

I was serious and I wanted him to know as much. Did he care? I doubted it. He rose from the chair and walked out. The others trooped off after him.

Alone, I assessed the situation: some kind of a video message sent back to the UK would be progress, I supposed. David would see it, and if 'negotiation start' then there would be clarity at last. I couldn't guess how long it would take, but the process would be apparent to all. I assumed David would stay in Africa for as long as it took to secure my freedom, and that Ollie would want to come out to join him.

I undressed, got into bed, tucked the mosquito net all around, and reflected on the evening's exchanges.

Perhaps I had been a bit over-combative with this Negotiator, given how important he was obviously going to be to my getting free. But then he didn't seem the easiest fellow to rub along with.

Evidently he had found the idea of women with 'sick heeds' to be strange and unsettling, if not outright distasteful. Did he think that Somalis were somehow immune to mental health problems? Or could there be a sort of taboo here that prevented such illnesses from being recognised and properly treated? I knew well enough that even in Britain a sort of stigma still attaches to anyone who is classified 'sick in the head', that they can be dismissed – 'half a person' at best – to be feared and ostracised because they simply aren't comprehensible to the rest of us. And from the little I had gleaned of the status of females in Somali society, I had the feeling that any woman suffering from mental health problems here might not receive a massive amount of compassion or understanding.

At any rate, the Negotiator hadn't thought much of what I did for a living – plainly he was more interested in impressing his own importance on me, the fact that he was no mere 'pirate'. I didn't much care. I knew that my job had armed me with a quite particular set of transferable skills. For a start I had learned how to 'read' people's personality traits from their smallest behaviours, to observe them when they didn't know they were being observed. I could usually tell when I was being lied to (or being told what the person imagined I wanted to hear). I had developed quite deep reserves of patience, and a pretty good facility for building rapport with people who might look 'difficult' or intimidating to the rest of us.

Above all, my training in social work had prepared for me for situations that were awkward, uncomfortable, scary, even down-right dangerous. I knew how to handle people from whom others might recoil. And if nothing in my past could have prepared me fully for this current predicament . . . still, it crossed my mind that certain aspects of my professional training could be a kind of salvation to me now.

8

Like a lot of people I found the path to my vocation in life by a bit of serendipity. In 1989 David and I were living in Andover, Hampshire. Ollie was three years old, settled in at nursery, and I was looking for a way to make myself feel useful again. I began to volunteer locally at Enham Alamein, a well-known residential centre for people with physical disabilities, founded originally as a place of rehabilitation for badly wounded servicemen. In December 1992 our little family upped sticks to Bishop's Stortford, but there I kept up my volunteering, helping out at a local multipurpose day centre for people with learning difficulties as well as physical impairments. I picked up a range of handy skills, from Makaton to driving a big tail-lift bus. I also encountered people who were struggling with a variety of difficult clinical conditions. For three years I worked with a man who had Asperger's syndrome. He could become aggressive quickly, but I seemed to be able to defuse his tempers just by being patient with him, talking him back round.

One night I mentioned to David that I had begun to feel just about as competent as a professional social worker, that I could probably do the job. His response, quite seriously, was: 'Why don't you?' My instinctive reply was to bring up all the possible obstacles to such a plan, not least among them the time that I'd have to spend getting qualified. 'None of that matters,' he said. 'You should do it. Go for it.' So I did. And David's support for me remained every bit as staunch as his initial and crucial encouragement.

I got my diploma in social work and chose to specialise in Mental Health. I had the benefit of a really excellent mentor or 'practice teacher': a smart, tough woman who had seen a lot of demanding patients and situations, and who impressed on me the importance of treating the people I would deal with as individuals, always respectfully, and without passing judgement on them, since they simply couldn't be held to the same account as those of us who aren't afflicted by these desperate conditions. I was to accept them for who they were, and to remember that we are all, to some degree, the products of our upbringing and environment.

My mentor had on several occasions been attacked by patients, and I came to view physical threat as something one would be lucky to avoid in a career of this kind. I had training in specific techniques for 'de-escalating' situations of potential violence, and I soon learned how to anticipate trouble. More than once, visiting someone in his or her own home, I found my intuition telling me, 'I need to get out of here . . .' However, to do the job you have to be prepared to confront and manage people who are disturbed and in distress. Lashing out, verbally or physically, might be the only thing they know how to do when they are confined to a hospital, frightened, confused, desperate to be free. The easiest option for an institution in such cases would be to have three big male orderlies fall on top of the patient and restrain him or her. But nothing is ever truly solved or made better that way. One has to try to build communication and trust – however long that takes, and however much one's nerves are strained in the process.

*

In my first social work job – with an Assertive Outreach Team for people in the community needing focused support – I met Jason, a nineteen-year-old with a serious anti-social personality disorder. He was from a comfortable middle-class home but had always been 'a handful' for his parents, who could never control his tempers and came to realise they were dealing with something far worse than mere 'naughtiness'. Jason was capable of startling violence at home. He made his parents' life hell, and at their imploring I found him a place to live, in a flat within a managed group home. He was a complex young man, but I had a reasonable rapport with him. He was someone for whom you had to get the medication exactly right, in which case he was certainly manageable.

But late one afternoon I got a call from Maggie, the group home manager: Jason was causing a disturbance, playing music loud. Could I please come and help? I wasn't in a position to refuse, so I got a message to David that I would be home late that night.

On arrival I went with Maggie to Jason's flat and immediately it was clear to me that he was unmanageable, and hadn't taken his medication. He then admitted as much. Any one of a number of things might have upset him in the first place, but I knew we had to get him to a hospital doctor, and that it was my job, using the rapport he and I had established, to make him see both that I was concerned for him and that going to hospital was in his best interest. 'I can see something's bothering you, Jason,' I told him. 'This is not the "you" that I know. Maybe we should go get you checked out, get yourself back on track . . .? What do you think?'

At first he seemed to comply. Knowing him to be fussy about his appearance, I was encouraging him to get his overnight bag packed with all his sundry toiletries and hair gels. At which point he pulled a knife on me.

I felt a cold flush go through me, but at the same time I heard an inner directive: *Keep calm. Think.*

'Come on, Jason. This is not you. Let's talk . . .'

Maggie's reaction, though, was to inch towards the door, offering to go and make all three of us 'a nice cup of tea'. I felt this was a cop-out and I was angry with her, but I couldn't let that show in my voice as I continued to try to talk Jason round. Sure enough, Maggie exited, leaving me in the small flat with Jason and the knife. I knew that screaming and shouting were no good. Nothing could be gained by hysterics. But there was no room for error either. I had to be 'in the moment' and try a lot of calm, careful persuasion.

'I know you're angry, Jason, but we have to talk. You're eloquent, you can tell me how you're feeling. You don't need a knife. You don't want to use it. Why not put it down . . .?'

He took to pacing up and down the room, muttering to himself, still resolutely clutching the blade. As I sat there I kept on urging him that he was a good guy, that he had other options, things to look forward to – for instance, the possibility of moving to another flat that he liked better, an option that could very well be jeopardised if he were to stab me.

Two agonising hours ticked by before Jason abruptly walked past me towards his kitchen and, in doing so, set the knife down on the side of my chair. I took it and darted to the door where I found Maggie waiting for me, and told her pretty sharply to get on the telephone. In orderly fashion I helped Jason collect his things and got him into an ambulance and away. Afterwards, I was a wreck. I got home to David at 10.30 p.m., and he had a glass of wine waiting for me. 'You want to talk about it . . .?' he asked calmly. He was brilliant – just as on the many other occasions when my working days, if not always blighted by the threat of violence, none the less quite often called for tense and exhausting levels of concentration.

*

I was ready for a new challenge when in 2004 I went to work at the women's ward of Kneesworth House Hospital in Bassingbourn: something of a place of last resort for women with difficult conditions who couldn't be supported elsewhere. Kneesworth was a medium-secure unit and the twenty-two women there had all been 'through the system', usually culminating in court appearances and rulings that their problems would be best addressed by care, treatment and secure rehabilitation.

The women I worked with were profoundly unwell. Some of the most challenging cases, inevitably, were women with schizophrenia. There will probably always be a proportion of the public that views people with schizophrenia as dangerously unhinged potential murderers, which is simply not the case. Danger to the public must always be weighed up with great care, but thousands of people can live with the condition in the community, so long as they are managed well. At Kneesworth we helped to get women back into their communities and to disburden them of the long-term stigma of being outcasts from society. But, of course, the consideration of whether these patients can make such a return safely depends on a number of factors.

Anna was a patient who, some years previously, had made a violent assault on a family member. I worked with her very tentatively, meeting her on a daily basis. For a year she kept her distance from me. Then I was advised by a nurse that Anna was suffering from a fixed delusion that I had somehow wronged her, and she might pose a physical threat to me. Anna eventually told me as much: 'Don't think I don't know about you. I'll take your eyes out.' And so I had to be on guard around her. The system was that whenever I went 'on ward' I rang ahead, and would be escorted to the nurse's office. One day I called and found the line engaged and decided, fatefully, to risk it.

I let myself onto the ward with keys, came through, rang the doorbell. The nurses in the office saw me and waved. I waved back. Then Anna appeared from around a corner, shot me a look, and I knew I was in trouble. She disappeared from sight and while I was hastily looking for routes of escape Anna strode up and set upon me with scissors, stabbing at my head. She got in two or three connecting blows before I was able to grab her, shout at her, 'Anna, no! You don't want to do this.' Then the nursing staff appeared and fell on her, hauling her away to a secure room. All the other patients flocked to my side. 'I'm fine,' I assured them, as blood trickled down my head. Then I was taken to hospital.

David got a phone call at work from one of my colleagues: 'Now, it's nothing to worry about, but Judith's been attacked with a pair of scissors.' He made it to the hospital in double-quick time and was as brilliant as ever. But this was a different order of scare than we'd had before, and I was just as worried as he was.

My manager urged me to accept some trauma-counselling sessions, because I needed to get over the incident and get back to work. I was prepared to shrug it off, to work with Anna again. But after the attack on me Anna had to have one-on-one protection from the other patients, and eventually she was returned to the high-security facility from whence she had come.

Hearing this tale, some might shake their heads and consider it a sorry and hopeless case. But the real sadness is that only two months before she attacked me Anna had made a remarkable bit of progress.

Anna did not know that I had made contact with the family member she'd attacked, who still bore the scars yet harboured no ill will towards Anna. Anna, in turn, had expressed remorse to one of our nurses for what she had done, with terrible violence but in a moment of utter blinding paranoia. I treated it as a responsibility and a privilege whenever I met with the families of patients, and I had come to realise that I was quite often the first person a family had ever spoken to about their loved one's illness.

On the basis of these encouraging signs we were able to take Anna out of Kneesworth one day for a family visit. I found the experience heartbreaking. It gave you a glimpse of who this woman could have been, were it not for her awful illness. Some amends, at least, were made by that visit: it was a good day's work. But the minute Anna climbed back into our van – which represented hospital to her, confinement, two entire decades of her life – the veil descended, and she was lost to us again.

*

I believed in what could be achieved at Kneesworth and felt we worked hard to provide a worthwhile service. Our successes were relatively modest. We knew that not everyone was going to 'get better' but that some people could still make extraordinary improvements, even when they had been removed from society for so long. The difference could be as small as a patient who always sat in a corner and never looked at you one morning raising her eyes and saying, 'Hello.' Such processes can take months, years even, and they can represent giant steps for the individual out of a world of silence and confusion, fear and distrust; steps in a journey back to human society.

At our hospital we were just a small part of such journeys but it was our duty to do our work properly and professionally, to give the patients hope that they could get better. Because there is nothing as bad in life as to have no hope, to believe you have been defeated, and to give in to that. I wasn't prepared to countenance that fate for the women I worked with at Kneesworth. And now that I found myself in confinement, four thousand miles away under a hostile sky, I would not accept it for myself.

9

At dawn the *muezzin* performed his newly enhanced job of stirring me awake while calling the pious to prayer. Woodsmoke was in the air again; I knew the morning's fires were already ablaze outside. And suddenly it came to me why this smell was so familiar: I remembered it from my time in Chililabombwe, thirty-five years previously, when fires would be lit in the locality at the same early hour, the woodsmoke then threading its way through the trees and hanging in the air over the arboreal canopy . . .

Looking up groggily to the plastic ceiling I winced to see I had company. A little colony of insects – mainly cockroaches and bluebottle-like flies – had gathered at the top of my mosquito net, in spite of the efforts I'd made to tuck the mesh tight all around the bed before I slept. The bugs had still found a way to invade, but now they were trapped and entangled by the net. I hadn't the energy to unpick and expel the intruders; I just turned over, with a shudder, and managed to drift back to sleep awhile, for a couple of hours, until Smiley Boy entered with his customary 'El-lllllo!'

Onto the table left behind from the Negotiator's visit, Smiley Boy set down another dish of greyish potatoes – two large tablespoonfuls, peeled and cubed and boiled. I really hoped this wasn't going to be my everyday diet. The Boy took away my bowl from the previous night, but also set down a flask of hot water and a packet of loose-leaf tea. I gathered this was so I could make tea for myself; but I'd yet to develop a taste for the Somali version of tea, and couldn't see myself acquiring one any time soon.

I ate resignedly, knowing I had to take whatever sustenance was offered. As the sun rose some light crept through gaps in the decorative breezeblocks set high up in the wall, creating a lovely pattern that inched gradually down the opposite wall. Barring the *muezzin*'s contributions, this was the only gauge I had of the passage of time.

I slipped outside to use the toilet and saw that Hungry Man – one of that Triumvirate who seemed to be the 'sergeants' of the group – was awake and moving about. But the other pirates were asleep, around the compound and, I assumed, inside Rooms 2 and 3 of the terrace that seemed to comprise their 'mess'. The door of Room 4, which I had taken for Pirate HQ, was resolutely shut.

Back in my room I began my day's walking, but it wasn't long before the Negotiator entered, flanked by Vain Man and Fat Man, who adopted his favoured stance, leaning against the wall and glaring at me, sidelong. Another pirate, one of the 'corporals', came at the rear, wearing a bright blue vest with yellow piping and CELTIC printed, incongruously, across the chest. (He walked with a noticeable limp.) The Negotiator took a red mobile phone from his shirt pocket and fiddled with it.

'OK, we take video. This is proof you are alive. And here is what you must say.'

He handed me a piece of paper on which I could make out a scrawled quartet of statements: *I am Jude Tebbutt. I am British. I am in Somalia. I am being treated well.*

He then positioned me in front of the wall, but didn't seem to like the image he was getting on his screen. He beckoned to Vain Man, who unpegged the curtains hemming the walls – and I saw for the first time that two sets of windows lay behind them, one facing the door, the other on the left-hand wall. A startling sunlight streamed into the cramped space, though it was diffused just as quickly when Vain Man reinstated the curtain pegs. I was directed to stand by the side window, for lighting purposes. I was wearing my blue-grey-silvery headscarf, *de rigueur*, but Vain Man indicated for me to remove it. The Negotiator nodded.

'You're sure? I thought you weren't meant to see my hair . . .?'

On this occasion pieties were set aside. They filmed two 'takes' of me reading the prepared statement: the first seemed to suffer from bad sound recording. The Negotiator showed me a playback on the little screen, then moved smartly for the door.

I called to his retreating back, 'So what happens now?'

'This is gonna be sent so we get money, yeah?'

'When will you send it?'

'Soon. And we will start negotiations soon.'

'How much money will you ask for . . .?'

But he didn't favour that with an answer, just swept out, with his entourage. I knew I had to accept I had no control over anything going on beyond the threshold of my small cell – and that would include whatever ransom was being placed on my life. But since money was so clearly all they wanted, it reassured me to think this matter was basically resolvable. We had money: for a long time David had been saving our pooled salaries – for our retirement, so we could travel and enjoy a decent standard of life. And, painful as it would be, he would know how to handle this negotiation. He would be guided, I was certain, by the British Embassy in Kenya, who seemed to me the most likely first recipients of the video.

A cloud in my mind, though, was the thought of the video airing on British television news, and my mum seeing it – seeing me, marooned in these dire straits. Hearing the news of my kidnap from my sister Carol would have been quite sufficiently traumatic, but visual evidence would only frighten her further. I had to stick to the thought that as long as David got the video – and he could only be waiting for it, in high anxiety – then from here the process could, in theory, run like clockwork.

My thoughts turned back to the task before me – how to get through another day in this room, my drastically reduced universe. But I was feeling upbeat as I walked my circuits. *This won't be so bad. We'll have an incredible story to tell at the end of it – a grim one, yes. But we'll be able to call ourselves survivors.*

*

I walked on what I guessed to be the hour, and for half an hour at a time, up until nightfall. I continued to prise small stones out from under the linoleum, collecting them in a pile in the corner of the room. Soon I had quite a rockery building up there.

My walking regimen could, no doubt, have struck another party as terribly monotonous. But I looked forward keenly to each and every walk, finding it therapeutic. The action calmed me, helped me to feel in control. I didn't see it as simply plough-ing the same furrow ad nauseam. The routine and the order were good for me: twelve paces by nine, twelve paces by nine . . . I swung my arms and watched my feet as I planted them, each tread exactly the length of a square of linoleum. Walking was rhythmic, meditative: it put me in touch with myself and was remarkably effective at driving any thoughts of the pirates from my mind. In my head, I was walking home. And at the end of each day I was exhausted, so aiding restful sleep.

Still, I wondered too if I could try some slightly more vigorous exercise, without having to get down on the floor with the insect life. Another thought occurred to me: at home I took a Pilates class every Tuesday evening after work. Shouldn't it be possible to imitate, however roughly, some of those exercises here? Ordinarily I needed a couple of weighted balls to work with, but when I took a pair of full water bottles out of my 'Bosaso' box and hefted them in my hands, they seemed to make an adequate substitute. Ordinarily I did my Pilates lying on a mat but I really didn't fancy the floor here; so I got onto the bed and tried out my core exercises, neck rolls and so forth. Now and then a pirate looked in through the door and beheld me in disbelief. But I was pleased with my own inventiveness.

With the passing time I realised that I was waiting in anticipation for the *muezzin*'s regular calls, as if there were a hidden connection between us, he my unwitting assistant in the business of establishing a roughly dependable form of timekeeping. By my count his cries rang out five times a day: the first with the rising sun, the second around 'lunchtime', the third in the latish afternoon. Not long after that third cry, in the fading of the light, I was delivered a bowl of boiled rice. Like my breakfast, this evening meal was noticeably small. Aside from that surreptitious gift of samosas after my arrival, they were feeding me about as sparsely as they could. Whereas I could see, from my glimpses of life outside in the compound, that my guards were eating pretty well, and more regularly. I had a notion that I should try not to let my thoughts linger on food, lest my hunger grow even stronger.

But I couldn't help straying now and then. I imagined myself pushing the trolley round the aisles of my local Waitrose, filling it steadily with the makings for delicious meals I could prepare for David and me. With some mental effort I shifted the focus of this little fantasy away from the food itself to the idea of the shopping list – and from that to constructing in my head a precise three-dimensional model of the supermarket as I made my imaginary tour. It didn't do me nearly as much good as a bacon sandwich would have done. But it passed the time.

The penultimate *muezzin* call of the day, at twilight, was the most welcome to me – it signalled that my day was nearly done. There was one more walk to do, but I had a special motivation: there was a lamp hanging in the covered walkway, powered by the portable generator, but it snapped off not too long after nightfall, casting us into pitch darkness, and I wanted to be in bed by the time it did that.

As I approached the end of my last walk there was a satisfaction in feeling so wearied that I was ready to fall onto the bed. I requested and was granted a last toilet visit – not from any great need so much as to take a moment to gaze up at the night sky and the stars. It comforted me to know that David, Ollie, my family, were out there somewhere, under the same vast canopy, and with luck I would be back with them soon.

The stifling heat of the day meant that my skin was continually drenched in sweat. But I quickly established that the provision of water for washing was a system that required punctual observance on my part. I was issued with an empty plastic petrol container that would be filled for me each morning, at my request, from a pump outside the compound. But I had to stick my head out of the door, shake the can and attract attention. Then I would have to set the can down, as the pirates would not take it from my hands. And then I would wait for the order to be filled, rarely with any special haste.

But thus, come the evening, I had water and I could disrobe and wash, cleanse myself as best as I could. It was a matter of dignity, and for this sliver of the day I had to have some privacy, some respect shown to a fundamental need. By tone of voice and gesticulation I managed to make it clear to the pirates that they shouldn't enter my room after dark. 'I wash – you no come in! You see naked woman if you do!' The door stayed open, only the curtain hung, but I'd succeeded in getting my message over: no one wandered in. Still I felt wary, vulnerable.

I peeled off my clothes, draped them over the back of a plastic chair – some additional cover from prying eyes – and sat down. Then I poured cold water from the oil canister into a big wide green bowl they had given me, and I washed my feet and body in that. I used just a little precious soap, which I didn't want to waste. There was a limit to how well I could tend to myself, of course. My body was scored all over with scrapes and scratches, spots and blood blisters. I was a mess, frankly. But I refused to resign myself to that. With my washing complete, I understood that come the morning the offending water would – in accordance with the Islamic strictures of these pirates – have to be disposed of down the toilet. (The green bowl was too wide and heavy for me to manoeuvre out through the door, and so I decanted the water into a third receptacle I had been given – a black plastic bucket – and conveyed it that way.)

The light outside snapped off but within a minute I was in bed with the sheet pulled up to my chin. I talked to myself a little, mantra-like: *Well done today, you got through another one. Tomorrow, same again. Remember, this is temporary, not for ever, it won't be long till you're out of here. David and Ollie are waiting.*

In the dark I wasn't entirely alone, of course. And I hadn't long to wait before I felt the first little insect scuttling across my hands or my face. I wondered about sleeping with my arms outside the sheet, so that I could bat them away. But on the whole it seemed better to get myself inured to their presence. I could manage – as long as there were no snakes.

*

I had my routine in place and I was resigned to the communications over my release taking a few days, maybe a week or so. In the time left over I tried to be vigilant and collect some workable understanding of my surroundings and my captors. Every visit to the loo, every glance around the compound, was a sort of intelligence-gathering. I tried to log the faces of the various pirates and sort out in my head who was who: who was 'friendly', and who not. Any sort of rapport seemed worth encouraging. *You do this sort of thing all the time*, I told myself, *only with very difficult psychiatric patients. Here you've got less chance of finding common ground. You know nothing of their culture beyond their devotion to prayer. But if you keep looking you'll find something to work with . . .*

The Triumvirate conversed together, hugged and laughed and play-fought with each other, and, most importantly, seemed to dispense orders (as well as cigarettes) to the younger 'run-arounds', who would come up to them and take instruction. They clearly enjoyed the confidence of Fat Man and the Negotiator. So my view was that I had better show respect to them.

Hungry Man would smile at me and give a thumbs-up, which I mimicked, since I could do nothing else. Kufiya Man also appeared quietly pleasant. When I saw him bare-headed I realised that his scant hair was in tufts and patches, alopecia-like, which loaned him a vulnerable air. But the third member of the Triumvirate, Vain Man, was at all times aloof and vaguely surly.

Marvin popped his head round my door with some frequency, his expression amiable, which was vaguely reassuring. Another pirate I noticed was short, solidly built, quiet and something of a loner. I never saw him without a cigarette in his mouth, be it morning or night, and so I dubbed him Chain-Smoker. I could rely on him, though, to show me a friendly face. There was one, though, who was large and muscular, dark-haired, with a small nose, somewhat Caucasian features and a coffee-coloured complexion, pockmarked with acne scars across his cheeks. He gave off a tough, rugged air, as if seasoned in piracy, and he carried a heavy machine-gun with a tripod fixing. Unlike with some of the more nervy young runarounds, I was quite convinced this man could kill somebody. He was a scary character.

In the early hours of the morning I'd taken to sneaking out to the toilet without asking, or donning my regulation headscarf, since the pirates slept so soundly overnight. But this came to an end on an occasion when I was tip-toeing back to the room and saw Scary Man, his eyes open and glaring at me from his recumbent position. Wordlessly he hefted up his machine-gun with one biceps-bulging arm, and pointed the muzzle at my head. I got the message.

*

I was nearing the end of my fifth day in the compound and was sitting on a plastic chair, trying to think hopeful thoughts, when a tall shadow crossed the threshold – followed by the unmistakable, rail-thin figure of the Navigator, a broad smile above his red-tinged goatee. I stood up to say hello. I hadn't seen him since that moment I'd been brought ashore to the car on the headland, whereupon I'd assumed he and Money had been charged with getting rid of the skiff. I hadn't expected to see him again, but here he was.

He took my hand between his and shook it – an unexpected formality, and I found his bony hands a bit off-putting. But given his politeness, and knowing he spoke my language, I had no shadow of a doubt that I ought to 'play nice' with him.

'So sorry I had to tell you "Mombasa", that you see David in Blue Room Hotel,' he said. He was smiling, none the less, as if it had been a smart ruse. Still, it was good of him, I thought, to start off by owning up to the lie.

'So why did you tell me that?'

'I tell you so you don't panic. But . . . I feel bad.'

'Bad? Why bad?'

He did indeed look abashed. 'Ah, I feel bad from when I give you trousers? On boat? I think, "This is not good . . ."'

Well, perhaps he has a heart, I thought. It sounded like a fair stab at contrition for his part in my kidnap. And I certainly needed a sympathetic ear around this place, where my status seemed to be closer to meal ticket than human being. *I'm going to want this man in my corner,* I decided. *For however long I'm here.*

'Well, it's done,' I said. 'And I'm here. And you're a pirate, just like all the rest of these men, aren't you?'

He shook his head, adamantly. 'No, no, I, like you. I was *taken* by pirates.'

I wasn't sure what he meant, but he sat down and, falteringly, told me his story. He was a fisherman, and two days before I was kidnapped from Kiwayu he had been out at sea on his own boat, early in the morning, planning to dive for lobster, as was his usual practice, when the Leader's pirate group sailed up alongside him, waved their AK47s and commanded him to get on board their boat. They had wanted his knowledge of the local conditions – the coastline, the tides and reefs – and they wouldn't take no for an answer. In other words, he was a pirate conscript.

It sounded plausible enough. At close quarters his skin was as weathered as I imagined a fisherman's to be. I was sorry for him. I asked if he had family, and he spoke of a wife and children. He dug a mobile phone out of his pocket and showed me various photos on it, one of his wife, extravagantly framed by graphics of heart-shaped red roses. (The lady herself looked stern and unhappy.) Did he have any idea, I asked, how his family was managing without him?

'My brother, sister, family – they take care.'

'And you, how did you come to learn your English?'

He only smiled and shook his head. But I sensed that, given his language facility, he couldn't have been a fisherman all his life.

*

Now that we were reacquainted, the Navigator looked in on me regularly. Sometimes it was no more than putting his head round the door with an 'OK? How are you?' At other times he came in and sat for longer: usually after the pirates' 'lunch hour', and then again in the evenings. He would spend an hour or so talking in his stilted English, and I didn't mind these idle chats. I was lonely, and our poor conversations were better than nothing. I found that I could ask him things, and he answered. I had been keen to know the time difference between Somalia and the UK, and he readily told me it was three hours. I also wanted a few basic words in Somali to ease my communications with the other pirates, and he advised me that 'thank you' was *mahadsanid* and 'good morning' was *subah wanaagsan*. (I duly tried these out on trips to the toilet, with any pirate who was awake, and was met with raised eyebrows.)

I had become conscious every night that there were men outside the compound, below my window. I could smell their cigarette smoke, hear them on their phones. I asked the Navigator what they were doing. 'They guard you,' he said, 'in case other pirates come, try to take you away, for themselves.' That was an alarming prospect: without doubt I felt safer for the moment with the devil I knew.

There was an apartness to the Navigator that affirmed my belief in his account of his plight: he didn't fraternise with the other pirates – except for Marvin, whom he would sit and eat with, usually at different times of day from the rest of the gang. I spotted them on guard together at night, too. So I wasn't surprised when one afternoon they came in together to see me.

'My friend, he, like me,' the Navigator said. 'We are both like you.' And they both crossed their wrists as if they were handcuffed or tied. The Navigator explained that Marvin was the captain of a fishing boat that had been captured by the pirates six months before him. 'Good man,' he insisted. 'He good man, my friend.'

They came in again the next day. I had been walking, and the pirates had been munching away outside on what seemed to be their early-afternoon snacks of bread, melon and bananas. But then I picked up on something different through the doorway: laughter and kerfuffle, the pirates gathered in a bit of a huddle and having a chat that sounded argumentative and purposeful.

When the Navigator and Marvin then entered they were giggling together and waving about something that looked to me like a bunch of watercress. On closer inspection it was a lot of wilted green leaves. At first I hoped they were for me.

'These leaves come from Kenya,' the Navigator explained. 'We say *khat*? Somali men like to chew *khat* from Kenya.'

'Really?' I said. 'Why don't you just grow it here?'

'Ah, no, no, can't do that. These *special* leaves . . .'

It seemed so, for they popped a few leaves into their mouths and began to chew, vigorously, cheerfully. I was offered a leaf of my own, but I couldn't see the appeal and declined politely.

*

As the days dragged by and I heard no news nor saw sight of the Negotiator, unease crept over me. Wasn't anything happening about the video, about communications and negotiations? I'd expected a greater urgency. One morning at dawn as I crept back from the toilet I made sure to glance to the doorway of Room 4 – 'Pirate HQ' – and with a start I recognised the Negotiator's sandals were sitting outside. *He's here! Has he got news?* I couldn't imagine any other reason for his presence. *If he doesn't come to me I'll ask to see him.*

Thankfully I didn't have to wait long before he entered my room, clad a bit more casually than before in a white vest and green sarong. We exchanged good mornings. Then he smiled.

'You have a young man in Nairobi, asking for you?'

'Excuse me?'

'A young man is in Nairobi. He fly out, for you, he waiting for you. Your . . . nephew?'

I was baffled. The idea that my sister Carol's teenage son Cameron might have flown to Kenya on a mercy mission for me was massively implausible.

'Sorry . . . do you mean *Ollie*? Is it my son?'

The Negotiator shrugged, looked non-committal.

'How did you hear this? Who told you?'

'I just know this. I hear.'

And he got up and left. My mind was in a tumult, I desperately wanted to believe the scrap I had been fed – and it seemed plausible. After all, David surely wouldn't have stayed on Kiwayu, he needed to be somewhere with good telecommunications and the internet, which would be Nairobi. Ideally he would be working with the British Consulate there. And it was natural that

Ollie would have flown out to be with him. But why couldn't I know more? I was left in the dark to wonder.

Later on the Navigator appeared, looking as if he had news he was happy to share with me.

'Your husband is in Nairobi, with your son. I hear this. He tries to get money for your release.'

'The Negotiator told me that too. But how do you know this?'

He, too, could give me no grounds for belief. But in my excitement I took this to be a corroborated account, and hung my hopes on it. *My god, that's it. Wheels are turning. Negotiations are open between David and the pirates. They've said they want x-much money. David's with Ollie and he's arranging it.* And I was pleased to think they were together, helping each other through what had to be a terrible, nerve-straining struggle. But now I had the happiest imagining in my head: once I was released the three of us would be reunited in Nairobi, and we would travel home to England together. That was a joyous thought.

And that was where I intended to keep my focus, so steering clear of a particular mental pathway I didn't wish to go down. It was to do with David, with the last image I had of him, his tussle in the dark with the armed pirate – the Leader, as I assumed. Anxiety shadowed my mind over whether David might have been hurt or incapacitated before the pirates fled the *banda*. What if they had hit him too hard, bashed him about the head with a rifle butt, left him unconscious and bleeding, maybe even semi-comatose?

What I told myself – what made sense – was that the Leader had seen David last, and had there been any problem of that sort he would have surely told his masters/superiors, Fat Man and the Negotiator – because they had to know that if David came to any harm then their chances of extracting a ransom for me were severely impaired. But ever since Kiwayu the pirates had made clear David was the person they wanted to contact. And so David had to be OK.

There was another factor – call it a superstition. But after all our years together, the close marriage we shared, some inner part of me was sure that if any harm befell David, even if he and I were apart at the time, then I would feel it, sense it. I would know in my bones, somehow. And I didn't have that feeling now. I believed with every fibre of my being that he was out there, working for my release.

*

It was Wednesday, 21 September, when the Navigator loped into my room carrying a mobile phone and a piece of paper.

'Phone call! Is for you! You listen . . .'

In haste I took the phone, clamped it to my ear, and the first voice I heard was the Negotiator.

'You speak to this Englishman. You tell him what it says on the paper.'

The Navigator gave me the handwritten note: I scanned it quickly. A new voice came on the line, clipped English tones.

'Hello, Judith. Are you there?' Immediately I assumed this could only be the British Embassy calling.

'Yes, this is Jude Tebbutt.' I read out what I'd been told to. 'I am alive, I am in Somalia, and I need help please.'

'Judith, is there anything you are allowed to tell me about yourself from your past?'

Racking my brain for the basic forms of self-identification, I told him my date of birth.

'Yes, but is there anything you can tell me from your family history, something that only your family would know about you?'

'My husband will know I was born with a hole in my heart? And I'm partially deaf.'

'But that only your family will know – the name of a pet you once had, say?'

His repetition of 'family' was confusing me, since the automatic thoughts that word evoked for me were of David and Ollie. *They just have to ask David*, I thought. Finally it twigged with me that he wanted some detail from childhood, something only my mother and my siblings would know.

'We used to have a black-and-tan terrier,' I volunteered. 'His name was McGill . . .' That seemed to suffice.

'Thank you. Are you being treated well, Judith?'

'Yes, but I'm desperate to go home and see my husband and my son, who I believe are in Nairobi? I don't know where . . .'

The man didn't address my implied question, only moved on to ask me for the addresses of the houses where I'd grown up in Ulverston, then for the names and ages of my siblings. I had no difficulty recalling any of that.

'How are you getting on without your hearing aids?'

'Not very well, I'm afraid.'

'We're looking out for you, Judith . . .'

Then the Negotiator's voice butted back on the line. 'OK, thank you, that's enough for you, my friend.'

The line went dead and the Navigator relieved me of the phone. I was perplexed but basically glad to have done something to contribute to my own release effort. *At least that's settled. Someone in officialdom knows for sure that I'm here – that I'm alive.*

*

Later that day I had a visit from the woman I had met on my first day in the compound, accompanied by the Navigator. She was wearing funereal black robes from head to toe but in her hands she was carrying, freshly washed and folded, the grey-pink-silvery number she'd worn – and on which I'd complimented her – when first we met. Smiling, she proffered the garments to me. 'You wear,' the Navigator prompted.

I accepted them with a nod and a '*mahatsanid*'. I was moved to ask the Navigator, 'What is this lady's name?'

The Navigator spoke to the woman and she smiled at me and said, clearly, 'Amina.'

I shook out the folded dress. Then Amina gently took it from me and helped me get into it. I soon realised she'd made some alterations to the cut, taken it in a little to fit me. She was a big lady with a big chest, which she patted as she gestured to me, helpfully pointing out the disparities in *décolletage* between us. I could only smile, in the midst of my grim situation, to be having this quintessentially female 'changing-room moment'. Once I was into the *jilbab* dress, Amina pulled the cape-like *khimar* over my head, though I was rather less keen on assuming full Islamic regalia. And then Hungry Man strolled into the room, and seeing me in the new ensemble he grinned and cried, 'Ah, beauty Somali!'

That was enough to drain the amusement factor from the experience. Abruptly I pulled the *khimar* off and over my head. Amina and the Navigator looked puzzled.

'Me no Somali, me English,' I explained. Then, thinking better of an argument about cultural identity, I waved a fanning hand before my face. 'Too hot, yes? Too hot to wear on my head.'

They seemed to accept that point. Inside, though, I was seething at Hungry Man, and how I must have looked in his eyes. *You're not getting used to seeing me like that*, I thought. *That is not who I am.* But the apparently simple act of a change of clothes felt to me like a stealthy confirmation that I had some-how ceased to be Jude Tebbutt – wife, mother, social worker. Amina's clothes stripped me of that, reduced me to a cipher, to mere chattel: 'Woman/Prisoner, in Somalia'. And it frightened me to think how swiftly my true identity could be erased. I had the same basic interest in my appearance – in expressing a little of myself through how I looked – as most other Western women, and so I shrank from this concealing, homogenising religious uniform.

I could live with the *jilbab* dress, plus the stricture of the head-scarf: given the heat, the long days and the amount I was losing in perspiration, any change of clothes had to be welcomed. And so Amina's *jilbab* became my new day wear. The clothes I'd taken off – my first prison-issue dress in splodges of red and black – I decided would be my 'going-away outfit'. I wanted to be pre-sentable when I saw David and Ollie, and I wouldn't mind them seeing me in that dress, whereas the *jilbab* felt unnatural to me.

I had spied Hungry Man washing his own clothes out in the compound, with sudsy water in a big stainless-steel dish, a box of washing powder at his side bearing the brand name 'Omo'. I now asked the Navigator if I could have a cup of Omo, and he brought it for me, though he seemed oddly hesitant. I did the job, using the bucket water that was brought for washing my body. Then I hung my laundry to dry over one of the plastic chairs. Even in the heat this took hours, but when it was done I put the dress in a black binliner. My room had recently acquired a new furnishing, somewhat superfluous to requirements: a coat-stand, burgundy coloured with bright gold knobs. But now I had something worth hanging on it.

*

Looking for more ways to refresh my physical-exercise routine, I had another thought that seemed to me rather inspired, whatever anyone else might think: a 'virtual hula hoop'. I started to practise a series of hip rotations that I felt would be sufficient to keep an imaginary hoop (red-and-white-striped, as I pictured it) twirling around my waist for at least five times at a go. I would then reverse the motion, and try five times in the other direction. I was quickly absorbed in the process, mentally as well as physically, though I called a halt whenever I reached fifty spins in all.

I had grown accustomed to the daily afternoon commotion that seemed to herald the pirates taking delivery of their *khat* leaves, from Kenya – the highlight of their day, it seemed, for they tumbled out of their various rooms, some dashing in from positions outside the compound. One day I decided to take a better look and made a toilet visit as they all huddled under the covered walkway. I realised there was a dealer at the centre of the hubbub, a man with lots of Afro-perm-like curly hair, toting two blue plastic bags bulging with *khat*. Vain Man appeared to be in charge of a process of bartering with him, trying to cut a bargain, weighing one clump of wilted leaves in his hand then another, finally deciding on a favourite, while the others chattered keenly. And then he took it on himself to dish out portions. Once the excitement receded and the *khat* man left, the pirates retreated to start chewing. I was inclined to look and see which of them took no interest, and I could see that the Triumvirate never chewed, nor Smiley Boy (who never prayed either). But for the others *khat* seemed to make them chatty, lively. The Navigator told me he chewed so as to stay awake until nine o'clock at night, whereupon he retired to sleep in Room 3. *Khat*, then, was both a perk and a necessary stimulant. I could see why they resorted to it, though I remained resolutely untempted.

I would have dearly liked some regular daily treat of my own, but I had nothing. My lack of interest in Somali tea drew attention, after Hungry Man came in one evening bearing the usual flask of hot water and paused to check my yellow packet of tea, looking puzzled by why it was still so full. He summoned the Navigator, who pressed me to explain that I just couldn't drink the stuff. He and Hungry Man shook their heads sadly, and took the flask and the packet of tea away. Inevitably, nothing else came back in its place.

I kept on trying to 'think positive'. But at times, in passages, this just couldn't be sustained – not when I was alone in a dark room on a plastic chair, so hot and claustral that I felt as though I were sitting fully clothed in a sauna. Sweat ran down me. The discomfort was such that at times I sat on the floor with my back to the wall, seeking its coolness, despite the curtain in the way.

While I persevered with efforts at 'meaningful interaction' with the pirates, it was hard going amid the strangeness of this alien environment, where I recognised precisely nothing, found nothing familiar or comforting. Listening to these men, my gaolers, laughing and conversing outside my door – and not in some semi-familiar language where a foreigner might pick up on the odd word or two, but in a truly indecipherable tongue – I really felt I was lost to the world.

I could take nothing for granted, had to keep on guard against giving offence. In the course of one short traipse over to the toilet my headscarf came undone and slipped from my head. Limping Man happened to be close by. At the sight of my hair he went ballistic, raising an angry din that sent the Navigator darting to my side, and not in sympathy. 'Hair, hair!' he shouted. *For goodness' sake*, I thought, *what is* wrong *with you men?*

Not long afterwards the Navigator and Hungry Man deemed it necessary to come to my room and tell me again, sternly, that I was never, not even for a moment, to go bareheaded around the place. After that I decided to keep the peace, take the *khimar* from where I'd hung it on the coat-stand and throw it onto my head for visits to the toilet. However, often in the rush I threw it on back to front.

I could suffer it all, every indignity and discomfort, for the belief that my ordeal couldn't last. But in my loneliness I could only run and re-run through my head the tale of what I hoped was happening a thousand miles away: David and Ollie, in Nairobi, working with the Consulate, bargaining with the Negotiator for my freedom. I didn't like to think about how they were feeling; nor about my family back in England, and how on earth they were coping.

A bit of me, I knew, was still in shock, and also rueful. How could this have happened to us? Why? Why the bloody hell did we go to Kiwayu? Why didn't we pick Zanzibar, as we'd meant to in the beginning? Why hadn't I stood my ground on that choice? To imagine where we could be if we'd only done things differently was more than I could bear. I had to dig deep, stay in the here and now, keep my mind on the next hour ahead – rather than falling back into self-pity and wishful thinking, those twin traps, from which nothing useful could come.

*

It was a Saturday, 1 October, early afternoon, and I was sitting on a chair facing the door, a walk just completed. The Navigator rushed into the room waving a phone – and not his usual black handset but a flashy red number. At his back just about every other pirate in the compound came piling in, an invasion, and the crowd in the room was two or three deep with me at the airless centre.

'What on earth's going on?' I asked the Navigator.

He grinned and thrust the phone at me. I pressed it to my ear and heard the Negotiator.

'I have your son on the phone.'

It was, as they say, as if my heart had missed a beat.

'Hello? Ollie, hello?'

But the line went dead. Breath bated, I handed the phone back to the Navigator, gesturing forlornly. 'Dead.' His brow furrowed, he darted from the room.

I was left looking at the throng of expectant pirates who clearly intended to share in whatever conversation I might be about to enjoy. My stomach churned in hope. The Navigator returned, pressed the phone upon me. Again the voice on the line was the Negotiator's.

'OK, it is your son. You have three minutes, no more.'

The line clicked and buzzed.

'Hello? Ollie, is that you?'

'Mum, yes, it's Ollie . . .'

To hear my son's dear voice, after all these dreadful weeks, had my heart pressing hard against my chest. There was so much to say – and yet I could barely speak. But Ollie sounded full of urgency.

'Listen to me, Mum. I can't speak for long, this has to be short, and there are some things I have to ask you. Are you ill? Do you need medical attention?'

'No, darling, I'm OK, I'm being treated well.'

'Have they given you bottled water?'

'I've got that, yes.'

'Have you got a pen and paper, Mum?'

'No, they haven't given me that . . .' It sounded as if Ollie were working his way down a pre-prepared list of things he had to verify. He had a system: evidently he had taken advice.

'Do you have a routine, something you do every day?'

'I do, yes, I'm walking round the room every hour.'

'That's good, Mum, stick to the routine, routines are good. Keep walking – you're walking to freedom.'

I had to smile at that lovely, spirit-lifting thought.

'Now listen, Mum, we're trying to get you home. The family is doing all we can, and we will get you home, you're just going to have to be strong . . .'

Then I heard the line cut out, and 'That's it, over.' The Negotiator was back. I could feel myself trembling.

'OK, now negotiations will start. Then I will come back and see you.'

He hung up. The Navigator reclaimed the phone from me and I saw him pass it to the Leader, who pocketed it. The pirates trooped out of the room, the show was over, but the Navigator grinned at me. 'Your son! He phone you!' For the moment I wasn't interested in his pleasantries. I wanted to get my thoughts in order.

Alone again, back to my walking, I replayed my and Ollie's brief exchanges in my head, incessantly. He had sounded so much in control, focused and mature, as if he were directing the effort to 'get me home'. But where was David? Our conversation had been incredibly rushed but, still, I was kicking myself for not squeezing in a question to Ollie about how his dad was doing. And Ollie hadn't mentioned him, which was, on reflection, strange.

My secret fear reasserted itself. What if David was languishing in hospital somewhere, still injured from the night of my kidnap? What if he had been struck too hard? His skull could have been fractured. This dark scenario mushroomed in my head: if David were incapacitated, and Ollie was in charge of things, having to rely on 'the family' – my family, in Cumbria – then there would be no quick fix. My family had no money to spare, and nothing to prepare them for this experience. I could be stuck here for a long time, not weeks but months.

I had no idea when Ollie and I would speak next, but I had to take the Negotiator's word that 'dialogue' had opened and I would hear from him soon. I felt my very sanity depending on it.

*

Later that day I saw Ollie's close questioning – as monitored by the Negotiator – yielding immediate results, when Smiley Boy entered my room bearing a little assemblage of items for me: a thick exercise book, a pen, a packet of tissues, and a slim battery-powered torch. In my straitened circumstances this was quite a care package, and my spirits were raised again.

The book covers were patterned with red roses on a yellow background, bound in cellophane. Inside the front cover the days of the week were given in English, along with a blank timetable grid: 'Lesson 1', 'Lesson 2', etc. Inside the back was the same formula in Somali. The pages were ruled, like any good school-book, and there were 170 of them. The thought did occur to me, how many of them I would use up before I was free.

I planned to put this to good use. My first thought was not to bother with any sort of diary – my days were too similar – but just to take advantage of a chance to employ my mind and occupy my time. My days were busy enough, after all, with walk-ing and thinking. Writing, then, could be my evening pursuit. I decided not to open the book until after evening mealtime, between the third and fourth *muezzin* wails.

The torch was another godsend. During the day I could just about cope with the gloom made by the closed, curtained shutters in my room. The pitch black of night was a different order. I needed to feel strong, and sitting alone in blackness after 6 p.m. was not conducive to strength. But now I had a means to light the dark.

Once night had come down I flicked on the torch and sat over the book. I decided to number each page as I wrote, and then I began with gusto, simply writing out trivial lists of things: girls' and boys' names, A–Z, as many as I could think of. Without reading glasses I struggled to see well in front of me: it would have to be close work, the torch's narrow beam trained hard on the spot directly before my nose. But I scribbled away with my face nearly on the page, like some Dickensian clerk squinting over a ledger by the light of a guttering candle. No matter the challenge, I was determined to get some words down on paper.

For the day's final walk I experimented with my new torch. While my battery lantern shed a bit of light there were a couple of corners of the room that remained steeped in darkness – and I didn't want to go there, almost superstitiously. On a base level, I was worried about treading on too many cockroaches. But I found that if I moved the lantern to the corner opposite the door, and pointed the torch to the opposite corner of the room, the illumination levels improved slightly. I knew I would be stepping on fewer bugs in any event, since they began to inch from out of their dark hiding places towards the room's new light source.

*

The next morning the Navigator brought me the news that I would receive another phone call later in the day. I was cheered. It might mean progress, perhaps a breakthrough in 'negotiations' –

at the very least a chance for me to address some things left undone during the previous day's call. That afternoon could not come quickly enough for me. Finally the Navigator came in bearing the Leader's red phone like a totem. Once again the room filled with eager pirates, some of whom hunkered down on the floor, while others kicked their heels. The Navigator, the Leader and Marvin perched themselves on the edge of my bed, as if affirming their seniority. But all of them were grinning and giving me the thumbs-up sign, seemingly as eager in their own ways as I was for news about how this piece of business was proceeding.

With the phone to my ear I heard the Negotiator: 'OK, I put through. You have three minutes . . .' What followed was another rigmarole of lost connections and the line going dead. But I stayed patient, sure it would happen, determined to use my time well.

'Hello, hello, hello?'

'Yes, Mum, it's me.'

'Hi, Ollie darling, how are you?'

'Mum, we've only got three minutes. But, listen, we're still working on getting the money.'

'And where's Dad, Ollie? How is he? How's he coping with this?'

'Mum, there's something I have to tell you. Dad didn't survive his injuries . . .'

In my head, in my heart, it was as if a clock had stopped.

'Injuries? What do you mean, injuries?'

'He was trying to protect you, Mum. He was brave to the very last minute . . .'

No. It just wasn't possible. Ollie simply couldn't mean what he seemed to be meaning.

'Ollie, are you telling me Dad is *dead*? Is that what you mean?'

I was staring, stricken, across the room. The sight I saw clearest was the Navigator's face – and the effect of the word 'dead' upon him had been immediate. His grin vanished.

'I'm so sorry, Mum . . .'

The Navigator muttered something to Marvin, but loud enough for the rest of the room to hear. Sharp intakes of breath, mouths opening, eyebrows raised – startled faces looking from one to another then back at me. Ollie's voice filled my head.

'We've just got to remember all the good times we had with him . . .'

Even as my whole being seemed to reel away, in horror, I was wondering who had counselled my beloved son, advised him to use these very considered words, so grave and wise and grown up, to deliver to me the worst news in the world.

'We're still working on getting you home, Mum. I've met with the family. They all send their love . . .'

I didn't know what I was saying any more, or what I could say. Some of the pirates, meanwhile, were getting up and making their way out of the room.

'I love you, Mum. I need you – I need you to get through this, to stay strong. It's just a matter of time, Mum. We'll get you home . . .'

The instant I heard 'home' the line went dead, and the Negotiator's voice returned.

'That's it, no more.'

'Did you hear that?' I said to him, trying to force my voice out through the dreadful fog in my head.

'Hear what?'

'My husband is *dead*. You killed my husband.'

'Who tell you your husband dead?'

'You were listening, weren't you? You heard my son. My husband's dead. And you have got to get me on a plane out of here, tomorrow, because I need to be with my son. You've got to fly me home tomorrow.' I was frantic now, desperate. I could hear the pleading in my voice. 'You *must*, you have *got* to do this – I've got to get back to see my son.'

'We will check that out tomorrow, and we will start negotiations.'

'I beg you . . .'

'We check it tomorrow. No decision.'

The ground had gone beneath me, and I had fallen, so hard I couldn't bear to look at the injury. I would give anything to reverse the spool of time, or prove that I'd been told another lie. But it was Ollie who had told me: he would only ever tell me the truth.

And in this squalid room I had barely space to move or breathe for the presence of the strange, unfeeling, mercenary creatures who had wreaked this catastrophe on us. Had they really known no more than I had until now, about how my and my family's lives had been ruined?

I looked around the room and I jabbed a finger from one face to the next.

'You, and you, and you – all of you – you killed my husband. My husband is *dead* because of all of *you*.'

Whether they were shamed, or embarrassed, or had simply lost interest, the stragglers too now started to file out of the room. None of them had taken part in my abduction. But I was staring hardest of all at the Navigator, and Marvin, and the Leader, still sitting on the corner of the bed. The Leader – the last man to see David alive – looked back impassive. He was the man David had struggled with. It had to be him. Money wasn't strong enough. It was him.

'You – you're responsible. Aren't you? You killed my husband, didn't you?'

I looked at him hard and he looked back. It was a stand-off. But I would not let him stare me out. Finally he got to his feet and sauntered out.

*

In the aftermath there were comings and goings to which I barely paid attention, but the next thing I knew was that Marvin and the Navigator were standing over me, now joined by Money, who grinned inanely.

'Go, leave me alone,' I muttered.

'Negotiator say we have to stay with you,' the Navigator replied. 'We stay in your room all night.'

'No, I don't want that.'

'I must, I must. Negotiator say you in shock.'

Hearing that, I wanted to tell the Negotiator everything I thought about him. But he wasn't there and I had to vent my feelings of disgust and hatred to someone. So I rounded on the Navigator.

'Did you know? Did you? That David had been killed?'

'No, no – I in boat, I did not know.' His tone was riled but still quite casual. I didn't want to look at these men and yet I couldn't expel them either. I threw myself down on the bed but I didn't sleep, merely lay under the mosquito net thinking, *This cannot be happening. I want to wake up. Please let me wake up.* I had nothing to cling to beyond the hope that if I could get through the night then in the morning I might be shown some compassion, permitted to go home to my son.

The pirates, who had insisted on intruding upon me for some idea of my own good, sat slumped against the wall and amused one another. I could tell they had been chewing *khat*. They chatted away, played avidly with their phones, swapped them back and forth to look at pictures, the little glowing screens illuminating the room's dark corner. The Navigator sparked up a cigarette. I shouted at him to stop. He didn't. Money looked over at me and laughed. Their blatant, crushing disregard seemed intended, somehow, to set the seal on the most terrible day of my life.

*

Dawn found me alone again, numb, emptied, desolate. I could feel in my chest the hard stone of a stark and awful realisation: *David's not going to come for you. You're not going to be saved – you never were. Your whole dream that he would sort this out – it was over before they even dragged you off Kiwayu Island. Nothing was true, nothing you were clinging to had any substance. David's gone.*

How could it have happened? What injuries had they inflicted on him? Why? I built scenarios in my head, bitterly. When they had raided our *banda* that night, perhaps they hadn't bargained on their victim putting up a fight. But they were carrying guns. And clearly their concern for human life was zero.

When food came I couldn't bear to look at it. I was sick to my stomach. All I wanted was news that I would be flown home, that some sense of shame had overtaken the Negotiator and Fat Man. But nothing happened, nothing changed.

My despondency, my loneliness, felt total and consuming. I had no one – no one to talk to, no one to share an embrace or even the merest shred of comfort. I sat down and I wept.

After a while I realised I was causing a disturbance outside. Hungry Man glanced in, darted off, and in short order he was back, at his side the Navigator, who beheld me with the look of someone who had drawn the short straw for an unpleasant chore.

[128]

'Why you cry?'

'*Why?* You know why.'

Hungry Man tapped the Navigator and muttered something to him. The Navigator turned to me.

'This man, he says you maybe get a new husband? When you home you will look for a new husband?'

'No, I will not,' I said quietly, stunned yet further by this stupefying discourtesy. But the Navigator seemed to be of the same mind as his accomplice.

'Yeah, is no problem. Your husband dead – you go home, get other husband.'

He had to be cracked in the head to believe this, and I felt I had to disabuse him of it.

'No, no way. I don't want another husband.'

'Why not?'

He then launched into a complicated explanation – from what I could make out – of an Islamic custom he called *iddah*, how if a Somali woman was widowed then she observed a waiting period of four months and ten days, long enough to ensure she was not pregnant by her late husband. It also allowed time for some kind of cursory mourning, after which she was free to remarry, often to a brother-in-law if not a new man – a simple enough matter given that Somali men were allowed multiple wives.

None of this touched in the slightest on what marriage meant to me: the desire for a lifelong union with a soul's mate, 'until death us do part'. That was the marriage I'd had: I wasn't interested in a lecture on some poor alternative version. Wanting to hear no more I put my face in my hands and wept. But the Navigator seemed doggedly set on being 'firm' with me, to the point of impatience.

'Look: David die. Who else in your family die? Your father, where he?'

'My father is dead.'

'OK! Father dead, see? So, people die. No problem. Why you cry? Your father die – people die.'

I tried to look him in the eye and get something important through to him. 'Yes, people die. But when you've been with a husband for thirty-three years, that is hard. You understand? If you died, your wife would cry for you, wouldn't she?'

He mulled this over. 'Ah, yeah. My wife would cry . . .'

Undeterred, he set off on another story from his own experience, of how his firstborn son had died as a baby. It was a tragedy, clearly – one I wouldn't have wished on my worst enemy. But what he seemed to want me to appreciate was that his baby boy had gone to a better place. That belief consoled him. It was part of his faith-based philosophy: *You are here awhile, you live, then you die, and you go to a different world.* Hungry Man nodded in agreement as he listened. I'd always had a feeling he was especially religious.

But nothing the Navigator said, however personal to him or deeply felt, was going to bring me a morsel of comfort. Having no faith in any god, I couldn't take the consolation he had found. My credo had always been to try to make the best of life, because this life is all we have. So I couldn't pretend to buy the wishful idea that I would be reunited with David in some afterlife. He and I had had our life together – it had been such a good and happy one – but it had been cut off, violently, and far, far too soon, because of the criminal actions of this gang of thieves. And if the Navigator really believed all this had in fact been ordained by some higher power – that was, to me, somehow even more despicable.

10

I was sitting with David: we were at home together, on our sofa, facing one another. Everything about our situation was normal, familiar, reassuring – but for the fact that what David was telling me, calmly and quietly, was that he was going to die.

'Isn't there something we can do?' I pleaded. 'This can't just be it.'

'There's nothing. You've got to be brave. But you're going to be OK. And I'd rather go like this than have to tell Ollie I've got some kind of terminal illness. I wouldn't want him to see that, or you. This is all right, this is OK . . .'

'No,' I said. 'I don't accept it. There must be something I can do to stop this happening . . .'

And then I woke up again, in my Somali prison – very shaken, anew, by that endlessly renewable power of dreams to pass for reality. I had believed with all my heart that David was beside me, his presence warming, consoling, despite all the dark things he seemed to say. Instead I had to face the day alone – more truly and terribly alone than I'd ever felt.

*

I got up and I walked, because I felt I had to; there was no alternative. Otherwise I would curl up, cry, lose hope. It was an especially hot day, and beyond the door the compound seemed deserted. I didn't realise it at first, I was sunk down so deep in misery, but I was crying anyway – and then I saw Smiley Boy at the door, unsmiling, in fact looking panicked and annoyed. And then I could hear myself. I was moaning, chanting almost, like a mourning rite: 'David. How am I going to live without David?'

My shoulders twitched with my sobs. I was shaking my head, wringing my hands. I was a mess.

The Smiley Boy shook his own head, disapproving yet flummoxed. It had to be that the Navigator wasn't around and couldn't be summoned to give me one of his futile talkings-to. So the Boy summoned his initiative and wagged a finger at me, as if to say, 'Stop!' I couldn't oblige him. Finally he gave up, stomped out. I sat down on the bed and cried myself out, until I was spent, exhausted. I had to ask myself how much longer I could go on.

And something inside me answered: *You're going to go on for as long as you have to. Pull yourself together.*

*

I couldn't just turn off my tears, dam up the sorrow that threatened always to rise in my chest. But with the self-control I had to call upon I knew I had to find a way to cope, or else things, abysmal as they were for me, could yet get worse.

For instance, my crying brought pirates into the room, and certainly brought out the worst in them. They would be angry, would shout and gesticulate at me. The Triumvirate pirates didn't like my distress one bit. Money came in at one point, and his reaction was to wave his gun at me and make a contemptuous *pfft* sound with his lips. Smiley Boy would just guffaw whenever he saw me crying. Such reactions certainly succeeded in exacerbating the pain I was in. They were stunningly disrespectful – as if human life were negligible, sensitivity a foreign or useless emotion.

So I made an inward vow that I could permit myself only brief and controlled interludes of sorrow. If I was going to get out of this place – and I was – then I needed to be sane and strong. I had to avoid the despondent, racking tears of self-pity, because at the end of that road lay utter breakdown.

At first I taught myself to cry in silence: a suppressed weeping, so that, though tears rolled down my cheeks, I made no sound.

Other kinds of 'coping strategies' seemed to come to me without premeditation. I found myself pushing aside the thoughts of my loss to focus on the dullest practical matters, a kind of lateral thinking. *How am I going to manage our household alone? What will it mean to cook for one person? Do I hold on to our car? It's too big for one. Should I give up work? Or will I need work now more than ever ... ?*

I realised I was doing this so as not to dwell on the brute fact that David was gone and I would never see him again. It was an insuperable task to stop him entering my thoughts unbidden. If I put him out of my conscious mind he appeared in my dreams. And the simple thought of a world without David – when everything we had done with each other was for each other – was unspeakably bleak. Deprived of that great bond in life, what was I going to do for myself?

I was frightened of letting my mind run off in that direction, making me thoroughly miserable and depressed, which I couldn't afford. I needed a more defined mental discipline. And my working life, thankfully, had some examples to offer.

A few years previously I had helped to run a group for women with schizophrenia, some of whom suffered constantly from hearing voices in their heads that they couldn't switch off. I got acquainted with a body of therapeutic thought that argued that these voices *could* be silenced by basic techniques, such as addressing oneself to the voice: 'OK, I've had enough of you now, don't want to hear you any more. I'll talk to you later.' My colleagues and I discussed these techniques with our patients and certainly it worked for some of them. Now I believed I could make use of a similar discipline.

When my thoughts – about David, about home – threatened to overturn me, I instructed myself inwardly: *Stop thinking about that now. It's just not doing you any good. Think about something else – about how long before your next walk. Think about checking your blisters before you start. Think about that gecko climbing the wall over there. Where's he come from? Is it a he or a she? How do you tell . . .?'* In this way I could drag my train of thought onto a different track.

At work I had also become conversant with DBT, Dialectical Behaviour Therapy, a form of psychotherapy designed to enable patients to control their emotions, in essence by thinking of their brains as having a logical side and an emotional side, and working on means to give the logical side pre-eminence. What I now devised in my head was a kind of organising system for sifting my thoughts and putting them into compartments, so that I could tell myself, *It's just not helpful for me to have this thought in mind right now; it needs filing away for another time.*

Not only thoughts but also people went into my mental filing cabinet, and, sad to say, David was filed to the very back, because I couldn't bear it otherwise. Every day I thought about him – I gave myself a daily allowance of 'Thinking Time' when I could open the cabinet – but for a strictly limited period, after which he'd have to be returned to the drawer. If it was an unnatural thing to be rationing my grieving, I was in an unnatural situation, feeling my very sanity to be at stake. In my heart I knew there would be a time to grieve for David, deeply and truly and properly. That time wasn't now: it couldn't be done. I had to focus on surviving, on getting back home to our son.

I knew my discipline wouldn't be watertight, and it wasn't. Sometimes the emotion just broke free, I couldn't ward it off, the tears came, and I would hear the nearest pirate scampering off to get the Navigator. But I practised and practised, and chided myself for lapses, and very slowly I got better at it.

A few days after the fateful call with Ollie I was pacing the room, allowing myself to think about David, and how he would have managed if he had been with me in captivity. I had a sense that, for all his great strength of character, he didn't have those 'coping' strategies which my working life had armed me with. He was someone who had to be in control of his environment. I couldn't see how he would have accepted or tolerated the condition of being kept hostage. He would have looked for ways to escape, ceaselessly, yet without any hope or prospect, and that would have made for a battle in his head. I was sure, too, that it would have crucified him to see me being treated so poorly, when he could do nothing about it.

In that moment I suffered a sudden, drastic lapse of drive and concentration, my mental defences were breached and the dark thoughts rushed in on me. *If David couldn't cope, how will I? I can't get through this, no, it's hopeless, I won't be able to bear it.*

And then the strangest thing happened. I felt the gentle pressure of a clasp on my hand, and in my head I heard David's voice, true as life, as clear as my dreams: *You're going to do this. I know you will. You're much stronger than me.*

The moment passed. I knew it had taken place nowhere but in my head. I was alone in the room. But I had felt a presence, strongly, undeniably. And the presence had brought a message, a reminder of what I knew David would have wanted me to do – not to give up, no way, but to fight on. Ollie had urged me to do the same. And he was in his own ordeal, having to cope with the death of his father, the kidnap of his mother, and the huge burden that had been placed on his shoulders. So fighting on was what I was going to do – for him, and for David.

*

All the anger and resentment I had felt towards my captors before I knew of David's death were as nothing to the hatred I now harboured for them, with the truth finally out. And this was a new feeling for me, disconcerting in its virulence. I had never hated anyone before – I didn't honestly recognise the emotion, much less that it could be so strong. It was hard for me to so much as look at these people, who had caused David's death and so ruined my life and my son's. But then they seemed essentially oblivious. From my cell I could always hear laughter and shouts in the compound, the slamming down of dominoes onto the floor where the pirates sat in the shade. I thought, *How dare they? How dare they enjoy themselves, after what they've done, what they're doing?*

And yet my logical mind told me an uncomfortable, undeniable truth. If I was to get through captivity, if the days were to be manageable, I had to get along with them. I couldn't waste every day confronting them, rebuking them, remonstrating with them. It wouldn't do me any good, not emotionally nor in terms of my material well-being. I had to be methodical, businesslike, ensure that there were pirates I could deal with, to whom I could make requests, so I could obtain whatever small conveniences were allowed me.

I was trained in social work to be non-judgemental. I had worked with, supported and helped people who had done dreadful things: women who had murdered their children, men who were rapists or child molesters. The nature of the job was to set aside any instinctive aversion to the person and look for a way to create a relationship. And I still had that ability, even in a situation where the victim of the offence was me.

Something I cottoned to quickly in the days after I learned of David's death was that both the Leader and Money had disappeared. This couldn't be an accident, in my view. They had been together at the scene of the crime, and they knew I knew that – as did the pirate leadership, who had surely decided now to get them out of the way for a while. The business of piracy was kidnap and extortion, grave crimes in themselves, but the Leader had added murder to this gang's offences.

As for the Navigator, he had protested that David's death was none of his doing, he hadn't known about it. The former was clearly true, at least. Every day he looked in on me, still trying to present a friendly face. And I knew that if I didn't deal with him then I would have to revert back to the square-one strategy of trying to make myself understood by noises and gestures.

More than ever before I needed to know the time of day – the exact time. Relying on imagined divisions of the day between the *muezzin*'s calls to prayer was no longer adequate. So on one of the Navigator's drop-ins I asked him if he could get me a clock, in order that I could time my walks properly. There and then he unstrapped the digital watch he was wearing, a black plastic Casio, and handed it to me. This was uncommonly good service. Then again, I'd noticed that whenever I asked him for something he had to first take that request to the Triumvirate. This time he might have found it less trouble to resolve the matter on the spot.

From then on, knowing the three-hour time difference between Somalia and the UK, I made a decision about my breakfast. Although it was delivered invariably around 7.30 a.m., I chose not to eat until 9.30 a.m. – in the knowledge that back in

England it was 6.30 a.m., and Ollie and Saz would be getting up in their flat in Watford, thinking about a bite to eat for themselves. And so I ate my grim potatoes in solidarity with them, and in time for my ten o'clock walk.

The watch helped me synchronise my 'Thinking Time', too. I thought of work a lot: my colleagues, their routines, mine. I'd look at the watch and wonder: *12 noon Somali time is 9 a.m. UK time. That's when the social workers have their handover meetings. They'll be going into training room.* I knew where everyone sat, visualised them taking their usual places . . . *Then if it's Thursday, from ten to twelve is the drug and alcohol group . . .*

My job was important to me. I resolved I would go back to work. *If I'm back by December I'll take that two-week holiday and then I'll go back in. It'll be difficult but I'll do it.*

I thought of my mum, her routine, her Saturday out with friends – how I had missed her ninetieth birthday just past, for all my urgings to the Negotiator that I be freed in time for that anniversary. But I had to keep clear of things that were too strongly emotional. I had to be regimented, resolved and cold.

My exercise book became an important measuring tool – I resolved to use just a page a day. Would I fill it before it was time to go? If so would I be given another? Did I need to make this one last?

I carried on with my list games – TV programmes, artists' names – and tried to devise some quirks. If I were running a cake shop, what sort of wares would I bake to sell? Angel cake, banana cake, cheesecake, and so on. And how did I make them?

I would write out an especially long word and try to make smaller words from the letters within it; then count how many times I had used particular words. For whatever reason, 'rage' and 'sane' seemed to recur with regularity.

I also began to write motivational messages to myself along the tops of the pages and down the sides, so I could flip through and see them always. The ones that occurred to me were things Ollie had said to me in his calls: *I love you, I need you, be strong; It's only a matter of time; Keep walking to the future.* I found them truly sustaining, and a kind of driving force. I read them every day. Sometimes, at particularly dark times, I would read them every half-hour, and repeat them as I was walking round the room. Each step I took, I told myself, was a step towards Ollie, towards home and freedom.

*

I hoped against hope that Ollie was managing to make some headway in the negotiations for my freedom, and I was desperate for news. The Navigator told me to expect a visit from the Negotiator within the week, and I clung to that. But he didn't come, though I pestered the Navigator about this every day. 'He away, out of the village,' was a standard answer. I gathered that internet access was rare and at a premium, and the Negotiator needed to be online in order to do his business. But, as with nearly everything the Navigator told me, I couldn't accept it as the unvarnished truth.

Despite the Negotiator's no-show, the Navigator claimed one day to have better news for me. He came in grinning and said, 'Money ready, you go home soon.'

'How do you know this?'

'Big Man tell me. Money ready.'

As much as I wanted to believe, I just knew that couldn't be right. I had utter faith in Ollie, but I couldn't see how he had put everything in order and to the pirates' total satisfaction so quickly.

Then one morning I woke to the Navigator kicking the end of the bed. He had brought my morning potatoes, and he plonked the dish down on the table. 'You eat quick! Negotiator is here!'

This is it, I thought, exhilarated. *Better eat up. It could be your last food for a while. And get your things in order, ready for the road, for the airport if needs be.*

Not long after, the Negotiator appeared at my threshold, wearing his green sarong and a white tight vest, with a chunky gold necklace. He picked up a plastic chair, put it against the wall by the door and sat, looking at me levelly.

'I hear from your son.'

My heart surged, hoping he would say, 'The money has come through.'

'Very disappointing,' he said, shaking his head. 'He not raise enough money.'

My high spirits drained away. 'That depends, doesn't it, on how much money you're asking for?'

His silent gaze indicated this was not a matter he wished to discuss with me. 'Don't worry,' he said finally. 'He and I will speak again. When we agree, the minute money come – you go home.'

It wasn't, on balance, the worst progress report. He got up to leave, but I badly needed to feel I'd got something tangible out of his fleeting visit. I told him I wanted to be able to say a few more basic Somali words, other than just 'thank you' and 'good morning'. Could he be of any help in that respect? He thought a moment, nodded, went away and came back with a small book.

'This is my dictionary. You have this. You can take it home, if you like.'

He could stick that offer: I wanted no such souvenirs of this experience. But I held my tongue and thanked him. I knew I could make good use of his dictionary while I was stuck here.

*

The dictionary was no easy thing to browse, and I wasn't about to sit down and devour it from cover to cover. However, I managed to locate the Somali words for days of the week (*isnin, talado, arbaco*, and so on). I wrote them out in my book, spoke them aloud. Pirates who glanced in seemed intrigued by this, and I was able to lure a couple of them into practising this translation exercise with me, taking turns over the recital of the Somali and English words. In the course of this they appeared to take some pride in teaching me a few additional terms: from 'good night' (*habeen wanaagsan*) through the items in my room ('table', *joodari*; 'mattress', *miisad*; 'curtain', *daaho*), to the much needed 'toilet' (*musqusha*).

These sorties across the language barrier did seem to encourage a bit of civility, as was borne out when the Navigator brought Hungry Man in to see me, bearing a little bottle of tablets with directions written in English.

'My friend,' the Navigator gestured. 'He wants you to tell him, what this is for?'

'He wants me to translate? OK.'

The medication was for a prostate condition, worryingly. But as I accessed the dictionary to find the corresponding term in Somali, the Navigator explained that the pills had been prescribed for Hungry Man's father. And Hungry Man performed a little mime for me, of his father bending double and urinating with great difficulty – a more explicit demonstration than I required. Through the Navigator I told him how many times a day his father had to dose up, and I wished the old man a speedy recovery.

*

I was paying a new close attention to my surroundings. For the first two weeks following my kidnap I had seen everything as temporary, too unpleasant to think about. Now I knew in my gut I was going to be here for a longer haul. I was going to have to settle in. And I wanted to start observing, noting what was around me, memorising everything I could – physical details that could be useful in a court of law.

I had always had good powers of observation and recall, but my work sharpened them further. Part of my job was to do risk assessments for particularly difficult patients who were requesting home visits. I had to assess the viability of these requests, to visit the premises where the proposed visit would take place. And for that purpose I developed a near-photographic memory. Where did the house sit on the street? Was it detached or terraced? By what door did you enter? How many doors were there? Could someone abscond out the back? How long was the garden? Was there a gate? How high was the hedge? Low enough to jump over? . . .

One of the room's double doors was always open, so I could see the far wall of compound. I would sit at an angle to the curtain so that when the wind blew it open I could see briefly what was going on. But I was increasingly intrigued by the windows in my room. Was there still a world outside?

Often I could hear children laughing, as if in a schoolyard. There was a time every day when a goat went past, bleating, a small girl's voice chatting away to it. I was keen to try to sneak a peek outside, but afraid of someone seeing me.

A highly useful phrase I gleaned from the Somali dictionary was *Daaqad furayya fadlan?* ('Window open, please?'). I made a point of trying this out on whichever pirate brought me my potatoes in the morning, and if I got lucky then a set of shutters would be opened, the curtains then redrawn and pegs reinstated.

My main target was the left-hand wall window that could be seen only obliquely from the door. As I went round, I would 'worry' the middle peg in the curtains slightly so that it loosened and finally fell off. I checked no one had heard, made another circuit, then I'd peek through the slit, furtively. I had two headscarves, and I dropped one on the floor between the chair and the table. I'd pretend to be picking up the scarf to disguise my peeking.

Through this window I could see buildings close by, surrounded by high thatched fences, with corrugated roofs. To the right one building was very long. If I was lucky I glimpsed the young girl leading her goat under the window. Immediately in front of me was a corrugated gate into a compound, where the house had a red door. To the right of the window there was another corrugated gate and one afternoon I watched a young boy trying to open it, succeeding after a long struggle.

It wasn't a visual feast through that window. But it became a big part of my world. I didn't want anybody outside to see me in case they told the pirates I was looking out. At the same time I wondered: did some of them already know I was behind the curtain? Were the villagers fully aware there was a white woman in their midst, that pirates were operating next door to them?

Whatever the truth, I intended to keep up my peeking. It brought a pleasing sense of doing something the pirates didn't know I was doing: a little oneupmanship. *You think you've got*

*me, that you can break my spirit, but you won't. That's going to
remain intact.*

*

Amina continued to visit me whenever she called into the
compound. We would bow to each other, shake hands. And now
I could greet her in Somali. I was happy enough to see her,
always. And yet she had become a puzzle to me. For all the
kind gestures she made to me covertly, I wondered how, as a
woman, she could go on being party to my imprisonment, knowing that my husband was dead and my son struggling to barter
for my freedom thousands of miles away. Couldn't she do more
to help me?

The Navigator told me she kept a shop in the village and had
been engaged to cook for the pirates and, rather less fastidiously,
for me. So there was no point in pretending she wasn't up to her
neck in this criminal operation. She also laundered and pressed
the pirates' clothes – very professionally, too, since the men were
routinely clad in shirts and trousers with sharp creases. (Hungry
Man, I noted, seemed to be alone in insisting on doing his own
ironing.) The pirates evidently saw her as a matriarchal figure,
and she would shout at them cheerily and share jokes.

I had to accept Amina was profiting from my captivity: it had
to be a good earner for her. Was it one she couldn't say no to? I
couldn't really see what else she would do for a living. Life for
Somali women looked to me like an awful lot of work and
subservience, from dawn through to dusk. Religion seemed to
deprive them of much say over their lives. They worked hard with
their bare hands, and no mod cons, leaving things to dry on sun-
baked stones. It was a way of life that probably had persisted for
generations, and didn't look likely to change any time soon.

Even if Amina had had the slightest urge to help me out of my predicament, I couldn't imagine what she would do, or to whom she would protest. In the end I had to take the view that, for all her smiles and the small favours she sent my way, she probably looked on my being held here as strictly business. And that was a bit sickening. It depressed me to think about how corruption could spread, become habit-forming, once immoral behaviour became part of a community's accepted way of life.

One morning as I came out of the toilet I was stunned to see – in the company of the Beautiful Woman who was delivering the pirates' breakfasts – a young black boy of six or seven years, blindly following in tow, bearing a stainless-steel dish with a lid on it. The boy and I exchanged bewildered looks, and I had an urge to cover my face with my scarf – it didn't seem right to me that he should have to clap his young eyes on any part of the iniquitous set-up inside this compound. After he had gone I felt indignant that he'd been drawn into this sordid world, made to help feed these thugs who wore guns on their shoulders. I told the Navigator what I had seen, and with an appalled expression on his face he denied it hotly. 'No, no, that cannot be.'

I didn't see the boy again. But whatever the Navigator really believed about the need to keep minors shielded from criminality in their midst, the fact remained that he was either kidding me, or kidding himself.

*

My days felt changeless, interminably long and monotonous, hot, sticky and unventilated. I walked on and on, barefoot, for half an hour on the hour from 7 a.m. to 8 p.m. – unless faintness came over me or the painful twinges of my blisters became unmanageable. Even then, I would try to walk on the edges of my feet, just in order to keep with the programme.

When I wasn't walking I counted: the 170 sets of vertical patterns on the curtains around the room; the 110 nails through eyelets that kept the curtains hung up; the 9 nails on one leg of my bed, the 5 on another. I practised yoga and deep-breathing exercises, cross-legged on the floor, and at times, peering down out at the coral-pink lino, I amused myself by seeing shapes within the patterns – an elephant, say, or Queen Victoria's profile.

In this way I served my time.

Gradually it seemed that the Triumvirate had taken over from Smiley Boy in bringing me my food, but the diet was unvarying – although my grey potatoes sometimes had tiny bits of green pepper interspersed, and my rice was sometimes bathed in a flavourless red water. Outside the pirates routinely feasted on aromatic hunks of meat. Once I asked the Navigator and Hungry Man if I might have a little of the meat juices from their plate to flavour my dish. But I was refused. If I passed them en route to the toilet they stared at me as they chomped away. I returned to the room seething inside, but I was adamant I wouldn't let them see me irked.

Every night at 9 p.m. I stuck my head out of the door and murmured *habeen wanaagsan* to whoever was posted there. Indoors I whispered my good nights to Ollie and to Mum, sent out good wishes and hopes that I would see them soon. (Talking to myself seemed a permissible vice in these circumstances.) Once in bed I never had trouble getting off to sleep for at least a couple of hours. But with regularity I would wake in the night and have to lie in the dark awhile until dropping off again. It was vital to me I get the sleep I needed in the hours of darkness – I feared the torpor of sleeping sunlit hours away, turning day into night and night into day, losing that connection to normality.

My dreams were usually vivid, often warm and wishful. One night I found myself restored to the comfort of our home. I was in the lounge, the wood-burning fire was on, David was beside me and we were watching television. Our cat Otis was nestled on my lap, I stroked him and could hear – could even feel – his purr. David and I hardly spoke; we didn't need to. Then I felt the dream fade, my eyes peeled open, and I realised my misery anew.

At such times I had to be brisk in my 'self-comforting', otherwise I wouldn't have left my bed, wouldn't have got down to what I needed to do to survive. *You've got your son, you've got your family*, I would tell myself. *You had a wonderful time with David. You couldn't have wished for a better husband. You were lucky.* That much was true, however painful, and – mostly – it helped to keep despair at bay.

*

Hungry Man continued to give evidence of a special devotion to his Muslim faith, but also of some kind of fledgling interest in comparative religion. As he took me for a Christian, he wanted to know how and where and how frequently I prayed. I demonstrated the traditional posture of kneeling by a bedside with hands clasped and eyes closed. This struck him as a bit funny-peculiar – and me, likewise, since I was genuflecting to a faith that held no meaning for me. None the less I cheerily told Hungry Man I prayed every night, that I might return to my family and to my son, since the thicker I laid this on, the more I hoped these men might begin to feel some collective obligation. The image of the motherless child seemed to me a universally plangent one, but I was careful, too, to refer to Ollie as the 'head of the household' in the wake of his father's death. The pirates had a settled patriarchal view of the world, and here I felt the pragmatic choice was to play up to that.

One evening another delegation trooped into my room, but without ceremony or threat: it was just the Navigator, Hungry Man, Smiley Boy, and a few other pirates, including one I'd dubbed Bambi (young, doe-eyed, almost pretty in a fragile way) and a diminutive fellow whose nickname in English the Navigator had identified for me as Mouse ('What you call tiny creature, four legs, long tail . . .?') One of the men now muttered something to the Navigator, who turned to me.

'My friends want to know about your son.'

'What do they want to know about my son for?'

'They say, does he like . . . football?' And he mimed a sort of net-bursting kick.

Ollie had never been especially keen on the game, but since that was what got them enthused I decided to tell a few white lies.

'Oh yes, yes, he loves football. He *plays* football.'

Faces lit up around the room. Here was a genuine interest and excitement. Smiles and cheery digs in the ribs abounded.

'What team he like?' the Navigator continued.

One day I'd noticed a pirate wearing an Arsenal shirt. It was the obvious choice. 'Oh . . . Arsenal?'

'Arsenal! Arsenal!' They were utterly sold. 'What other sports he like?'

I told them, truthfully now, that Ollie loved to swim and to take long bike rides, fifty or sixty kilometres at a time. But I wasn't certain they grasped the concept of the bicycle.

'He no have car?'

'No, he gets about on his bike. Or by bus?'

This seemed only to perplex the gang further.

'How many *years* he?'

'How old is he? He's twenty-five. So he's older than some of you.'

When I then had to explain that he wasn't yet married with children, this deepened the frowns and internal discussions.

'Why you have only one child?'

It was the Negotiator's gripe, back to haunt me again. Girding up my patience I told them, 'When I had my son I was very ill. Could not have another child – too risky? But God was very good to give me a boy . . .'

This entirely calculated remark got them nodding vigorously once more. Altogether it was a version, albeit warped, of a 'normal', 'friendly' exchange over the health of one's family; also another little trip for me down a cultural divide. Of course they asked me nothing about myself, and, had I a daughter, I knew they wouldn't have taken the slightest interest.

When they had gone, I found myself resenting the intrusion a little. Why had I talked? These men weren't entitled to know a single thing about Ollie. Nor could they even begin to appreciate the sort of person he was. On that level, I was glad I had lied to them. But I found, too, that I could forgive myself for what I'd said truthfully – because for me, as for any proud parent, there was a strong and simple pleasure in speaking of a beloved son, who had brought such joy and wonder to David and myself from the moment that he came along and changed our lives.

11

One important detail I gave the pirates was absolutely true: I was indeed very ill after giving birth to Ollie. My pregnancy was relatively uncomplicated, but I was monitored closely throughout on account of the medical history of my weak heart. Once my contractions quickened and David took me into hospital, my heart was under considerable strain, and what followed was twenty-two hours in labour. Finally the consultant came in, examined my readings, and declared that I had to have an emergency Caesarean section. The baby was wanting to be born, but I just didn't have the strength to push. Within two minutes I was whisked out of the room – David would tell me later that he had wondered if he would see me again. He was by no means sure I would pull through, and no one explained to him precisely what was happening.

From that point I remember little or nothing, but Ollie was born at 8.14 a.m. on 23 July 1986. As David told it, he was left pacing, anxiously, not allowed to see me, until the nurse came out and put Ollie, swaddled and crying, into his arms with the words, 'This is your son.' David found himself thinking: *Please, Jude, pull through, I can't do this alone.* And he shed some tears of his own.

I woke up the next day at 1 p.m. There was a crib in the corner of my hospital room. 'That's your son,' a nurse told me. 'Would you like to hold him?' Sadly I fell asleep again before I could manage even that simple feat: I was just too worn out. And I didn't see David until the evening.

Within days, still confined to hospital, I knew something was wrong. My stomach was sore, too tender to touch, and hot when

I dared to touch it. Ollie was proving a little fractious, not feeding, and I was fractious in turn. I had an infection. I needed a blood transfusion, and injections to break a blood clot inside the Caesarean scar that was turning septic. Ollie and I were in hospital together for two weeks in all before we were allowed home.

My post-natal experience was relatively good, but it was a more difficult time for David: he had been very shaken by our traumatic time in hospital, and it took him a while to adjust. Ollie, though, was a lovely baby. He didn't sleep as well as we might have hoped (the familiar parents' lament), but he was no trouble – happy, cheeky, engaging. As he grew he showed a keen curiosity, a natural inquisitiveness, even when very small. As soon as he began to talk, everything was 'why?' – putting David and me on the spot.

We were living in Chute Forest in rural Wiltshire, four miles from the nearest village, and David, very busy with his work, went off in the car every morning. So I spent a lot of time with Ollie in a somewhat secluded existence, the only mum with a small child in the vicinity. One thing we had taken from the standard advice about childrearing was that, when children are small, 'you get out what you put in'. So I made sure we had adventures. I had a little backpack and would take Ollie out yomping for the day in nature. I'd show him trees and flowers, touch his hand to bark and leaves and petals, explaining what these things were, encouraging sensory experience. At home I got him to help me turn the pages of books as we read, and I put his baby-seat up on the kitchen worktop when I was cooking or baking, so I could let him in on what I was doing, give him pieces of peel to hold. Years later I began to think he might choose a career as a chef: he loved to cook, and creatively at that, as did David. It was one of the striking similarities between them.

When Ollie reached school-leaving age his creative abilities were borne out by his gaining a place at a leading London art college, which thrilled David especially, as this was something he would have loved to have done himself. In due course we went along proudly to Ollie's graduation, where I whooped and whistled when his name was read out. We were both of us so happy that he had found a means to do something he enjoyed doing and that fulfilled his talent. He was living the life we had hoped for him. Now I could only imagine that on the night he got the phone call bearing the terrible news from Kiwayu he must have felt himself catapulted into an utterly different world.

At first I had the natural concern: how on earth was Ollie going to cope with the awful responsibility that had been thrust on him, and without David, the backbone of our family? But gradually I realised that he would have people around him for support – he had his girlfriend Saz and her family, his uncle Paul and aunt Maxine were kind and caring, my sister Carol would be there for him. Above all I knew Ollie to have a quiet strength of character that would enable him to handle this ordeal, to remain calm, not get hysterical. In fact I was pleased, relieved, that he was in charge. I had heard it in his voice on the phone – that control and assurance. So I had every confidence in his abilities. *He's David's son – he'll do it.*

12

On a Tuesday, 1 November, I was favoured by another visit from the Negotiator. He told me he had spoken again to Ollie, that Ollie was 'still getting money together'. And yet he seemed confident.

'Don't worry, your family are helping your son,' he told me.

I just knew this couldn't be the case. *Who is helping him? Where's he getting advice from?* I thought it best, though, to make it clear I had total faith in Ollie.

'I'm not worried. My son *will* get you the money.'

The Negotiator did not intend to dally but as usual I wanted to make the most of the conversation.

'I'm curious – I'd like to know more how piracy works in Somalia. How do these people become pirates in the first place?'

I had a theory of my own, namely that there couldn't be a great deal else to do for money in Somalia. As we'd travelled through the countryside, I'd seen no industry – this was a deprived country. The Negotiator didn't seem to want the conversation, though. He waved a hand. 'Just speak to any man here, they will tell you.'

'How can they? They don't speak English. Your English is very good . . .'

The flattery didn't work. 'Some other time . . .' he muttered, and left.

The Navigator – so adamant that he himself was no pirate but, rather, an unwilling conscript – nonetheless turned out to be keen to relate to me the latest news bulletins from the front line of Somali piracy. He came to see me one evening with a conspiratorial finger pressed to his lips, and spoke in hushed tones.

'There is American hostage taken tonight.'

'Oh no!'

He nodded keenly. 'Big Man take American woman, hold her in house. He will ask *millions* of dollars for her.'

'So, the Big Man has some other place where he can hold hostages?'

'Yes. Not this village. Different village.'

I had a notion. 'Why don't you tell Big Man, he could save some money, and bring the American woman here instead?'

A friend for me, I thought. *Misery loves company – we could get through this together. Who knows? It could be one of those lifelong friendships, Americans can be so affable that way . . .*

'No, no, no . . .' The Navigator broke my reverie, waving his hands, making clear that even if my proposal were serious he would not be relaying it to the Big Man. But then, perhaps wary of having disappointed me, he began to tell of several other Westerners being held in pirate bolt-holes across Somalia – as if to assure me I was not so alone, the Big Man's operation being only one of many.

'There are two men from Italy, they aid workers? They hostage, yes. And two women from Spain – young women. And a woman from France, old, she taken.'

'An old woman?'

'Yes, very old, and she is sick, she . . .'

He gestured with both hands as if he were pushing himself about on wheels.

'Do you mean she's in a wheelchair?'

'Yeah, she very sick. But they take her. Very bad. They take her away on boat, put her on donkey, donkey in forest.' He sounded aggrieved on this woman's behalf; and things did sound dismal for her.

'Is she being held near here, this woman? Are any other hostages near by?

He shrugged, shook his head. 'No. I don't know.'

I wondered about his interest in sharing information with me covertly. Was he trying to remind me of his oft-stated view that he and I were 'on the same side'? The little I gleaned of pirate operations was from him, and he had to expect I would remember our exchanges once I was freed. A grim, fleeting thought crossed my mind: maybe he tells me this because he thinks I'll never get out of here: 'dead women tell no tales'.

*

I kept up my efforts to rub along with the pirates via the dictionary. The Triumvirate was a special focus in that respect. They were, so to speak, the sharpest knives in the drawer: they must have had some education, for at one time or another I heard each of them say something in English. Vain Man was an awkward character, but the other two I could work on.

Some pirates, I noticed – Hungry Man and Kufiya Man in particular – would vanish for days at a time and then return. I asked the Navigator about this and he said, 'They go to see their families.' That had the ring of truth: the pirates were on their phones a lot, and you could tell when they were speaking to their families by the change in their manners. At such times Hungry Man would kiss the screen of his phone, a vaguely touching sight.

From the dictionary I dug out the words for 'family', 'children', 'home', and attempted to ask them about these furloughs. Kufiya Man nodded, 'Yes, yes, I go home.' Hungry Man confirmed the same, just as content as he was in going through numbers and days of the week with me, translating back and forth.

The stiltedness of communications was entirely understandable, of course. And yet sometimes it did occur to me that the members of the Triumvirate knew a little more than they let on. One day I asked the Navigator if the local *muezzin* used a microphone to amplify his loud summons to prayer. He frowned, seeming not to understand 'microphone'. I tried Kufiya Man on the same question. 'Yes, or else he wouldn't be heard,' he shot back. This struck me as a rather more sophisticated English construction than 'I go home.'

*

On another of his evening visits to my room the Navigator took out his phone and showed me a picture on the screen.

'Do you recognise this?'

The photo was taken in daytime, from out at sea, looking from a distance at a shoreline of sand and thatched beach huts. I started in sudden recognition. It was Kiwayu.

'This is where you took me?'

He nodded.

'Did you take this photo? From the boat?'

That one – as was his way – he did not deign to answer.

'How long were you in the boat before you took me? Had you been waiting all day?'

'We had to wait until midnight . . .'

He looked less happy now. As before, I got the impression he wanted to please me by divulging scraps of information, but if I pursued them then he instantly regretted his candour. But my need to know was great. If he was not 'one of them', surely it cost him nothing to disclose all he knew?

'Did the pirates know that David and I would be the only people staying at Kiwayu that night?'

He nodded. 'They knew. There was another man. He still in Kenya, stuck there, they leave him. Very bad.'

'So there were six of you, in all? Six men involved? But one got left behind?'

He nodded again.

'The weird thing is, there was just one couple staying there the night before us. So they were the only two there that night too.'

He looked rueful. 'That is a stroke of bad luck,' he said. Again, this seemed to me quite a phrase to use, from a man who liked to profess that his grasp of English was poor.

*

The slow but useful progress I made with the Navigator was off-set by the brute fact that there remained others among the pirates I simply couldn't deal with, and who unsettled and intimidated me, seemingly with intent – chief among these Mouse and, especially, Scary Man.

One evening as I stepped warily across the compound with my torch en route to the toilet I saw in the puddle of light a huge black beetle making slow progress of its own across the sand, working its way around rocks and stones. As a child Ollie had been keen on insects and read up on them in encyclopaedias. By taking a parental interest I was consequently able to identify all varieties of beetles, stags and scarabs and so forth. This was a goliath beetle, quite unmistakable with its big pincer claws and domed black-and-white-striped head. I followed it with the torchlight, fascinated. The pirates watched, bemused. Vain Man had his usual look of disdain. Hungry Man giggled.

Scary Man, however, got to his feet, marched past me and stood on the beetle – with a sickening crunch – then stared at me with his customary hostility. I wanted to shout at him for the sheer pointless callousness of it. Instead I shone the torch right in his face and then stomped off. But I could have cried, it was so mean and unnecessary – not to say redolent of my situation. The beetle's crushed carcass remained there for days, on view whenever I walked by.

*

One afternoon the Navigator entered, bringing with him a pirate whose face I didn't recognise at first.

He smiled. 'Do you remember "Man Number Five"?'

'No . . .' I said hesitantly.

Then this man stepped into the light, and a horrible feeling crept over me. It was indeed the long-absent 'Fifth Man' from my abduction. This was the first time I'd seen him since the nightmare of that midnight hour. His presence was unsettling, he was so gaunt and hollow-cheeked and unsmiling, with glaring, bulging eyes. I associated him with violence, with my being dragged out of bed, struck on the back with a rifle butt. I summoned my nerve, held out my hand to him as if we might shake. But he ignored the gesture, and leaned back against the edge of my picnic table, aloof.

In the days that followed he was even less affable. He came into the room not merely to stare in the manner of the others, but as if to unsettle me and put me on edge. If I was eating he would watch me, jab a finger at the food, then his own mouth, as if he wanted me to feel he might steal my poor rations. As I walked around, he would plant himself in my path. (I stepped around him.) At other times he would unshoulder his rifle and point it at me, drawing a bead on my progress as I walked.

One sweltering afternoon – of sauna heat, as I sweated and felt debilitated and drained – Kufiya Man came in, unpegged the curtains and opened the window, letting in flares of light like a halogen lamp. As I walked I felt the cooling breeze, a blessed relief. It lasted five minutes, until the Fifth Man stomped in, shouted at me as if I had done this on my own initiative, and shut me back into darkness again. Kufiya Man wandered back in a little later, and I gestured with a thumbs-down. He shrugged, but looked as if he didn't feel like reversing the decision.

*

Although I was not being harmed, there was a lot of bluff discourtesy directed my way, and precious little personal consideration of any sort. In the absence of kindness, then, I looked for ways to be kind to myself.

My feet were increasingly blistered from my walks. When the blisters then burst, I knew I needed warm water to wash them properly, so they might heal. Given the usual responses to my exceptional requests I needed a ruse. And I thought of the thermos of hot water that used to be delivered to me daily for my tea. That afternoon I raised this with the Navigator.

'You know, I think I'd like to start drinking tea again. Could I maybe have some this evening . . . ?'

The Navigator seemed to think this was a splendid idea. Smiley Boy duly came in before 6 p.m., beaming, with packet of tea and a flask that he set on my table. 'Tea!' he chirruped. A little later Amina entered with the Navigator and set down a shiny new-looking tea-strainer.

'This is for you!'

'Ah! *Mahadsanid!*'

Alone again, I exulted in my cleverness. When wash-time came round I knew I had first to make a token gesture towards the tea: so I spooned up some loose leaves, wetted them with a dash of water, then flung them out into my toilet bucket. Then I poured the rest of the precious hot water into my green bowl and lowered my feet into it – the closest thing to 'pampering' I'd known for months, and desperately needed. I gloried in the sensation, felt my feet begin slowly to relax. Once they were thoroughly soaked I massaged them, avoiding the blistered areas, feeling some pain, none the less, but some crucial relief most of all.

*

Ruses were a lifeline to me whenever I could devise them: they helped me improve my circumstances, however slightly, and made me feel I had my wits about me still.

Writing in my book was what I considered to be my private evening pastime. But the pirates routinely came in and checked what I had been scribbling, sometimes twice a day, sometimes weekly. What they were looking for, I couldn't imagine. But while they flicked through the front and back of the book, and saw all my fastidious A–Z lists, they never bothered to check the middle pages. Realising this, I got the idea of keeping a diary of daily happenings that began in the middle of the book and proceeded outwards. It would be secret for as long as the pirates didn't bother to look in front of their noses. And they didn't.

Writing was, of course, entirely dependent on adequate torch-light. And the first time I noticed the beam waning was a very angst-inducing moment for me. I asked for replacement batteries, and was intensely relieved when they came. An instinct, though, told me not to discard my 'duds' but to keep them handy. Since it was usually different pirates who fetched things for me, I picked a moment a few days later to replace the duds in the torch, summon a pirate and complain that the torch was dead. Again he brought me new batteries. But I stashed these, put my perfectly serviceable ones back, and contented myself knowing that I had 'spares'.

*

The idea that the pirates were protecting me from something beyond the compound walls dawned on me gradually. It wasn't, of course, a concern for my actual well-being so much as their need to protect their valuable asset. There were times when my request for the toilet was refused on the grounds that there was a plane passing overhead. I couldn't hear anything, and I could hardly believe I could be spotted from the air. However, they took this very seriously.

The Navigator had told me of 'other pirates' who might be minded to snatch me, but that I was safe inside the compound. I was reminded of this when he came to me and said in his familiar hushed tones, 'If anyone try take photo of you, you tell me, straight away. You come get me. Or it will be very bad for you. Very bad.'

I was spooked. 'Why?'

He wouldn't explain further, yet he was adamant. Thinking it over, I decided that if one of the pirates illicitly snapped a proof of my presence here then they could, if they were wily enough, claim to the British Consulate that they had taken me, and so open up a different channel of negotiation. Fat Man and his gang had already invested much time and money and effort in my capture and upkeep. I could see they would be nervous of some other party scooping me up and making off with the proceeds.

Obviously this was why the compound was a veritable arsenal of weaponry – not simply to control me but to meet outside aggression. The pirates routinely stripped and cleaned their guns, like a decently drilled militia. Each man had his own assigned firearm, 'personalised' by little rags of assorted colours that were tied to the barrels. Even Smiley Boy came in to me one day waving a rifle and making *pew-pew!* sounds, like a kid playing with a pointed stick. I really hoped he knew how the safety catch worked.

One day in my room I nearly jumped out of my skin on hearing a volley of gunshots close by, and I stuck my head warily out of doors. Vain Man was firing his AK47 against the compound wall, quite freely. The Navigator hastened up to me to explain.

'No problem, no problem, we practise . . .'

I could see Vain Man was aiming at a notional target. Another pirate, though, was just discharging his rifle into the air, exuberantly, as if he were celebrating a wedding in Canaan, and since he clearly didn't appreciate gravity, or the idea of bullets falling to the earth with terminal velocity, I prudently returned to my room.

'Practice' became a weekly affair, but thereafter the pirates got in the habit of warning me in advance. One particular day, though, proved different. It was two o'clock, and I was walking, when suddenly I heard lots of gunfire – lots of different-sounding guns, and beyond the compound walls, though not far off. There were whistling sounds, then *tap-tap-taps* like short bursts of fire. I looked out to see pandemonium on the terrace and in the yard: scurrying, commotion, confusion. Vain Man had taken charge, was barking orders, organising people. He sent assorted pirates running off in various directions out of the compound, and posted Hungry Man and Limping Man outside my door. I wasn't surprised Hungry Man had been kept from any front line: he seemed a non-martial sort, happier sweeping the compound or ironing his shirts pristine.

Shortly the Navigator rushed in on me, carrying a rifle and a sort of combat vest with square pockets that bulged with boxes of ammunition. His rifle looked old and battered, its strap tatty and threadbare. The Navigator had never been one to join in the group cleaning and disassembling of weapons. Now he looked out of his depth, scared, visibly shaking.

'What's going on? Is it other pirates?'

'No problem, you stay here.'

I wasn't going anywhere. But equally there was quite clearly a problem. 'Are you OK?' I asked.

'Ah, I never had gun before. Never fire gun.'

He rushed out again. I looked to see Hungry Man and Limping Man sitting on the worn earthen steps to the covered walkway, but Hungry Man waved me back and out of sight.

As the sounds of what was evidently a gun battle kept growing louder and fiercer, and seemingly right outside the compound, I could feel terror rising in me. I no longer felt remotely safe. It sounded to me like, despite previous assurances, this 'safe house' was being raided. And if I wasn't shot and killed in some insane crossfire then I would be retaken, by some new set of violent, hostile, trigger-happy goons.

Utterly gripped by fear I sat on the floor by my bed, crouched with my hands over my ears against the din from outside. Gradually I slumped down and curled into a foetal position, desperately wanting this to end.

There, in the panic of it all, my mind wandered and strayed into wild imagining. I had a vision in my head of an invading band of pirates, pulling the room's window clean out of its frame, climbing in, hefting me up into a fireman's hold and carrying me off, like a chattel – a daylight replay of my living nightmare on Kiwayu. It was as if I could feel myself bouncing about like a rag doll on some man's broad shoulder, being dragged through bush, scratched by thorns . . . For a time that I couldn't measure, these figments appeared to me as absolute reality. And yet part of me knew all too well I was slipping away; I was 'losing it'.

I had to fight, mentally, calling on whatever solid moorings of consciousness I could, to pull myself round. *You're here. The ground underneath you is what's real.* I could feel my spread fingers scratching the gritty floor, a real and harsh sensation: I knew I had retreated to the corner of the room, and was pulling up the linoleum. I put my fingers before my eyes, saw they were red raw. I could hear the guns still. But I was no longer hallucinating. My fears were real, but no longer enhanced by fevered imaginings. If I was scared I was also sobered. *This is bad. But you cannot lose your mind, you mustn't.*

I stayed huddled, the gunfire continued. But gradually it seemed to turn sporadic, and then to abate. I could hear footfalls, troops returning to the compound. Another pirate looked in, bearing one of the big rifles with a tripod fixing. Bizarrely, round his waist he wore a bright orange chiffon sarong, sequined flowers sewn on it – the strangest battledress one could imagine.

'Is OK now,' he said.

Vain Man led a larger group back through the compound gates. He wore the look of a conquering hero, proudly silent amid the excited chatter of the others. Whatever had brought about this 'contact', it was clearly over. I breathed more easily.

The Navigator, no doubt greatly relieved himself, came to see me and to explain. What was going on, he said, was a skirmish between rival local clans. A neighbouring clan had trespassed on this village, and tried to seize a patch of grassland for their goats. The village had had to muster against this aggressive intrusion – successfully, it seemed. I asked if anyone had been hurt.

'The other clan, some of them wounded. In their arms and their legs. And I think some die.'

Just like that, I thought. *All over some pasture for goats.*

'But none of these pirates got injured.'

He shook his head.

*

Unease and restlessness rose up in me with a vengeance, the more precarious my situation seemed. I felt dangerously in the dark about external matters, found myself starting to think, *Maybe nothing is happening. Maybe I'm here for ever . . .* It was hard to hold back such thoughts, however briefly they came, since I had no solid evidence, no trustworthy advice, to shore up against them.

One afternoon the Navigator came in, affecting his conspiratorial air, and started to tell me yet again that I was going home because money had come through.

'People in Nairobi, they know you, they give money.'

'But *no one* knows me in Nairobi,' I snapped. Still I wanted to grasp at hope. I was so desperate for some real, honest news of what was happening to me. Could there have been some separate effort on my behalf by the British Embassy, initiated, maybe, by the Englishman I spoke to all those weeks ago? The Navigator insisted, 'People give money.' But it seemed to me I was being told whatever occurred to them, as if it might keep me quiet or incurious.

'I don't believe you,' I said. 'I want to speak to the Negotiator. I need to know exactly what's going on.'

I was stroppy, because I felt I could push him as I couldn't the others. He went off. Amina came in not long afterwards and I tried to grill her too. 'We hear nothing,' she said. The Navigator came back and said, 'Negotiator come this afternoon.'

'I hope so,' I shot back.

The Negotiator eventually came with Fat Man, who wore a face as black as thunder, followed by his creepy Sidekick. Amina and the Navigator were in tow. I decided to put the Navigator to work as a translator.

'Ask the Negotiator, is there money coming or not? I want to know.'

The Navigator started to relay something in Somali. But it was Fat Man, not the Negotiator, who responded, irately. Instead of his usual slack, hostile stare he came forward, stared hard at me. Thrown offguard, I was determined not to blink. Finally he turned away, spat out some words, angrily. His Sidekick mirrored his anger as they stomped out.

The Negotiator looked at me levelly, gravely. 'You've made the Big Man very angry. He say you *shot* tomorrow.'

'What?' I blurted out in shock.

'You hear! He say we shoot you tomorrow. We *fed up* of you.'

'Well, I'm fed up of you.' I regretted that comeback instantly, knew I should have bitten my tongue, since the gravest threat had just been uttered against me. And yet somehow I couldn't believe my situation could get worse. The look on the Negotiator's face, though, was horribly convincing. He turned and left, and the Navigator followed. The threat stood: a sentence of death had been passed.

My mind reeled. Was it to be summary execution? In the morning, was I going to be stood up before a firing squad? Blindfolded, or allowed to face the executioner? Or just pushed down to my knees and despatched with a bullet in the back of the head? Who would pull the trigger on me? How would Ollie get the news? Would they return my corpse or dump me in the desert ...?

Amina stood there looking at me still. There was something solicitous in her face, as if she saw my upset without quite understanding it.

I looked at her, helpless, feeling tears welling in me, and with my index finger I mimed the universal gesture of a straight slash across my throat.

'Me die tomorrow.'

'Oh no, no, no!' she said. She sat down on my bed and beckoned me to join her, then took my hand in mine and stroked it, looking consolingly into my eyes. She knew, for sure, that I was desperate, scared, in misery. And for that she extended some comfort to me, as if it were instinctive.

We sat there for some time, an hour at least, as the sunlight through the eaves of the room faded and darkness began to close in. We did not speak. Finally she patted my hand with hers.

'*Berri*,' she said. Tomorrow. And she pointed to me. 'You eat.' Did she mean my last meal? I couldn't be sure. Then she left, and I was alone. It had gone 5 p.m.

Soon afterwards, I smelled the food for the pirates. My congealed rice was delivered at 6 p.m. I was battling in my head: how easy would it be for them to shoot me and get rid of me? I had to draw on my logical mind, expurgate the emotions. *Close the negative drawer, open the positive, take out what helps you, what makes sense. You were kidnapped for money. If you're dead you have no value any more. They've spent a lot of money on you already: they need a return on that. In the cold light of day they'd not be so stupid as to shoot their meal ticket . . .*

Still, I hardly slept that night.

The next morning at 7 a.m. I commenced my walking, and my food came. I ate at 9.30 a.m., imagining Ollie at breakfast too. But I was living on the edge of my nerves.

The Navigator entered and I looked up at him. He didn't smile. 'Big Man not happy. But he not kill you . . .'

So, it was to be another 'normal' day, after all – not the day of my judgment, just one day nearer my release. I was better off, too, for having framed a strong argument to myself: that however they might intimidate me, they would be fools to kill me.

Still the precariousness of it all was in my thoughts not long after, when the Navigator came again to my room with the air of carrying a message.

'Bad news,' he said.

'What?'

'The old French lady – hostage? She die.'

I found this perturbing. 'Oh my god, really? You mean she died in captivity?'

He nodded. 'Very bad. She sick, she need tablets, they not give to her.'

That was a sobering thought. Clearly, there was more than one way to die as a hostage in Somalia – neglect, lack of care, misunderstanding. In a place of limited resources, these, too, could be lethal. I was neither elderly nor disabled, but my body could not be immune to the effect of continued privations.

In the course of my night-washing routine I had begun to notice that sheets of my skin were peeling away from my body. My flesh was sagging loose: I could count folds where fat had once been, unwelcome evidence that I was shrinking. Undoubtedly I was losing more weight that I had realised.

And yet I felt no inclination to lodge a protest for improved food rations. I was quite certain – on the evidence of past (and very modest) such requests denied – that I would be ignored. And, at bottom, I just didn't want to afford these pirates any more pleasure in the act of refusing me – in the smug sense that hunger was a tool by which they could exert further control over me. I had to assert that I could manage. I knew that I could survive, at least, on little food. What felt more important to me was water – not to mention my book and pen, my means of mental engagement. But in other respects – in the physical sense – it seemed, somehow, that I was losing a degree of interest in 'me'.

My body just looked tired: it wanted so badly to go home. It had spent too long under the wrong skies, in this alien, hostile environment where nothing was natural. The French woman's tragic fate had given me a hard reminder to do all I could to look after myself. But I had no realistic hope of my rations improving. It seemed to me that mental strength and the correct manage-ment of my energies were the decisive elements I had under my control.

*

I was weary of cold-water washes, of feeling perpetually sweaty and ill-smelling without any relief. My headscarf had grown grubby and stiff with perspiration, but when I asked for a little Omo detergent to wash it, this was refused me. In the end I performed the task myself at night with soap, and put it on wet. But all these sensations were increasingly loathsome to me.

And then one day my ears picked up on a low hiss from out-side, then a *drop-drop-drop* on the tin roof above me. I went to the door and I could see it was raining. I had smelled it before I saw it – that reviving smell of rain falling on dry earth. Pirates were crowding under the cover of the overhang, but I asked if I could go to the toilet. They looked at me as if I had sunstroke. However, I had a plan. And I took my time there and back, for it was such a joyous moment to stand and be exposed to torren-tial rain. I was content to be soaked, to feel cold. The pirates laughed at me, evidently suspecting I was losing my mind. But I was quite clear that I wanted to be in the rain for as long as I possibly could. It made me feel alive again – whereas in that room the sensations felt more akin to slow death.

*

One evening, a surprise: Kufiya Man came into my room carrying a transistor radio, the most intriguing sight I had seen in a while. He wore a big smile and, encouragingly, seemed to want to engage with me.

'Ah, radio?' I said.

'Oh yes, very good,' he replied, with a thumbs-up. I had no idea what he was listening to, but that didn't seem to be the point.

'BBC very good, yes?' he said. 'BBC World Service?'

'Oh yes, World Service!' I gave him my broadest smile.

At that he lifted the radio and began to fiddle with the tuning knob. Suddenly an English-speaking voice broke forth, the familiar RP intonation of a nightly BBC newsreader. Kufiya Man handed me the radio with a look of triumph. I was amazed, and feared that I might cry.

'Not for me, no?'

'Yeah!' he said, beaming. Then he sauntered out.

I sat and listened for perhaps half an hour, to *News Hour* and then *World Briefing*, stunned by how the business of the great wide world was suddenly cascading into my narrow confinement. To be able to hear my own language, and news from home, felt like a lifeline, a friend in isolation, clarity and coherence after so much dark and confusion.

Whereupon the Fifth Man stomped into the room, carrying his usual cloud of rancour, and snatched the radio away. He barked something at me and walked out with my prize. *It was too good to last*, I thought, deflated.

In a little while Kufiya Man was back, and seemed bewildered to find me empty-handed.

'Radio?' he asked.

'Gone', I said, shrugging, pointing outside.

His brow furrowed. I got the impression his view was that, as he had joined me together with the radio, no other pirate should then tear that asunder.

He must have gone out and registered a complaint on my behalf, because later that night, as I was preparing to wash at 8.30 p.m., Amina entered, all smiles, and from under her *jilbab* she produced another transistor radio, this one with an earpiece dangling from a socket. Then she hugged me, which I appreciated.

I couldn't get reception from the radio that night, but I awoke the next day with new hope. I had been managing for so long with so little, pen and book and torch, rudimentary things that were hugely vital to me in structuring and getting through a day. This radio was therefore an incredible luxury.

I tried periodically to pick up a signal; and around 1 p.m., to my delight, the set came to life with the voice of James Coomarasamy and the World Service *News*. Mindful of conserving batteries, I turned it off again when I walked. Later, around 7 p.m. to 7.30 p.m., the signal turned frustratingly inaudible. But I was cheered: my days had acquired a new, essential, unmissable element, one that opened up my world.

That night Amina and the Navigator entered, along with a new face, a young girl in a blue and black *jilbab*, carrying a handbag. Amina had brought me extra batteries for the radio. I explained through the Navigator that it was working fine, but that I was very glad of the spares. I was more intrigued by this girl. She appeared to be about sixteen years old, with a shy look, her head down, eyes averted but for occasional quick furtive glances. I said to the Navigator, 'Who is this?'

'Ah, this Amina's daughter.'

I said to Amina, 'Your daughter is lovely.'

Amina smiled and said something to the Navigator, pointed to her daughter then to me, then gestured with her hand, the thumb and pinkie finger extended, turning in the air like an aeroplane swooping about. The Navigator guffawed.

'What did she say?'

'She say when you leave here, you take her daughter with you. For your son.'

What a thought that was. Still, liking Amina as I did, I wanted to be sure I responded with care. 'Oh no, my son is twenty-five years old.'

'No care! No problem!'

The next day I saw Amina again in the compound and when she saw me she again made that gesture in the air with her hand, grinning. I supposed it was going to be a running gag.

*

In the early hours of the morning I felt the ground shake. I awoke in darkness to harsh vibration, discordant noise. My bed was being kicked, very purposely so as to wake me. As I stirred I was dazzled by the harsh glare of torchlight in my eyes, and for a moment I could see nothing else in front of me.

Then I found some focus and realised the Navigator was standing there. He didn't say a word, but held out a black bin-liner, and pointed sharply at my things around the room, then prodded a finger down into the depths of the binbag.

'You want me to put my things in there?'

He nodded. 'We go,' he said.

'Where are we going?'

To that, no answer. And so anxiety came spiralling down on me again. I got out from under the mosquito net and began to fill the bag with the sum of my worldly goods – my book and pen, my radio, my torch, a little bottle of shampoo. When no one was watching, impulsively, I plucked off the six pegs that were holding my curtains together: it just seemed to me that they could prove a handy addition to my cache. Then I was told to sit, and they took down the mosquito net, folded up the blue-and-yellow mattress, gathered up my water receptacles. In the dark I could barely make out the figures flitting around me: the effect was phantasmagorical. But Vain Man was directing operations, ensuring everything was stripped down and carted. Silence prevailed. No one spoke. The pirates' feet seemed to be soundless on the floor. Actions were seamlessly orchestrated, one man's job to pick up and bear off this, another that.

Then I was led out into the compound. As usual most of the pirates were asleep, either undercover or outside in the compound, their sheets wound up and around their heads, like shrouds. The door in the metal gate was opened, I stepped out and there the Fat Controller's four-wheel-drive awaited me, its door open. I was bundled inside, clutching my black bag. Pirates got in the back beside me, with their guns.

The car rolled away, headlights off, moving slowly through the village. Through the glass I saw a restaurant, a hairdresser's, a donkey tied up, houses with four-wheel-drive cars parked up outside. All was quiet, dark, deserted. After a little while I noticed piles of stones along the sides of the track, seeming to lead out of the village. We were headed that way, but not at speed. Once we were past the dwellings the car lights went on. But soon we entered another settled cluster of houses. We hadn't gone so very far, and seemed to be nearing our destination. I knew now I was going to be confined to new quarters. I'd got accustomed to the compound, got settled there. This new disruption was frightening to me.

It was an eerie feeling, knowing oneself to be transported somewhere 'in secret', and a kind of mental torture, too, because I could feel the natural, surging instinct to scream out, 'Help me!', to anyone who might listen and come to my aid. Or else to try to bolt from the moving car – something, anything, that could alert some other sensible person to my plight.

But I didn't dare do any such thing. I had contemplated escape once, right at the start, in the mangrove swamp, but not since. It had been hopeless then and it had been hopeless ever since. My prison wasn't just whatever hole of a room I was confined to. It was this whole village, and its surrounding area. My prison, indeed, was all of Somalia. And from that there could be no escape.

13

The car pulled up before a narrow gate of blue corrugated iron with a tiny shiny padlock, in a frame of flimsy wood set amid a perimeter fence of misshapen branches and shrubbery secured by wire. The pirates got out first, and Hungry Man led the way, scratching around in the pocket of his shorts as if for keys. He pulled out a bunch and tried the gate with each of them, without success. I watched this folly glumly from the car's back seat. I checked my watch. We'd left the 'Big House' at 2 a.m. Now it was 2.20 a.m.

At last the gate was levered open, I was taken from the car and we trooped into the compound. They used the light shed by their phone screens to show me the way, across a small yard towards a poky dwelling with a corrugated-iron door. Fearful already of what I was going to find there, I asked for the toilet. One pirate pointed, swung the weak light around in another direction, towards another door. I fiddled in the dark with a bolt, flung it open – found another hole in the ground, with a tree seemingly growing up through it. Conditions here, I could tell, were much cruder and more rudimentary than the place we had left.

When I crept back out from the toilet Vain Man ushered me into a dark, dirty, chilly room. In it was nothing but a table at the end and a bed base of wooden slats on a frame, standing unsteadily on an uneven concrete floor. The roof was tin, the walls appeared to be pale clay with occasional knobbly protrusions. There was one shuttered window, about twelve inches square. I felt desolation creep over me.

A quartet of pirates came in and set about desultory efforts to 'make up the room'. The Navigator carried in the mattress and threw it onto the bed base. I put sheets on the bed as they tacked up the mosquito net. My bucket and bowl and container were brought in, plus a chair that had been carted across from my previous room too. But there could be no masking the squalid, ramshackle appearance of this place.

'Why have I been moved here?' I asked the Navigator.

He shrugged. 'I not know. I just told we must move.'

The thought of being stuck here for the foreseeable future was so dismal that I had to try to shut down my emotions, assert the logical side: *OK, so the first task is to make it through to morning. In the light of day you can assess the situation anew. You'll walk, you'll get into your routine – you'll manage.*

Two more mattresses were dragged into the room and I realised I was to have company for the evening: the Navigator, the Fifth Man and Bambi threw themselves down. The door was pulled shut, enclosing us in airless darkness: I had a horrible feeling we would be in unpleasantly close quarters here. Of course in a room scarcely fit for human habitation we also had company of the six- and eight-legged variety. In bed I pulled the sheet up to my chin as always, but it wasn't long before I felt the repulsive sensation of creatures scuttling across my face and neck.

*

Surveying the room in the light of dawn was a stern test of my spirits, from the moment I opened my eyes to see a gauzy mesh of grey cobwebs on the ceiling above me. The walls, I now made out clearly, were fashioned from dried wattle and daub that had been plastered onto the branches of trees, some of which protruded through this render.

After the first shock to my system of the kidnap from Kiwayu I had tried to practise resilience: I knew I had reserves to draw on, and I was sustained too by a particular hope – in retrospect, a nearly naive optimism. But then had come a second shock, the dreadful news of David's death, which had thrown a shadow over me and shattered my dearest hopes. None the less I still had my resilience, my faith in our son, and my dream of getting home to him. However I felt in my bones that this move was yet another shock: one that made the thought of getting through the days all the more daunting.

I would have to hold onto my structure: my walking and exercise, my set times of eating and sleeping. The floor was nine paces long, and my challenge hadn't changed: to walk that floor a dozen times daily until I fell into bed from weariness. I had to keep telling myself, 'You'll be leaving soon. It's just a matter of time.' But looking around this bleak place it was a lot harder to believe that. If I was to be here now, did the Negotiator know? Could I expect to see him, to have calls with Ollie, to be informed of what, if anything, was going on over my release? Everything I had understood to this point had been thrown into disarray.

I needed to impose myself on my surroundings somehow. Looking around the muddy walls, in particular at the spurs of hard tree bark that poked through sporadically, I decided to put these to good use, as ad hoc clothes hooks. I hung up the bin-liner that contained my carefully washed and preserved red-and-black dress, and as I commenced my walking I nodded to it with each passing circuit. *That's your going-away outfit. At least keep that clean.*

I got some sense of the pirates' new modus operandi when Vain Man and an elderly man arrived at the compound by car, bringing food and water for the pirates and for me, along with plastic bags of *khat*, which were doled out near-religiously.

When I looked out to the yard I realised that the only other permanent structure in this compound bar my room and the toilet was a small, round house, its roof thatched in the African style, to the left of the gate. That house looked to be so cramped – indeed the whole place appeared so jerry-built – that I wasn't surprised I'd been required to share my room with pirates overnight.

I tried to engage the pirates in a few other small tasks that I hoped would make the room more bearable. I asked for Marvin's help to move the green-and-gold-topped plastic table, and a filthy rug that sat underneath it, the shifting of which disturbed a veritable colony of cockroaches. In the yard Hungry Man was being his usual fastidious self, busying himself with a broom, and I asked him if he would help me clean out the room. He loaned me the broom and I swept, and then he brought in a large bucket of water, which he splashed around the floor with a scoop. This meagre effort at houseproudness was a little 'connection' of sorts, and the outcome was a clean floor.

Later that morning Vain Man came and took my door off its hinges, propping it against the outer wall while Hungry Man fetched a green curtain and nailed it up over the doorway, leaving a two-foot gap at the bottom for fresh air – which also gave me sight of the gate and the African House. Realising this, the pirates reconsidered. Vain Man decided to drop the curtain right to the floor. I had to have fresh air, and I decided to put my case to Hungry Man rather than Vain Man: smiling, I gestured as to clutch my throat and made a ghastly choking noise. He took my point, and refixed the curtain one more time to leave six inches at the bottom. My small victory, though, proved short-lived:

come the afternoon torrential rain came, lashing at the curtain, and the pirates hastily reinstated the door, pulling the curtain over the top so it wasn't exposed. And so gloom resettled itself on my dingy and cheerless habitat.

*

There was a second delivery of food and water late afternoon, and around five o'clock my evening portion of rice was brought. I saved it for after my walk, and ate by torchlight, since there was no other source of light come the evening. However, one of the guards came in and made me move to the furthest corner of the room, in case someone outside might notice the light through the window.

I counted seven pirates in the compound. There was no sentry at my door. Most of the time they all seemed to be in the round house. Two of them had been assigned the big tripod-mounted machine-guns, and they were stationed with these weapons trained on the gate. The other pirates toted their standard-issue AK47s. Those who weren't part of the detail for sleeping in my room had a particular ritual come the evening: they dragged an old car bumper from the side of the yard to a position in front of my door, and propped it up with sticks, then threw their mattresses down and their coats against it so they had a crude kind of backrest.

Around 8.30 p.m. I insisted on my usual washing time and would close the door, with the words, 'Washing now.' But as soon as I was done the pirates crept in and got onto their mattresses. Their presence was hugely annoying, as they fiddled continually with their phones into the small hours. Sleep was next to impossible given the lights of the glowing screens and insistent tapping. They were wired on *khat*, of course, and they knew they could get through a shift and then sleep the rest of the day. But I didn't have that recourse. I was desperately afraid of turning nocturnal in my habits. That way led to unreality, and I needed to be as sharp and alert as possible.

*

The move had shaken and dispirited me, and I couldn't hide that from myself. I was edgy, no longer knowing what to expect. Hour by hour the awfulness of the place seemed to exact a price on my morale and my psyche.

My room was hot and dark and felt to me like the lair or domain of whole clusters of beetles, ants, arachnids and even amphibious life. Continual noises and small rustlings made me start and think, 'What could that be . . . ?' I found a frog in the corner of the room one afternoon, and brushed him out. But when I began to see insects emerging through the walls I recoiled and wondered if I could believe my eyes. These invaders were large, bright-red caterpillars, their bristling movements so dis-concerting that I could hardly bear to look at them.

The floor of the toilet heaved with insect life, and I couldn't set my foot down anywhere without a crunch. Big ants, an inch long, roamed over my feet and up my legs as I squatted. In the dark I couldn't be sure what I might touch wherever I put my hands. The branch growing up inside the toilet was especially crawling with life. Unfortunately I found I needed to hold this branch for support in getting to my feet, and whenever I did so I got a handful of squirming arthropods for my trouble.

The corrugated-iron roof exaggerated the heat of the day. In the mornings the pirates tended to open my door in and pull the curtain out over the doorway, so at least I got the benefit of some breeze. They constructed a shaded area for themselves out of branches with matting draped over them, but more often they seemed to lurk in the African House, and so I found myself strangely isolated. In the Big House (as I now thought of it) the covered walkway outside the rooms meant that one always had a sense of life outside, pirates talking and laughing. But in this Horrible House (which seemed the most fitting appellation), I had to lie down on the floor and look under the curtain for the smallest sign of life or activity.

One day, as I sat in the room sensing that nothing was happening outside, I wondered what the pirates might do if I flicked the curtain over the door, to give myself a little more air but also something more to look at beyond the enclosure of four walls, and the cockroaches crawling over the bed. Somehow they must have had a preternatural sense of my initiative for no sooner had I dared to do this than they came running out of the African House and shouted angrily at me. I retreated to the corner of the room, lay down on a mattress and protested weakly in Somali, '*Kulul* [hot].' But they threw the curtain down and closed the door on me. I had to believe the punishment was temporary, that they understood I would be in danger of asphyxiation unless the door was opened soon.

I had to keep my head together, my mind occupied. I took to virtual driving, beginning by picturing myself clambering into our car on the drive in Bishop's Stortford. I could feel and smell the leather seats, the steering wheel in my hand, the power in the vehicle as I turned the ignition, indicated, reversed up the slight incline and out, and then drove off down our street. Long drives seemed to make sense to me. I routinely headed for Cumbria, towards the M11, then A14, M6, A509 – until I imagined myself approaching the Cumbrian fells.

As a hostage my world had shrunk: I had adapted to a cramped, confined space, with great discomfort. To a degree I was amazed that I could 'manage', 'cope'. But I worried, too, that I would get accustomed to it, accept it – because to do that would be to say goodbye to my self-worth. I had in any case been robbed of my outward dignity and reduced to some desperate measures. Lying on a filthy floor shared with cockroaches in order to peek out under a curtain was a debasing activity, but I did it, and decided it was not so bad, in return for at least seeing what was outside – even just my captors praying on their mats. In myself, though, I thought: *Thank goodness David is not having to witness this level of deprivation I'm being subjected to.*

*

In this Horrible House I soon got used to waking up in the morning and discovering different, if familiar, faces in my room and in the yard outside. Clearly the pirates were rotating my guard, and I supposed they were hardly more comfortable with this squalid setting than I was. Certainly their moods seemed not a great deal more elevated than mine, exemplified in my mind by the miserable face of Limping Man. One day he appeared so disconsolate that I thought to engage with him just by reference to what was emblazoned across the front of his vest. 'Celtic very good team,' I offered. But he just blanked me, scowling. I ought to have remembered that he was one of the pirates on whom efforts at friendliness felt especially wasted. Another of these was a pirate who made a point every evening of stealing my plastic chair from the room so that he could perch himself on it for the duration of the night watch. He was too belligerent a character for me to argue with; and he was called 'Chair Man' in my mind henceforward.

The Fifth Man was one of the contingent routinely required to sleep overnight in my room: a close proximity that I supposed he resented, since he seemed to have such a problem with me generally. He was perpetually threatening, and he made me uncomfortable. Yet, for this very reason – also, perhaps, for a challenge – he was a character I felt drawn to work on, to try to improve our relations. I had an inkling that he was intelligent, and knew a little English too. I had encountered many more 'difficult' individuals during my working life, and I had always been able to find some way to connect to them.

My charm offensive began with regular smiles in his direction whenever I passed, smiles he fixedly didn't return. I would often see him washing his clothes in the yard, just as all the pirates had to in this compound, deprived of Amina's laundering services. But the Fifth Man did this chore with some rigour: he always wore short-sleeved white shirts, and seemed to want them pristine. I'd walk by him purposely at these times, offering compliments on his 'very good' scrubbing, which fell, again, on deaf ears.

One afternoon, though, I observed him attempting to hang up his newly washed grey jersey shorts on the compound's washing line: a forlorn task, as the shorts were heavily soaked and kept slipping down onto the sand. After a few goes he gave up and slouched off to the African House. I had an idea. I shouted for the toilet, gathered up the clothes pegs I had 'borrowed' from the Big House, went out and pegged up the Fifth Man's shorts securely. How he would react to my intervention seemed to me a test: a make-or-break moment. When I came back out from the loo I saw the Fifth Man standing pensively under his pegged shorts. He turned to me – and offered a smile and a thumbs-up. Later, when his shorts had dried he came in and returned my pegs, with an air of civility quite new to our relations.

I had for a while been mulling over the thought that none of the pirates ever seemed to refer to each other by name – at least not that I had heard. Possibly this was a form of criminal self-discipline. Certainly I had accepted it until now. But I wondered what it would cost me to make an enquiry or two. When the Navigator looked in on me one afternoon I decided to make the obvious start with him.

'You know, I've been wondering – what is your name?'

He looked at me warily, then whispered, 'Ali.'

'Ali! I see. And what is your second name?'

He frowned, paused. Had I overstepped the mark? 'Sorry,' I said. 'Is that wrong? Not allowed?'

He whispered again, 'Mohammed. After my father.' But he glanced at the door, furtively, as he said it. I thought I might as well try to press the advantage.

'I'd really like to know the names of other pirates. How do I ask them what their name is, in Somali?'

'In Somali, "What is your name?" is "*Magacaa?*"'

'Right, and if I wanted to say, "My name is Jude. What is your name?"'

'*Magacay waa Jude. Magacaa?*'

This seemed to me like quite a breakthrough, and it was underlined when Ali took it on himself to name for me one or two other members of the group. His friend, who I thought of as 'Marvin', was in fact Abdullah; and 'Smiley Boy' was Mohammed.

Now when pirates looked in on me or crossed my path outside I took to asking them to tell me their names. Some of them merely laughed at me. But others answered my request. I had hopes in respect of the Fifth Man, having laboured to earn his respect; and when I asked him for his name and pointed to my book, he nodded, took up the pen and inscribed IBRAHIM.

*

My renewed forays over the language barrier yielded another bonus: Kufiya Man came back to the Horrible House after a visit to his family, bringing with him a little printed A4 booklet from home which – he explained through Ali – was for me. The booklet was titled *Al-Imrah* and inside it offered a series of 'lessons', paragraph-length dialogues in Somali and English, suitable for a language class. As ever I was grateful for anything to divert me, and for something to read in particular. The first thing about the booklet that really struck me was that handwritten on the back cover were several runs of digits that looked to me like telephone numbers, and also a name: JAMAL.

The next time Kufiya Man visited my room I decided this was a moment to extend the intelligence-gathering operation I had been conducting in the field of names.

'Is your name Jamal?' I asked him.

He was visibly taken aback. 'No, no,' he muttered and hastened out again.

I wasn't to be denied, though. When Ali next called on me I tried him out. 'The man with the beard and no hair, who wears the *kufiya*? Is he called Jamal?'

'Yes,' Ali nodded. 'And the big man who eats a lot? He is Gerwaine.' I smiled politely in thanks, exulting inwardly at this bumper yield of fresh data.

When next I saw 'Hungry Man' I addressed him clearly. '*Mahadsanid*, Gerwaine ...' He looked askance, shook his head, said, 'No, no', and stomped away. I wasn't sure I hadn't taken a step too far in my curiosity. Quite possibly the pirates were phobic about disclosure of their real names, and if I was armed with this identifying information then, arguably, it gave them reason to be leery of granting me my freedom down the line. But on balance I thought it was worth that risk to keep building on my efforts at 'rapport'.

As for Jamal's *Al-Imrah* booklet, browsing some of these lessons did indeed prove diverting, if at times also a little disturbing. One, for example, was presented as a conversation between two boys about the ethics of international aid and development, and was set out roughly like this:

BOY 1: My friend, what do you think of the many foreign aid workers in our country?
BOY 2: I am told that they come to help us.
BOY 1: No, you're wrong, my friend. They come here to turn us against Islam. We must not listen to them, or others of that sort, as they are Western people who only wish to spread Christianity . . .

Other lessons treated other kinds of issues, albeit with a similarly decided line emerging from the to-and-fro. 'What do you think of breastfeeding?' was one topic, from which it was established that mothers were obliged to nurse so that their boys grow up big, healthy and strong. Nothing was said on the matter in relation to girls, but then I had the sense, as often before, that the culture wasn't much bothered with girls anyway.

Not, then, the most engaging reading matter, but at least it was something. One evening as I sat on the mattress and browsed the book, Bambi sidled into the room, and sat down next to me silently, as was his way. I put the booklet down beside me, wondering what might happen. I smiled at Bambi. He smiled back. Then he picked up the book and started to read, seemingly without the need for my torch. I shone some light on the page for him and made to give it to him but he just shook his head, cheerfully, and refocused on the 'lesson' before him.

*

If ever it slipped my mind that I was among pious Muslims, with a strong attachment to rituals and customs, and very vehemently held ideas about purity and defilement, it was usually brought back to my attention in emphatic fashion – and most often by Vain Man, though he was by no means the most conspicuously devout member of the group.

As always, when I walked the twenty steps to the toilet, I had to get myself fully clothed and modestly covered, and then back in my pit of a room I took most of it off again. I hated the headdress: the more times I put it on, the less 'me' I became, the less of a woman I felt, the more I was reduced to a faceless captive. Under the headscarf my hair was horribly matted and ill-smelling. Worse, Amina's grey-pink *jilbab* had got so filthy and malodorous from daily wear that one day I had to surrender and put on my going-away outfit. I knew I had to carry on complying with headwear regulations. But doing something you absolutely loathe, being forced into that mould, is bitter medicine to swallow.

I ran into further difficulties to do with water.

In the compound of Horrible House I had noticed a very big plastic bucket filled with water from the well. It sat in the open without any obviously special significance, and so one day as I was coming back from the toilet I blithely washed my hands in the bucket. This was observed by Vain Man, who flew into a rage, shouted at me, and kicked the bucket over, sending the water everywhere.

I had no idea what my offence was, but Ali came forward, muttering smartly, 'This is very bad, very bad.'

I said, 'Well, please tell him I am sorry, I didn't know.'

But Vain Man continued to glare at me, as more water was fetched, this bucket now clearly *verboten* to the Western female.

I well understood the particular sanitary routine by which I had to treat hand-washing water differently from body-washing water, the former being safe to fling out into the compound, the latter calling for disposal down the toilet. In the Big House I had observed the distinction scrupulously – in part, because I had first to step out onto the terrace in order to perform either action. In Horrible House, though, the compound was just outside my door. And one day I tipped my body-wash water out of the door – an act that, once again, was observed and occasioned pirate uproar, with Vain Man once again the most clearly lividly incensed, and Ali once more delegated to caution me.

'You must not do that,' he barked. 'Very bad.'

'But the water's just soaking into the ground,' I said. 'What's so bad about that?'

'You must put in toilet, you must! We Muslim, we keep our water separate! You must apologise!'

There was nothing else for it, and so of course I expressed my regret. But their concern for purity seemed to me to go beyond the fastidious, even the doctrinal. In the case of that bucket of common well water, it was hard for me not to feel that they were especially concerned to share nothing of their own with me. Even in these most unhygienic circumstances it was as if I was considered to be the chief contaminating presence. It seemed to me telling, somehow, that I was never given anything from anyone's hands, other than by Amina – an exception that, on reflection, appeared to fit.

One night I had a strange and curiously satisfying dream in which I found myself walking through the village with Amina and her daughter and realised that, very calmly and reassuringly, they were helping me to escape. They took me to a house where there was another young woman, and together they sewed and chatted and laughed together, and I shared their company. Outside the house was a beautiful garden with a vegetable patch, where we walked. Then Amina left me with the other woman, who fed me, then gave me a *burka* to put on so that I was entirely covered and concealed but for my eyes. The woman and I then wandered out together, to a market place, where we shopped for food and I was at liberty in my voluminous, cloaking black garments. I was free at last.

It was a brutal thing to wake from such pleasant real-seeming dreams, and to wake in such a place as Horrible House: the feeling of desolation was quite overwhelming. I had to take a deep breath, near to tears, knowing I had dreamed and wishing to dream again, as soon as possible. Even to walk awhile outside the walls of my gaol would have been a huge blessing to me. For that I would have willingly donned a *burka*.

*

Probably the worst aspect of my predicament was to have no contact with the Negotiator, no visits, no idea what was going on. I had my unshakeable faith in Ollie, but I could only hope the wheels were turning, since on the pirates' side I had very reduced grounds for confidence. At times I felt there was a dilatoriness, a lack of urgency, as if they were toying with my situation while having other fish to fry, so that I could languish.

I would often ask Ali if the Negotiator actually knew I was here. He told me the Negotiator 'not come any more', that he had 'gone away', was 'busy working on boat'.

Oh god, no, I thought. *He is the only hope I have that things can work at this end. And now that system's breaking down?*

'So who is Ollie going to talk to, if not him?'

'Your son, he talk to another man, different man.'

'What do you mean? Who?'

'Big Man not happy. Ollie not dealing with him, not picking up phone. He talking to other man, dealing with that man now.'

Incoherent as it sounded, still it felt like terrible news. I lost faith, yet again, in the story with which I was sustaining myself. The Big Man – the Fat Controller, as I'd come to think of him – was in evidence at times. I glimpsed him in the compound, con-ferring with one or other members of the Triumvirate. I had got used to seeing him in big tent-shaped shirts, but now he seemed to have abandoned button-up shirts in favour of tunics in garish colours – one was red, green and yellow in black-lined shapes like crazy paving. He would have been ridiculous to me were it not for the implicit threat he carried around with him. But in one unguarded moment I let slip my private nomenclature to Ali.

'Big Man coming tomorrow,' he told me.

'The Fat Controller? Oh, right . . .'

I had said this without thinking, but Ali snorted. 'You call him . . . Fat Controller?'

'Well, yes. Because he controls you, and he's fat.'

Ali was mildly amused by this. My sense was that he wouldn't be reporting me to the Fat Controller.

Although I no longer had the Negotiator's updates Ali would pass on to me scraps of information he claimed to have heard from the Fat Controller. It was never positive, but nor was it ever entirely convincing and, sometimes, blatantly bogus.

One such occasion was when Ali said to me, 'Big Man speak to Ollie and Ollie say there is no money. He give up, can't get money. Big Man say you will be here for one, two year.'

'You go back and tell Big Man that's a load of cobblers,' I snapped back to his grave face. 'That will never happen. He's lying to you. My son's not going to give up on me. You can bet your life he's working his hardest to get me out of here. And I can guarantee you – he will come up with the money.'

Of course I still had not the slightest clue what sort of price was on my head, but then neither did any of the pirates in subordinate positions – a realisation that came over me gradually, since at first I had imagined them to be 'thick as thieves' over all the fine details of the ransom demand. But the truth became clear to me one evening as Ali sat on my bed fiddling with the sim card from his phone. Abruptly he said to me, as if I would know, 'How much money we get?'

I was nonplussed. 'Do you mean, how much are you *paid*?'

'No,' he replied, pointing at me quite sharply. 'For you, how much we get?'

'Oh, the ransom?' I asked.

'Yeah, yeah,' he nodded. 'Gerwaine tell me 2 million.'

'Not a chance,' I told him. 'If it's that, then we're all going to be stuck here for an awful lot longer.'

He looked a little dejected. I couldn't help but notice, too, that he had used 'we' rather than 'they' as a pronoun for the pirates.

'Ask the Negotiator. He'll know,' I volunteered, seemingly helpful. But I saw clearly that he could no more enquire along those lines than I could.

*

The shutter on the window in my room was grey metal, with a new bolt, but it didn't sit snugly in the frame and so I was able to glimpse outside through the resultant chink. I could see the outskirts of a village over a shallow sand dune. One morning a man in a skirt and vest came with a bucket and spade, and skimmed the top of the sand off a dune, put it in a bucket, then disappeared. Another morning two men dug a hole so deep they vanished from view. The next morning a truck came along and tipped huge boulders onto the ground with a great thud. Then the men manoeuvred these into the pit. I had no idea what they were doing.

To the extreme left I made out a large-leafed tree affording some shade to a patch of fenced-off desert tended by a woman using a hoe to dig furrows. She would do this with one child tied on to her and three or four others watching. Some way behind the tree was the village, with an obvious track. I saw villagers, some very smartly dressed, pregnant women and young children, even the smallest girls in *hijab*.

In the background on the left-hand side were low corrugated-roofed houses with thatched fences around them. In front of the houses were two thatched-roof corrals for goats. To the right was a large bright-painted building that I suspected was a school. As early as 6.30 a.m. there would be a young woman washing stacks and stacks of stainless-steel bowls and saucepans, using sand as an abrasive, while babies and children played in the sand with sticks. This building was clearly a focal point for all the goats in the area as they would congregate in front and the women would shoo them away, although they would sometimes seize a goat by its back leg and milk it before dismissing it.

*

The radio remained my friend. I never changed the band from the World Service, and perhaps the one boon of the Horrible House was that I could get reception around 7 p.m.

I would listen to *The Strand* media programme, note their recommendations for books and exhibitions, and write them down for future reference: things to do when I got out. *Witness* was also a fascinating show, in which people offered their first-hand remembrance of notable events from the recent past. I was especially struck by one report of the struggles of coalminers and their wives during the strike of 1984–85: the camaraderie in adversity, as well as the bitter feelings towards scabs.

I began to listen to a slot called *Heart and Soul*, a series of interviews with people of religious faith, some of whom had experienced political struggle and huge adversity. These were amazing, inspiring stories of human determination and strength, of people in troubled places around the world fighting for basic rights, sometimes suffering in that fight. The humanity of these stories was very comforting. Listening to them I felt: *If they could get through that strife, then I can too.*

I listened to the story of a Filipino, a former Catholic priest and Christian Aid worker with an English wife, who had taken up a challenge to combat violence and political corruption in a small town where he stood for election as mayor, despite death threats and an enforced separation from his family. Another man with a powerful story was a human-rights activist in Zimbabwe, who fought for recognition of a massacre of civilians by soldiers and paramilitary police, only to see his home raided, his family abused, and himself thrown into prison.

Incarceration was a common theme, and a meaningful one for me, as I sat, hungry and dispirited, listening to the tremulous reception on a filthy mattress on the floor of my insect-ridden cell. One piece of testimony hit me hard. A man who had been imprisoned unjustly was asked how he had got through his days knowing the odds were so stacked against him.

'When you're incarcerated,' he said, 'if you can be sure that there is someone still out there who is shining a light for you, standing up for you, fighting your corner – if you're sure of that then you can get through anything.'

This, I knew, was what my son was doing for me. Ollie was my light. Calm came with that thought: *I know he'll do it, whatever it takes, so long as I keep my side of the bargain.* That gave me inner peace. That feeling got me through another night. Then morning came; it was another day; food arrived . . . And I thought, *This is a day closer to going home.*

*

It was 26 November: my brother's birthday. The Fat Controller entered my room, carrying the plastic chair, Ali beside him. I sat on the mattress staring up at him. The Fat Controller said some gruff words to Ali, who turned to me.

'Big Man say you get phone call today from Ollie.'

My heart leapt. I had waited so long.

'You must tell Ollie, he must come up with money, or you be taken to the forest.'

'I don't understand. What is the forest?'

The Fat Controller looked yet more irate and frustrated even as Ali translated. They stepped outside, and I heard raised voices. The Fat Controller was screaming.

Ali re-entered the room and sat down on the bed next to me – which was unusual, and I found I didn't care hugely for the proximity. But he seemed to want to impart something very important to me.

'You must tell Ollie to get money. Or you go in forest. Big Man take you there this afternoon. And I don't want you to go to forest.'

'You have to tell me what that means.'

'In forest, you have to drink water from the rain, in puddles? You eat beans, not good for you. In forest, you can't walk, you won't have things, you have nothing.' Ali said this in tones of solemn distress. He appeared genuinely bothered. 'I don't like this, I don't like this, I don't want you to go forest . . .'

Mulling this over hastily, I found it hard to believe things could get so very much worse for me. But I had to consider the possibility. At the same time the idea of another move, to a place exposed to the elements, struck me as poor judgement on the pirates' part.

'If I'm going to a forest I'll need different clothes, won't I? And won't it be harder for you to guard me?'

I wanted to sow the seed of what a logistical problem this forest might pose for them. But Ali didn't seem too interested in my arguing back. Later that afternoon he returned and showed me a video on his phone. 'See? This forest . . .'

What I saw was indeed a wooded area, and the face of a balding man, very round and clean-shaven, in a white T-shirt. He couldn't have been long into captivity. He sounded Italian, and very scared. 'Please help me, please . . .' he moaned.

Whoever was operating the camera panned right, where higher up on a rock stood a man with an Arab headdress around his lower face, showing nothing but his eyes, pointing a rifle at this poor man. That angle allowed a better view of the surrounding trees and foliage: I thought I glimpsed the mouth of a cave behind this gunman. The camera panned further right, allowing sight of a second hostage, a man with a full head of dark hair and thick beard. His face as he looked into the lens was a picture of terror.

Ali looked at me. 'These men are in forest. In forest there will be just two pirates, they guard you.'

I questioned Ali on this and established which two pirates these would be: Chair Man and Mouse. This felt to me like an additional and considered cruelty on the part of the Fat

Controller: he had chosen two men I didn't much like and had not the slightest 'connection' with.

It was frightening to consider the prospect of 'the forest'. I tried to use logic to come up with some positives. How long could they really keep me there? At least there were trees. If I ended up in a cave, it would be dark, but also cool. Perhaps I could go for a walk. Such were my mental habits in the face of a threat, but it seemed real, and I was scared.

Finally Ali came in with the phone. 'Big Man outside. After you speak to Ollie, if money not ready, you go to forest . . .'

And so I took my call from Ollie sitting on a stinking and stained mattress on the floor, watching a red caterpillar wriggle slowly out of the wall.

I told Ollie I was going into the forest, and that I was frightened. Even as the words came out of my mouth I felt disloyal, somehow, and annoyed with myself. The last thing I wanted to do was pile emotional pressure on him. I didn't lay it on as thick as they were demanding. But Ollie sounded calm and reassuring.

'Mum, listen, you are a valuable commodity to them. They are going to look after you, you can be sure of that.'

It was the best thing I could have heard in the circumstances: I knew he was right.

'It's hard for me to understand, Ollie, how much money they actually want, I try to talk to them about it . . .'

'Mum, do not talk to them about money. You must not enter into negotiations. I'm doing that, and it's going well, we're moving forward.'

Still I found it hard to control my emotions, after the hardness of the weeks in this squalid place. I found myself pleading with Ollie, knowing how difficult it would be for him to hear.

'Ollie, please, can you give me a date when you think the money will come through? I have to get out of here ...'

'Mum, I can't give you a date – I want to, but I can't. It's just not going to be as easy as I hoped it was going to be.'

I knew he was telling me a tough truth, and that it could be no easy thing for him. But I understood.

'You must trust me. I am doing everything I can, everything, to get you out. Everyone sends their love. We all want you home as soon as possible and we'll do it ...'

I was fully aware of what a low ebb I had reached. I told myself I wouldn't let it show again. Next time I would be controlled. I owed it to Ollie. He was in a situation where a son or a daughter or a spouse could easily have cracked under pressure. But he was being hugely mature, and in that way he brought me back on track. He asked me about my routine, I told him about my Pilates, my books and my lists, and of course, my walks.

'Keep walking, Mum. It's only a matter of time ...'

After the call I saw the Leader wandering around outside. Ali was there, Gerwaine, the Fat Controller: it was another of their conferences. Ali came in with Gerwaine, looking troubled.

'Big Man not happy. You have everything taken away. No radio, no books, no pen, no walk, no bed, no mosquito net, all go. And you drink water from the well. No bottled water, and food, once a day.'

So the threat had been recast: no forest, but new deprivation. I thought: *My god, I am fed up with this.*

I said to them, 'Keep your bloody radio, keep the books, the pen, you can have the lot. But I have to have bottled water. I want you to tell Big Man that if I don't get bottled water I am going to get sick and you'll have to take me to hospital. Is that what he wants?'

They met my outburst with silence and then left the room, pulling the door closed behind them so that I was enveloped in gloom. I sat down on the bed. I was shaking, sweating profusely, my heart beating hard, adrenalin coursing through me, turning already to anxiety and fear. They had driven me to distraction. But had I gone too far in pushing back? *You stupid woman*, I cursed myself, *why did you say all of that? You've cut your nose off to spite your face. You do need your radio. How will you manage without that?*

I was on my feet again when Vain Man appeared at the door, a discernible smirk on his face; and he seemed to puff himself up to his fullest and broadest so as to fill the space. He pointed out at the well in the yard from which the pirates drew their water. 'Good, good!' he laughed, not kindly. Then he flexed his right biceps and squeezed it.

'Somali women big, strong!' he cried. He jabbed a finger at my bony shoulder. 'You, pah! Small . . .'

His pokes at me were sharp and profoundly annoying but I stood my ground, steadfastly as I could. 'I'm not drinking that,' I insisted, quietly.

Time crawled between these angry confabs. I was left to stew, though I was aware of the Fat Controller outside, evidently seething and fuming and stomping about. Finally Ali came back in the room flanked by Gerwaine and Jamal.

'OK. Nothing change. You keep books, you keep radio, you can walk.'

I was relieved, and yet also wearied. What had the charade been for? Ali, in fact, wasn't quite finished.

'Also we go tonight.'

'Go where?'

'Back to Big House.'

I could barely believe it. So the outcome of all the threats was a small but important improvement. I packed up my things and waited. Later that evening, after I'd eaten, Ali came back. He said, 'Big Man not happy because pirates wouldn't take your radio, your things. They like you, so you keep.'

Whether this was true or not – whether the pirates had developed a sudden sense of gallantry, or I was being treated to a not terribly sophisticated good cop/bad cop routine – I was certainly happy with the result.

*

When the pirates came for me that night I was ready, and took my part in the hushed, busy activity of packing up my room. I filled my binbag and threaded my way out of the compound past sleeping pirates. This time I didn't recognise my driver, a young man. But I was unreservedly glad to see the gate close on the Horrible House.

As we neared the Big House I was struck anew by the height of the compound walls. It was an imposing building for sure, but preferable to where I'd come from, without question. I was brought back into the compound not through the metal gates at the front but through double doors that gave out onto the side street. Then I was ushered through what I realised was Room 4 of the terrace. There was nothing in it except a huge flat-screen TV, evidently rigged up to the generator outside, and a mattress propped against the wall. All this time I had imagined it was a crackling nerve centre of pirate operations. In fact, it was more likely a place for them to lounge around and watch football on telly.

Back in 'my' old room I noticed instantly that the table had been shifted to the far corner from where I had placed it. I was irked. *Right, that's getting put back tomorrow,* I thought. Grim as the space was, I had to live in it and I wanted it arranged as I saw fit. I replaced the pegs on the curtains and lay down to rest.

By 7 a.m. I was pacing around the linoleum floor again. Limping Man popped his head round the doorway and, for the first time, I saw a smile on his face. He was really happy to be back. I was just thankful for small mercies.

14

It was a reluctant companionship that I had with Ali, but it was the only one in the vicinity that was of any real use to me, and so I got accustomed to knowing how he was feeling. Back in the Big House he was soon complaining of a bad stomach ache.

'Is the food. Bad food here, I not used to it.'

'Tell me about it,' I said, sympathetic only to a point, since his rations were princely next to mine. But I advised him to drink boiled water, and to stop chewing *khat*, which I had to suppose was detrimental to the digestive system. I asked whether Amina could get him peppermint, and I wrote down the word for him and her as reference. But the pain seemed only to worsen. He said it burned in his insides, he couldn't lie out flat and had to sleep sitting up. He had stopped eating, and the effects were inscribed on his face: he looked gaunter than ever.

No sooner had I attempted these ministrations than I got sick myself, as if in solidarity. One morning I woke up with a fever, my head aching, forehead boiling hot, my throat on fire. I was shivering and found it a genuine struggle to raise myself off the bed. In my mind I was urging myself: *You've got to get up, you've got to walk, otherwise you're not walking towards home.*

But by the time I was sitting upright it was clear to me I wouldn't be walking anywhere for a while. My frail body felt heavy, every muscle ached, my feet throbbed. This hot, dark, sticky room felt like a dire place to fall ill, but ill I most certainly was.

I could hear pirates outside, laughing. I lurched to the door, stepped into the corridor, and they stared at me.

'I'm ill, sick. Get me Ali . . .'

I went back inside, but no one came. I attempted a walk, but I just couldn't get around. My feet were in agony, and I collapsed back onto the rackety bed. Again I dragged myself to the corridor, where the pirates were idly playing dominoes.

'I'm *ill*. I *need* Ali!' I looked hard at Gerwaine, clutched my throat to semaphore my discomfort, and pointed down the corridor to the room where I knew Ali would be sleeping.

'Please get him, get him now!'

'Ali asleep,' Gerwaine said simply, and looked away with apparent disregard.

'I don't care. You must get him.' I staggered back into the room and sat disconsolate on the bed. An hour passed. At one point I cried, with the sheer misery of how I was feeling: it couldn't be helped. With difficulty I used the dictionary and pen and paper to source and write the Somali words for headache, sore throat, painkiller, penicillin, hospital. At last Ali came in, and I could see how badly he was feeling. But I needed him to see the same in me. I could barely open my eyes. Sweat ran off me; I couldn't stop myself shivering. I gave him my scrawled piece of paper.

'I'm sick. I need medicine, a hospital.'

He read the note and said, 'There is no hospital here.'

'Pharmacy? Chemist?'

'No pharmacy.'

'You've got to help. I'm sick.'

My distress, the sheer state of me, seemed to have got through, and past a clear reluctance to act. Finally he said, 'I get you tablets.' Off he went. Jamal and Vain Man came in, looked at me, muttered between themselves. I knew I looked terrible.

When Jamal returned he had pills for me. It was a relatively rapid response, confirmation to me of their vested interest in not letting me slip below a basic threshold of well-being. But I had to swallow those pills in blind faith: they had no markings I could recognise.

As it was, by the next day I started to feel some relief. I slept a lot, unhappily, since I was frightened of getting disoriented in my routines, turning nocturnal. But I had to accept the bad shape I was in. I couldn't eat for a couple of days. But then to my great surprise the Leader brought me a mug of broth, which tasted fantastically meaty. Later he brought me a knuckle of goat meat on the bone: my sore throat meant it wasn't the easiest thing to eat but, my god, I persevered. Coming from this cold and self-contained man these were notable acts of consideration.

Although the feverish symptoms of my throat infection receded, they seemed then to mutate into a heavy cold. I asked for more medication, and was brought a little paper envelope containing four tablets labelled 'Cold Tap'. I assumed they were paracetamol, and I gulped them down. But the cold kept me confined to bed, inactive, feeling much the worse for the place I found myself in, and generally very sorry for myself.

I hadn't seen Ali since he'd reluctantly left his own sickbed to minister to me. I asked Mohammed where he was.

Mohammed said, 'He very ill. Big Man take him to hospital.'

I wasn't surprised to hear that they looked after their own better than me. With further questioning I established this hospital was five hours' drive away. I did worry, with Ali not being around and me in a vulnerable state. If I really needed anything there was no one but him I could communicate with. No one else really understood. Even if I used the dictionary and wrote words down I couldn't be sure. Some of the pirates couldn't read, even in Somali.

While I recovered I did make one useful discovery via the dictionary. While flicking through it idly I found myself paying attention for the first time to a list in the back of it, which gave the names of all the nations of the world plus their capital cities: Afghanistan/Kabul, Albania/Tirana, Algeria/Algiers, and so on. A new time-whiling game proposed itself to me. In my book I divided several pages into two columns, one of countries, one of cities, then covered one side with my hand and tried to make matches from memory, scoring myself out of 175. If not the most absorbing of puzzles on paper, the game quickly took on a mesmeric fascination for me.

*

It was evening and I was playing my countries-and-capitals game in my book when Ali reappeared at my door. He certainly looked a good deal improved, and was grinning from ear to ear.

'I back, I back,' he said.

'Good news,' I smiled. 'You're better?'

He nodded. 'Doctor give me tablets.' He showed me a packet. 'Then Big Man pay for me to be in hotel in town – a hundred dollars a night!' His value to this pirate operation was very clear.

Then he switched into conspiratorial mode. 'I have news.'

'What's that?'

'Big Man tell me in car when he drive me back. Money is almost there. In two weeks, you go.'

'Did he really say that? You're not just saying . . . ?'

'Oh yeah, really. In two weeks. Then you go, I go! I see my wife, you see Ollie.'

His enthusiasm was so pronounced, I didn't need any more convincing. I gave myself permission to dream. If freedom was really two weeks away then I would be home for Christmas – home, even, for my birthday on 12 December! Excitement bubbled up in me. After Ali left I sat and pictured scenarios in my head. Surely I was going to have to be delivered into Nairobi. It was the only hub I could imagine. Where was the nearest airstrip to here? No matter. I'd fly to Nairobi, where Ollie would be waiting for me. We'd get back to the UK on the next available flight – and in first class, if I could wing it, by any special pleading necessary. I thought too about what I would take with me, other than my books. Inside them were all the recommendations I'd carefully noted down from *The Strand* on the World Service: exhibitions to see, books I would read, music I'd listen to.

With my hopes high, the wonderful thought of my birthday, of Christmas, shared with Ollie back home . . . I permitted myself to open the drawer where I kept my thoughts of David, and to ponder how that homecoming, those festive occasions and celebrations were going to feel without him at my side. It made for sobering reflection; yet I knew it was the right thing to do. Whenever my ordeal was finally done I fully intended to put this place and these people behind me, but I would have to deal with the felt absence of David every day of my life.

*

My illness had depleted me badly, and even once the symptoms receded I found I wasn't physically up to the task of resuming my full walking/exercising regimen as before. To ease myself back I decided not to walk at all between 1 p.m. and 3 p.m. I wanted to be as fit and well as possible when I climbed onto that plane taking me home.

The climate turned a little more inhospitable as November passed into December. The days remained hot but the nights grew windy and the temperature fell, from 6 p.m. through to around 9 a.m. the next morning. I found myself shivering in the mornings until the sun seeped through. At night I would take a couple of the pegs holding the curtains that hemmed the walls, and use them to clasp the curtains by the metal doors into the room – a bit of improvised draught exclusion. And I slept with everything possible piled on top of my bed: *jilbab*, headscarf, even my going-away outfit.

I noted that in the mornings the pirates sleeping out of doors were wrapped up in blankets rather than sheets, and they kept the blankets round their shoulders as they smoked their first cigarettes of the day. I put in a request to Ali for a blanket of my own, but he didn't appear to treat it with great urgency. When I reminded him he only waved a hand. 'Yeah, yeah, it come . . .' And soon a week had gone by with no sign of the much coveted blanket.

One evening after my ritual washtime I had put my dress back on and was on the point of stepping to the doorway to shout out yet another most likely unheeded call for a blanket when the Leader appeared at the threshold, holding in his arms a package wrapped in a polythene cover. With something approaching a flourish he pulled from the wrapping an evidently brand new blanket – blue and pink, fleecy and cosy-looking. I accepted this base-level creature comfort gladly, and I was struck once more by the Leader's new interest in doing me small favours. Every time I saw him I was compelled to look him in the eye and hold his gaze, as if I might get some insight into his mind. Inside mine, the question was seared: *Was it you who killed my husband?* And however hard his outer shell, I sensed a wariness from him. He couldn't stand too much of my stare: eventually he would look away, or down to his feet. And I had begun to wonder if these considerate gestures in my direction were not, from his impenetrable perspective, some sort of raw, fitful attempt to make a form of amends?

*

The Leader's renewed presence around the compound had made for an interesting observable change, or clarification, with respect to the pirate command line. For one thing I had come to the conclusion that he didn't ever spend a night inside the Big House, and would rarely be there for a full day. Ali had told me that the Fat Controller slept elsewhere in the village – in what he described, to my envy, as 'a clean house'. I wondered if the Leader wasn't a house guest of the Fat Controller in said 'clean house'. I was certain he was being groomed, somehow, for a role in the pirate operation yet more senior than being in charge of the 'active service unit' that went out foraging to capture human bounty.

One morning, returning to my room, I got a glimpse through the door of 'HQ', Room 4, and I could see the Leader and Gerwaine in conference. The Leader was dressed rather in the fashion of a Maoist Red Guard, wearing a dark-green short-sleeved jacket and voluminously baggy pants that hung no lower than his calves – an outlandish outfit, to say the least. But there was nothing funny about the huge rubber-banded wedge of banknotes he was holding, fully six inches in depth, which he passed to Gerwaine who thumbed its shortest edge and then unfastened the float and began to count it out, as if dealing a deck of cards, into smaller piles. It was then that Gerwaine sensed my watching them.

'Oh, Somali money!' I blurted out, keen to sound innocent in my curiosity. Gerwaine smiled, took a 500-Somali-shilling note from one pile and waved in under my nose. *Pecunia non olet*, the Romans used to say, but these notes had a bad odour to them, and I flinched. Later that day Ali called in on me, nicely dressed for a visit to town, his shirt pocket stuffed with these 500-shilling notes, which the Leader had evidently distributed. (Each note, Ali told me, would buy him one cigarette.)

The Leader was certainly treated with something approaching reverence by the younger pirate 'runarounds', who kept out of his way, as opposed to how they thronged around the Triumvirate. The Leader was always punctilious about his prayers and seemed to come to the compound purposely to be with the other men at these times. I saw now that Vain Man, who didn't usually pray, was careful to do so when the Leader was around: he appeared to be keeping himself somewhat in line. In other respects Vain Man did not strike me as a man who held himself to the strictest personal standards. And he was someone I knew I would be especially glad to see the back of.

At least, as I had with several other pirates, I established his name. One evening as I was returning to the room from the toilet he beckoned me to sit down with him and a few other pirates who were lounging about. 'You spell your name?' he said to me in English. I darted into the room for my book and pen, and when I came back I said to him, '*Magacaa?*' He smiled and etched in my book, KAALIM. And then he displayed his penmanship to the rest of the group, as if serving notice of one more of his many abilities. I wrote my name, too, since he had asked, though no one paid it any mind.

If arrogance was Kaalim's least appealing trait, his brusqueness came a close second. Although I didn't feel actively menaced by him, he seemed to have a compunction to make things needlessly difficult for me. One day my lantern stopped working. I undid the casing and found the batteries had corroded. I stepped out to where the pirates were chatting, set down the lantern and said, with a shrug, 'Broken.' Kaalim came forward but only to shoo me back to the room with a disparaging flick of his hand. But a little later I received a visit from a recent addition to the pirate ranks, 'Tall Man' – a smiling, open-faced character, who seemed a couple of years older than the rest of the crew and stood several inches taller, too, at around six foot four. He had brought me a replacement lantern, which worked perfectly – until Kaalim then tried to exchange it again with the old, corroded one to which he'd pointlessly added fresh batteries. I refused to put up with this, made a protest that was registered, and got Tall Man's offering back.

But this was typical Kaalim: a fully paid-up member of the awkward squad. He had a cocksure, chauvinistic edge to him, and seemed always to want to be loudly at the centre of any masculine gathering. One early morning before I had received my blanket I had crept out to the toilet past him and some other pirates, and he must have seen I was shivering, for he opened up his blanket with a grin as if to say I should join him. The 'lads' appreciated his gag: he got the laugh he was after. For my part I'd have sooner cuddled up to a snake.

On another occasion his chauvinism was more actively unpleasant and disturbing. However, I was not the target of it.

I had got accustomed to Amina's daughter drifting into my room to sit idly while I walked. She was short and round just like her mother and it was difficult to engage with her initially. But after a while I grew used to her. She was like the standard shiftless teenager in that respect, and I was glad of her presence. On this particular morning she was playing music on her mobile through earphones, and she beckoned me over for a listen, laughing and jigging about delightedly. I imitated her, just for the fun of it. Then she showed me a photo on the phone, of the female singer, a beautiful woman with coffee-coloured skin, painted lips and long lustrous hair, her cleavage on show in a tight, red, low-cut, V-necked dress. I couldn't imagine what she thought of this particular vision of femininity, though I had a clear enough view of her culture's opinion. At any rate I resumed my walking, she her listening, until Kaalim intruded on us, and I knew straight away by his surly expression that he didn't like this scene one bit.

He strode up and stuck his hand between the girl's legs – an act that shocked me, and utterly startled the girl, who pushed herself backwards and shot out of the chair, screaming at him. He snatched the phone from her, but she snatched it back, irate, and wagged a finger at him while tucking the phone into a belt round her waist. Kaalim ripped the *khimar* off her head, took her by the shoulders and shook her. Still she bravely resisted, bashing him on the chest with her fists. But he only laughed. He was much larger and stronger than her, and finally he shoved her back onto the floor. As she grasped about for her *khimar* he stepped towards her.

'*Maya* [no]!', I shouted.

He stopped and stared at me with scorn. I backed off, worried now, but this had given the girl enough time to get up and run out. Finally Kaalim stomped off too, muttering oaths. I saw no one else for the rest of that day.

*

The one person from this nightmare I sensed I might feel agreeably towards was Amina. She had shown kindness and fellow feeling to me without my asking, and that had been precious. But even if I wanted to overlook her function and complicity in the pirates' operation, little reminders presented themselves none the less. One night she visited me with Ali, and as the two of them chatted a little between themselves she let out a big engaging laugh, slapping her thigh and dipping her head – whereupon I glimpsed something within the fold of her *khimar*, something glinting and shiny. She and I were 'friendly' enough that I could presume, so I came over to her, very carefully moved her headdress aside, smiling all the while and maintaining eye contact, for 'trust', and I could see she was wearing a quite fabulous pair of gold drop earrings, like mini chandeliers on her lobes.

I said to Ali, 'Tell Amina, she must be very, very rich! Lots of money!'

She laughed without any seeming irony. Her finery was an ill-gotten gain, perhaps, but there was no point in my pursuing that with her. She was consistently good to me. One afternoon she brought me a small ripened melon, plonking it into my hands with her familiar secretive index finger to her lips. I thanked her, she touched my face, smiled, and I did the same to her. Once she was gone I faced a quandary: how to get the delicious-looking thing sliced open, with nothing but a fork and a spoon at my disposal. There was nothing I wanted more. But if I bashed it on the ground then I expected it would splat rather than split. So great was my need that, unwisely, I stuck my head out of doors, thinking about a pair of scissors that I knew the pirates kept stashed in the low breezeblock wall. But as luck would have it Kaalim was exiting Room 4 at that same moment, and he shouted at me, and harried me back indoors.

'Knife,' I said. 'Need knife.'

'What? What?' He shook his head, indignant. Then he saw the melon, and glowered at me. 'What *this?*'

I indicated that I needed to slice it. He went out and returned brandishing a blade.

'*Mahadsanid*,' I said, a shade too soon.

With one blow he chopped the melon in half and scooped up one piece for himself. Then he glared again.

'Where get? Where?'

'Amina,' I said helplessly.

'*Amina!*' he spat, and walked out.

I scooped up my half and ate messily: it was such a treat, I was glad of half. Kaalim sat outside and noisily dissected and ate his confiscated treasure, spitting the pips. The downside for me was that I suspected I had got Amina in trouble, and that this could be the last of my secret privileges. Sure enough I didn't see her in the days that followed. I hoped at least I'd have an opportunity to say goodbye to her.

*

One of the unquestionable bonuses of the Big House over the Horrible House was the relative dearth of unwanted small intruders: roaches, flies and spiders were all in evidence, but not to the same sickening extent. However, a couple of visitors who never failed to disconcert me were two pointy-beaked birds that looked rather like ring-necked doves – grey with a subtle pink hue on their breasts. They made a habit of flying in under the eaves and then roosting on the opposite top of the wall, where there was no escape for them, and so they cooed and scratched about. Their presence perturbed me on account of a very specific and unpleasant memory from childhood, of a day when I was accidentally locked inside an aviary, and found myself terrified as the birds flew up and around me. The trauma was such that even the pigeons congregating in Trafalgar Square reduce me to a nervous wreck. Now I hated sharing my confinement with this pair.

When one of them flew suddenly across the room I must have screamed, for Jamal came running in, with his gun at the ready. I pointed frantically at the birds, to let him know I'd have no objection to his dispatching them with bullets. But he only grinned and said, 'No problem.' I didn't agree.

While I was now quite well inured to insect life I could still get a surprise in that department too. While playing word games with my torch one night I sensed something in my peripheral vision, shone the beam around – and lit up a large green praying mantis, unmistakable with its inquisitive head and two spiky forelegs. Again I must have shouted out, because in seconds Ibrahim darted in bearing his AK47. Seeing the source of the disturbance he took a broom that I had been using to sweep the room earlier that day, pushed his gun into my hands, and began to chase the mantis out of the room. I stood there holding this Russian assault rifle, thinking (a) how heavy it was and (b) how incredibly unprofessional Ibrahim was to let me have it. Ali then stumbled in, and doubtless found the scene most irregular.

I had to laugh. I was going home soon, and so a little slackness on the security front made no great difference to me or the pirates.

*

I had counted off the days as Ali had indicated. I assumed Ali was as inwardly excited as me at the prospect that 'he go' when 'I go'. And so I went to bed hopeful on 10 December, and rose as usual on 11 December, but in the faith that this was D-Day, departure day.

I waited for Ali to show up and give me my instructions – orders to pack, directions on where we were headed. However, the day very quickly began to seem disturbingly like any other. On my toilet visit I looked around outside, but Ali was nowhere to be seen. I glanced to the pirates' Room 3, knowing Ali always slept on the same mattress, just underneath the window.

Ordinarily the most fleeting of glances could establish his presence. But he wasn't there.

I didn't know what to make of it. Perhaps, then, Ali had been released from his particular bondage to the pirates and was headed back to his family. But it didn't seem that I was going anywhere, or else no one cared to tell me. I walked, alone, and tried not to dwell on my rising disappointment.

At night my rice was brought by one of the pirates who spoke no English at all. I looked up at him disconsolately.

'I go home?' I said. He looked at me as if my speaking was highly irregular, turned and left.

I felt utterly crushed, and angry at myself – at my sheer folly in believing some scrap fed back to me, purportedly from the Fat Controller of all people. Why had I bought into Ali's yarn this time after his assorted previous lies? There was an element of turning circles, of Groundhog Day, to all of this. Would I ever get home? How was I going to manage in the meantime without Ali in his communications and liaison role?

As ever I knew I had to pick myself up: *OK, so you don't go home today. Tomorrow is a new phase, then. Brace yourself to get through it.* But this time it took a very concerted effort.

My birthday on Monday, 12 December 2011 was a small and miserable affair. I had told Ali it was coming, but now he was gone. Late in the day I felt somewhat heartened to see Amina creep in. I got up to greet her, we shook hands and smiled as was our way. Then she put her finger to her lips, made her hushing sound and produced from under the folds of her *jilbab* a plastic bottle of Sprite lemonade. Later, when the deed was done, Amina crept back and spirited away the evidence of the empty bottle – my best and only birthday present.

*

So I returned to square one. For weeks previous I had been actively keen to receive fresh stores of water, batteries for my torch and radio, a new book to scribble in. Now the sight of new provisions cast me into gloom – made me fear there were no active plans for me, no word in sight from anyone about anything, just the drear sense that I would be languishing here a while longer.

I had been getting ready mentally never to see the pirates again. Now I had to drag myself back to the chore of inter-relating with them, seeking their favour. I had begun to notice a further symptom of their seeming wish to avoid most forms of exchange with me. Whenever I drained a small bottle of Bosaso water I would put the 'empty' down beside the front door, near my black wash-water container. Gradually I got used to a particular and peculiar sight, that of a black-skinned arm creeping round my open doorway, groping about, locating an empty bottle and snatching it away. What I figured out eventually was that the men wanted the bottles as receptacles into which to decant their brews of sweet tea while on night watch.

Right, I resolved, *if they want them they'll have to come in and ask.*

Instead of putting the bottles by the door I took to replacing the empties in the box that was my makeshift bedside table. The pirates soon realised that their groping expeditions were coming up with nothing. One night Bambi came in looking shifty and pointed to my box.

'*Biyo* [water]?'

'Ah, yes . . .' I said, pretending to cotton on, and fetched him an empty bottle. In no time at all the others were following suit. I called this another little victory, however meagre. I'd encouraged some good manners, a little more human interaction.

In an abnormal situation you do value the establishment of certain norms.

*

Ali had been gone for four days: I was dealing with his departure in the only way I could, by trying to stay occupied. I was writing at the table on the fifth night when he came through the door, and I could have fallen off my chair in surprise.

'Ali, I thought you'd gone home.'

He shook his head. 'No, no, they take me, looking for ships.'

'Ships? Are we near the coast here?'

'No, no. Ships far away.' He gestured. 'We go there in car, and we see four ships.'

'OK.'

'Yes, very bad.'

I had been puzzling a little over what purpose this viewing of ships would serve. His wary tone now suggested that the pirates were sizing up some new piratical venture.

'So, you and me – we no go? We still here?'

'Yeah . . . No go. Money not come through.' He shrugged.

I looked at him carefully. He certainly didn't look as disappointed as I had felt when my D-Day dream had turned to dust.

'I don't believe you,' I said finally. 'I don't believe the Fat Controller ever told you money was nearly there. I wasn't ever going home last week, was I?'

His brow furrowed. 'Yes, oh yes. We go home soon.'

'No, I don't believe you. And I don't like lies. I'd rather you told me I'm going to be stuck here for a year, so long as it was the truth.'

'No, we go home soon. You go, I go.'

David and Jude together on the morning of their flight from the Masai Mara to Kiwayu Island via Nairobi, 10 September 2011.

Jude and David by the airstrip in Nairobi, awaiting their plane to Kiwayu,
10 September 2011.

Jude tries out the hammock in the *banda* on arrival at Kiwayu Safari Village,
10 September 2011.

A beachside *banda* and communal building at Kiwayu Safari Village, seen from the sea: 'There was simply *nobody else around* . . . the silence was very pronounced, a 'peace and quiet' that felt just a shade remote, even intimidating.'

The beachfront at Kiwayu Safari Village, 10 September 2011. 'Rather than a perk, it struck me as a slight cause for concern, that we should be so much alone in this rather lonely place . . . The cove was picture-postcard beautiful, but quite deserted.'

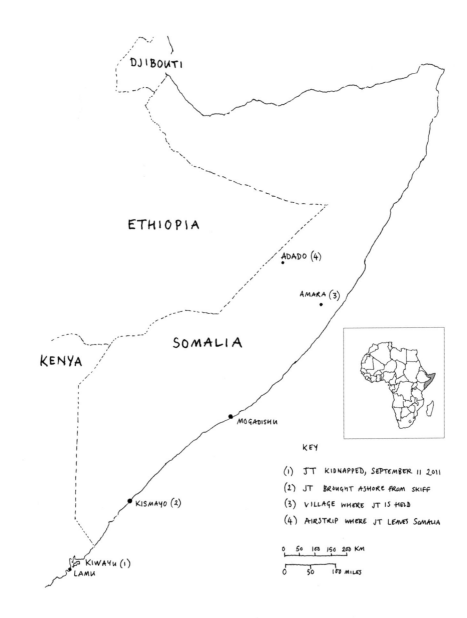

DJIBOUTI

ETHIOPIA

ADADO (4)

AMARA (3)

SOMALIA

KENYA

KEY

MOGADISHU

(1)   JT KIDNAPPED, SEPTEMBER 11 2011
(2)   JT BROUGHT ASHORE FROM SKIFF
(3)   VILLAGE WHERE JT IS HELD
(4)   AIRSTRIP WHERE JT LEAVES SOMALIA

KISMAYO (2)

0   50   100   150   200 KM

0   50   100 MILES

KIWAYU (1)
LAMU

'The Horn of Africa': map showing the location of Somalia within the East African peninsula, and highlighting the key locations where Jude was kidnapped, held, and finally released.

Armed police patrol a stretch of beach near Kiwayu Safari Village, 12 September 2011.

Metropolitan Police officers inspect the crime scene at Kiwayu Safari Village, Tuesday 13 September, 2011. In the centre of the group (wearing a grey suit) is Senior Investigating Officer Neil Hibberd.

The layout of the 'Big House' compound where Jude was held for two periods: September–November 2011, and November 2011–January 2012. 'Within those metal gates the first sensations to strike me were of searing heat and hard light bouncing off the thick stone walls of the enclosed yard.'

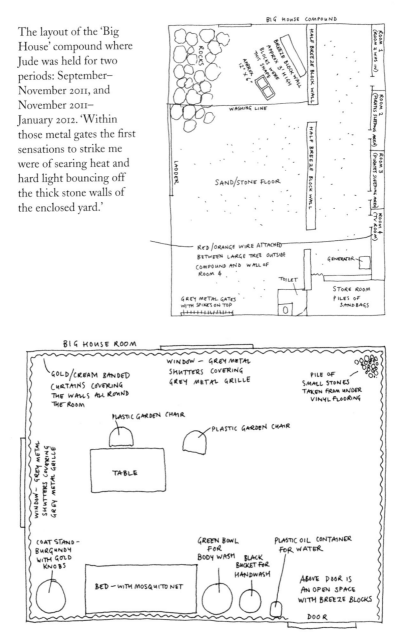

The layout of Jude's room, 'a gloomy room, maybe fifteen feet square, with a high ceiling' in the 'Big House': 'Nailed drape curtains masked the walls. There were no windows that I could see, and only a little natural light seeping in through breeze blocks set in the wall . . . The bed was of a size suitable for a small child . . . During the day I could just about cope with the gloom made by the closed, curtained shutters in my room. The pitch black of night was a different order.'

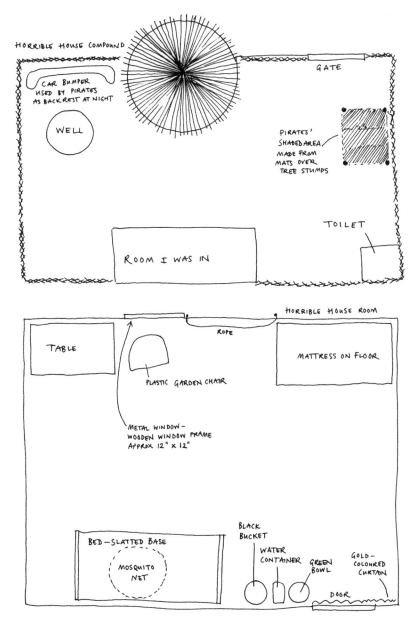

The layout of the 'Horrible House' compound where Jude was held for three periods, in November 2011 and twice in January 2012.

The layout of Jude's room in the 'Horrible House': 'In it was nothing but a table at the end and a bed base of wooden slats on a frame, standing unsteadily on an uneven concrete floor. The roof was tin, the walls appeared to be pale clay . . . There was one shuttered window, about twelve inches square. I felt desolation creep over me.'

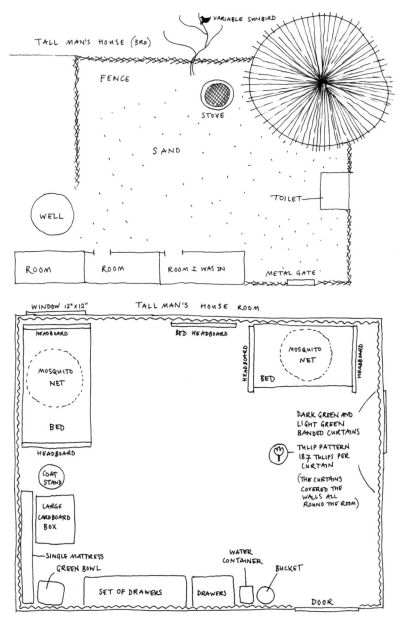

The layout of the 'Tall Man's House' compound where Jude was held for two periods, in January 2012 and again in February until her release in March: 'There was little to the fencing of this place that could have prevented me from slinking away . . . but the fencing was not the prison. The village was the prison. Somalia was a prison. I had nowhere to go.'

The layout of Jude's room in the 'Tall Man's House.'

Jude in a clearing outside Adado, awaiting confirmation from the pirates of her release, 21 March 2012. '[In] a clearing marked out by four big mature trees . . . hemmed by lots of tall shrubbery. Here, the pirate convoy had gathered . . . Mr Red trained a little video camera on me. He even asked me to walk around a little. I flat refused to play the circus act for him, and stood there, looking away from his lens, but for an occasional glare.'

Jude receives a phone call from Ollie while waiting to be taken to Adado's airstrip from the official buildings of the Himan & Heeb regional administration, 21 March 2012.

Jude is released into the care of her rescuers, then led to the light aircraft that will fly her out of Somalia to Nairobi, 21 March 2012. 'I just stood there, feeling the breeze, conscious of a small throng of people to my right snapping photos. I tried to shield my face . . . Almost by instinct my feet started moving me . . . And then I was inside the plane, the door was wrenched shut, Jack called out, 'Go, go, go . . . !'

The British High Commission, Nairobi (opposite), where Jude was taken directly after her release and reunited with her son Ollie. 'I was brought inside this palatial house, all light and fragrance, beautiful fresh flowers arranged on polished walnut tables, staff in stiff-starched white jackets. I was so glad of these surroundings. But really there was only one thing I wanted done on my behalf.'

Jude addresses the annual international conference of the Serious Organised Crime Agency (SOCA) in Seville, Spain, October 2012.

Jude, spring 2013, one year on from her release. 'I feel right now that David wants me to carry on. I think he would have been proud of me, of the way I got through my ordeal . . . My life won't be the same, but it is life itself, and its value is clear: it is all that we have . . . it must be cherished, respected, never ever taken for granted.'

I waved a hand in front of his face. 'Stop it. I don't want to hear it.' I turned away, unable to stomach any more *faux-naïf* fakery.

'You angry?' he said to my back.

'Not angry, no.'

He wandered out. I wasn't convinced he had my feelings at heart. Rather, I felt he wanted to be sure I wasn't about to make a fuss, to be 'difficult'. It seemed to suit the pirates to keep the temperature of my spirits at a manageable level. And to that end they would tell me anything – or, rather, have Ali tell me.

The next day I saw Ali again around 1 p.m. and he gave off the demeanour that nothing much had happened, really. I was finishing a little bit of potato I had saved from 'breakfast', as my 'lunch'. Ali mentioned that he was going outside for a walk.

'That would be so nice,' I murmured.

'You want to come?' he said with a smile.

'Yeah,' I stood up. 'Of course.'

His smile wavered. 'Ah, tomorrow. Tomorrow we do.'

I sat back down, unsurprised, and returned to my potato. 'Tomorrow never comes, Ali.'

'Yeah, you're right . . .' he murmured. That, at least, had the ring of honesty about it.

*

That night, after I had completed my washing and dressing for bed, Gerwaine surprised me by entering in haste as if he had something he needed me to see, concealed between his cupped hands. He opened them to reveal a dragonfly that he had nabbed by its wings. It had bright red eyes and a large triangular face, and he raised it up right before my eyes. I was mildly curious but

I didn't react especially. Part of me, I felt, was becoming shut off from sensation the longer I was made to endure my confinement.

'Ah yes . . .' I said. What else could I say?

He gestured for me to put my hand out. I did, and he set the dragonfly down there. I felt its little legs in my palm for a moment then off it flew. Gerwaine and I looked at each other as if in perplexity. All I felt was an envy of the insect. At least it could escape.

*

I was used to the pirates puffing away on their cigarettes but one afternoon I found myself staring at Ali's empty red-and-white packet of Sportsman-brand fags as he held it in his hand. I realised that for my Countries/Capitals game the packet would make a better cover-up than the back of my hand, so I asked Ali if I could have it, and I used it in just that manner for a couple of days.

Then, a eureka moment: it occurred to me that if I dissected the empty packet I could make tags, on which I could write out my countries and capitals, and so make a proper displayable, three-dimensional, cross-referable game. It would be a long task, a project, to produce three hundred and fifty or so tags. But time was what I had. So I asked Ali if he would make a point of saving his empty fag packets for me.

I needed more donors, and Tall Man was another smoker who seemed affable, so I got Ali to ask him on my behalf, and he too began to bring in empty Sportsman packs. (I thanked Tall Man in Somali, which he seemed to appreciate, and one day he brought me a packet of biscuits, a stunning consideration on his part.) Then other guards started to take an interest: I began to get donations in twos and threes. I took apart the cigarette packets: one of the top panels was the perfect size for my requirements, and I prevailed on Ibrahim to take the compound scissors, use that panel as a template, and cut the packs up into tiny little tags. Then I began to create my matched pairs.

It was a long endeavour for a fairly rudimentary product, but I was terrifically pleased with myself for having devised and designed it, and I had a schoolgirl-like immersion in it once it was done. I made it a routine that on a Monday morning I laid the two sets of tickets out from A to Z, and tried to match cities to the countries. On Tuesdays I did it vice versa. (Initially I found this consumed a whole morning.) When I was done I stashed the cards safely away in empty tissue packets. One or two pirates seemed to find my efforts nearly as absorbing as I did, Gerwaine being particularly interested. But anything that helped me get through the day was to be prized and clung to, and my Fag Packet Nations of the World Game was incredibly effective in that regard.

*

There were multiple ways in which I could keep my mind keen. My body, however, seemed to me less and less manageable. The long months of poor hygiene were taking a special toll. I complained to Ali that I stank, felt horrible. My bedding had gone unwashed for months. I was still not permitted to wash my clothes, and no one washed them for me. Meanwhile the pirates groomed themselves and each other and emerged each afternoon, laundered and fragrant. The Leader must have got wind of my grievances, for one morning he came in with a red-topped glass bottle of men's cologne for me, its brand name 'Maliki Star'. There wasn't much in it, and it wasn't my preferred fragrance, but I sprayed myself and my clothes as best I could.

There was, though, no masking the terrible physical condition I was in. My feet were blistered and bloodied from walking, and by the end of each day they had swollen, freakishly so, as if pumped full of water, the skin smooth but strangely 'cushioned'. My scarred ankles and toes ached. The swelling would recede somewhat overnight, but in the morning my feet had the look of Gorgonzola cheese, veins awfully prominent, so that I could trace them, dark blue and risen just as they were on my hands and arms – a frightening sight. As my hair began to come out in handfuls, my fears heightened and rattled me.

The night wash became a more alarming experience by increments. If I lay down flat and gingerly palpated myself I could feel my internal organs beneath my increasingly wraith-like skin: gut, bowel, bladder. There was not an ounce of fat on me, and I couldn't kid myself about the scariness of my weight loss. My hip bones jutted out, I could feel my sternum and ribs. I was emaciated; my body was subsisting on itself. And I suspected it would only get worse. In the shock of realisation I knew I was going to have to rethink my strategy about keeping fit. I ceased all exercise apart from the walks, for the simple fear that I would damage myself.

I was still walking home, though. Home was still there and I had to walk to it, had to carry on. Part of me knew I wasn't being too clever – indeed, bloody silly, on some level. I understood things could yet get a good deal more painful. But walking was so essential to my state of mind that I was going to have to make mind triumph over matter.

*

Monday, 19 December 2011 was, by my reckoning, my hundredth day in captivity: a gloomy milestone, compounded by the knowledge that I hadn't seen the Negotiator for quite some time. If

Ali said he was coming, and with news for me, it wasn't worth being hopeful. Still, I usually knew if he had been in the compound – I could smell his aftershave – but I had come to accept he was rarely there to see me. And then I saw him by chance.

I was returning from the toilets, early in the morning, and he had stepped out of Room 4, 'Pirate HQ'. He wore his sarong and vest, and I wondered if he had in fact slept overnight in the compound. His expression was dark, and yet I didn't think I could afford not to engage him.

'Good morning, how are you?' I said as I drew near.

'*Three hundred!*' he shouted at me in reply. 'Your son say three hundred! Three hundred not enough!'

I was taken aback. 'Why are you shouting at me? I can't do anything about that. Only Ollie can tell you about money, and what we can get.'

'Is not enough,' he snapped, convincingly irate.

I retreated to my room, thoroughly spooked. I was sitting down a little later, anxious and confused, when the Negotiator entered with the Fat Controller, who planted himself against the wall, Sidekick in tow. There was an air of the heavy mob, and the Negotiator looked hard at me.

'We are having problems getting the money. You have to think of some way to help your son get more. Do you have another bank account? Any other money that he not know about?'

I shook my head. 'We're not rich ...'

'Yeah, yeah, we hear that,' he snapped dismissively.

'Well, it's true,' I said wearily. 'So if it's a problem for you it's a problem for me. But I don't know what I can do.'

The Negotiator jerked a thumb at the Fat Controller. 'This man is getting tired, he get no money. You have to know, it make him very upset. Very angry.'

'I know, he wants this to end. I do too.'

'He is fed up. He could decide to sell you, to another pirate group, other Somalis.'

That idea rattled me, without doubt. The Negotiator saw as much. He leaned closer, his voice menacingly controlled.

'You know, in Somalia, anything can happen. You understand? There is no government here, no police . . . Do you realise, how easily you could disappear? This man could *make* you disappear. And no one would know.'

I felt as if I was being assaulted with low blows that I was too weakened to resist. It felt as if they were determined to drive me to submission, surrender.

'So, you must think', the Negotiator said, 'how you can get us more money.'

'What if I can't?' I blurted. 'Has it crossed your mind that whatever Ollie's offered is as much as he can possibly get?'

The Negotiator relayed that to the Fat Controller, who erupted from his slouching position, gesturing angrily, spitting. The Negotiator stood, calmly.

'He say if it's that, then we are done with you. We shoot you.'

And he followed the Fat Controller out of the door.

I had heard a similar threat once before. But that seemed a long time ago, when I'd believed we were much closer to a resolution of my plight. The passing of time had made that feel further away than ever. And now the antipathy, the contempt on the faces of these men made me feel worthless, like nothing – made me believe, indeed, that they could prefer to cut their losses rather than spend a single penny holding on to my tired bones.

I couldn't stop it: I lost all control of my thoughts. Turmoil ensued. In my head I saw them shoving me against a wall, pushing my blindfolded head into the dirt. I heard a rifle cocked and fired, at me, point blank. The end, of everything.

I don't know how long these images assailed me, but I stumbled backwards, retreated to the furthest corner of the room, diagonally opposite the door. I hugged my knees as the darkness came down. And the whole room began to seem to me a cavern in which I was being crushed, buried. I fought for my breath.

Gradually, through the gloom, I could make out a figure on the floor mere yards from where I sat: a person, lying prone, but not alone. From the shadows emerged a committee of scavengers, bald-headed, sharp-beaked birds – vultures – that clustered around the fallen figure. I could hear their cruel deriding caws. And I could see the stricken figure was wearing my pink-silver *jilbab* – because the figure was me. These vultures began to pick over my corpse, pulling and tearing at the dress with their beaks, until strips of fabric tore away, and then strips of flesh. A frail hand was raised and reached out to me for help. And there was nothing I could do.

I couldn't move from my corner – too scared, traumatised. But in my head I felt I had to. I had to rescue myself, to fight off the vultures, to save this body from desecration. Even if there were no hope, her dignity had to be preserved – my dignity. Otherwise how would Ollie recognise the corpse as his mother?

Somehow I did. In my head I hauled myself forwards, inch by inch, as if through mud, an odious sensation. I couldn't speak, couldn't shout. But as I drew nearer the vultures scattered.

Clarity of mind returned to me slowly, in patches. Gradually I regained awareness of the body I felt I'd lost. It had been a profoundly disorienting experience, unprecedented, and I was chilled to the bone. As soon as I felt able I told myself, urgently, incessantly: *They won't shoot you. They want you for money. You*

*can't panic. You can't let your imagination take control. That's how
you lose your mind, and then you're gone for ever.*

I convinced myself. But for some time afterwards I was
drained and exhausted, disturbed by the experience, the
awareness that my mind could go somewhere so terminally
bleak.

The Negotiator came back to me the next day, and no death
sentence was mentioned. Instead he told me I was going to speak
to Ollie, and told me again, tersely, that I had to tell him to get
more money, had to help him find a way . . .

I looked at him as evenly as I could. 'This is hard. There has
to be a compromise. I don't know if we can raise the amount you
want. I don't know how much that is. Will you tell me?'

'Ask your son,' he said dismissively, and left. When he returned
he told me Ollie wasn't answering his phone. If this was their
version of negotiation it seemed to have entered a rocky, fractious, precarious stage.

*

Amid the general dolour, incongruously, Christmas was drawing
near. Ali told me I could expect to have a Christmas-morning
phone call with Ollie. But I didn't bank anything on that pledge.
Then he began to try out on me a renewed version of his well-
worn 'I have news' routine.

'Mohammed tell me he heard Big Man organise plane, for
January – you go with two Americans, two hostages, in January.'

'Are they close by then, these Americans?'

'I don't know. But you go home on plane.'

More bullshit, I decided. After the excitement of early December, followed by the fall from a height of two truly hopeful weeks,
I wasn't going to buy Ali's nonsense again.

'Ali,' I said carefully, 'you keep telling me I'm going, but it never turns out I am. But I'm sure when everything's settled and I really am going then the Negotiator will tell me, and I'll speak to Ollie about it. But from now on the only person I believe is Ollie. So don't tell me anything about any plans any more, OK? I don't want to know . . .'

I wasn't sure he believed me or would abide by my wishes, but he seemed to see my point.

*

Come Christmas morning there was no phone call with Ollie, and no one could have been less surprised than me, much as I would have loved to have been proved wrong. But in the afternoon Ali came in.

'Negotiator speak to Ollie. Ollie ringing back tomorrow.'

Boxing Day it would have to be then. But Ali lingered, evidently with other things he had to impart.

'You must tell Ollie you are in the forest. And you are very ill – *very* ill. But there is no hospital, no doctor . . .'

I groaned inwardly: another threat, to force another pretence, and yet one more attempted fraud.

'. . . so you tell him, your leg is cut, very bad, wound it not heal, so you need hospital. And you no get food, things bad for you . . .'

I didn't need to think this over. 'No, Ali. I'm not doing that.'

Ali looked most unhappy at this. I felt I had to explain.

'I will tell Ollie things are bad, that I'm in the forest, that the pirates want their money. But you tell them I am not going to say to my son that I'm "wounded" or I need hospital or anything else like that. Because then he will worry, and I can't have that.'

'Why not? Why not? What is the problem?' Ali barked at me, gesturing angrily, in – to my eyes – a highly uncharacteristic manner. I was so startled I had to step away from him, from the sudden vehemence, which truly surprised me. He glowered still.

'I don't lie to my son,' I said simply.

And then he clicked back into shape, as if aware of how far he'd strayed 'off message', as written in the look on my face. But, as far as I was concerned, his mask had slipped: *He's not as nice as he makes out, this fellow.*

'OK,' he shrugged. 'I tell Big Man. But he not happy.'

I gave him a shrug of my own. 'I'm not happy, Ali.'

And I wasn't. I had given Ali the benefit of the doubt in terms of his own motives and intentions. And I wasn't about to stop dealing with him just because he had shouted at me. I couldn't afford to. But it had been a farewell to the notion that he was really 'on my side'.

*

On Boxing Day, then, I got my treasured phone call: my first contact with Ollie in thirty days. I told Ollie that I was 'in the forest', but I stumbled, as I couldn't persuade myself, never mind him. I genuinely hoped that in my tone of voice I was sending him a message that I was not ill, frantic, or otherwise very much more inconvenienced than usual.

'And Ollie, when you eventually come and get me, please be sure to bring a change of clothes for me. I've only got loose robes on, the sort Muslim women wear for their modesty . . .'

My instinct was that Ollie, hearing me burble on about changes of clothes, would find it difficult to believe I was in any kind of forest.

'We're still working to get you home, Mum, and we're getting closer, that's all I can tell you. So keep eating, keep focused, keep walking.'

I told him a little about my fag-packet game.

'That's good, keep your mind occupied, Mum, keep hope.'

'Have you seen your uncle Paul and Maxine?'

'Yes. They brought Christmas lunch round. We exchanged presents.'

I felt a real pang in my heart, to be so far removed from this simple shared family moment. But in my prison I wasn't treating it like 'Christmastime'. So I was just glad to hear David's youngest brother and his wife were being so supportive, as I'd known they would.

'I'd have hoped to have been able to call you.'

'I was hoping too, Ollie darling. But, listen, out here, it's just another day for me. We'll have Christmas when I get back. We can choose to have Christmas whenever we want to . . .'

When the call was cut off as usual, I felt pensive, but strengthened as ever by Ollie's calm and assurance. Gerwaine and Ali entered and Ali said, 'Everything OK, you stay here until you go.'

That was comforting. I thought: *However long it is until I go, it's relatively comfortable here. I know what to do. I just have to conserve my energy, look after myself, as best as I can.*

New Year's Eve was another celebration deferred. My company was the radio, and I listened to the end-of-year quiz on the World Service, sitting on my bed. What I did vow to myself – my resolution – was that in 2012 I would go home. *This year it happens. I will not be here in twelve months.*

*

The year 2012 was only days old, and I was taking my respite in a night's sleep, when my bed was kicked repeatedly and I woke to glaring torchlight in my eyes, then a slow-forming vision of phantom-like figures flitting around my room, Ali standing by with a black plastic bag ... *This wasn't the deal*, I wanted to cry out. But we were on the move. I went through the motions once again, as if automated, and I was shepherded outside to the car, my insides churning. It wasn't long before I recognised the grimly familiar route the car was taking – back to the Horrible House – and my spirits plummeted. There was a rotten inevitability to the latest setback, the newest broken vow. I should have known better, but somehow I had just stopped concentrating – yet one more unwelcome lesson for me.

15

I didn't suppose the pirates were a great deal keener than me on this enforced return to the wretched Horrible House, and the reduced short-straw rota for guarding me. For my part, I got myself resolute again, 'spinning' the situation in my head as if I were open to persuasion: *It's squalid, yes, but there's nothing here to surprise you any more. Be stoical, get on with it.* Though I didn't trust the pirates one bit, I trusted Ollie unreservedly. And since he had told me, 'We're getting closer', then it had to be true.

While I had been away, though, the insects had reasserted their dominion in what was 'my' little room. And the level of infestation that met the eye seemed to unsettle even the pirates. At the first opportunity Kaalim went off and came back with some industrial-strength bug spray. I was escorted into the African round house and there I waited for about half an hour while Kaalim fumigated, and the noxious gases then dispersed. When I returned it was like a scene of killing fields – dead bugs, supine, at all sides, on the floor and across the bed. I needed another loan of the house broom in order to sweep out all the shiny, dark, clustered carcasses. But I completely approved of the extermination order.

As much as ever before, I longed to improve my personal hygiene, too. But I got a modicum of relief in this department by way of two startling discoveries. In the morning I noticed some cardboard by the door, the flattened and discarded box of a radio just like mine. In light of the wobbliness of my bed I thought I might use this cardboard as a wedge under one leg, and so I picked it up – to reveal underneath it, grail of grails, a black plastic comb. It was clearly a man's item, with all its fine teeth broken off, but five of the thicker teeth remained. And so, thrilled, I sat down on the bed and attempted to comb my hair. I longed for the sensation of those teeth untangling and parting the strands cleanly, but it simply wasn't possible given the matted mess on my head. I was too vigorous – some hair came out, and I scraped my scalp painfully. None the less, I took a quiet satisfaction in this new addition to my meagre grooming rituals, offering, too, a new way for me to help the morning hours pass.

Then I spotted another object lying discarded on the floor by the table – on closer inspection, a men's roll-on deodorant. Marvelling at my fortune I snatched it up and put it to immediate good use then, freshly scented, I stashed it away in my water box. Alas my blessing was short-lived: soon Gerwaine came in and hunted about the room, evidently looking for something, eyeing me suspiciously. Once he started sniffing in the vicinity of my person there could be no doubt what he was after. I played dumb. But in the evening time he returned and made a beeline for my box. Once he'd found what he was after he grinned, triumphant. *Bugger*, I thought.

The pirates had long and obdurately – and, to my mind, quite unnecessarily – denied my requests to launder my own clothes. But I had targeted Gerwaine, so fastidiously Mr Clean in his habits, as one who might be susceptible to renewed pleading. So I asked him if he would permit me to wash Amina's *jilbab*, and he indicated that would be OK by him. The job was hard work, the big *jilbab* heavily unwieldy once soaked. But I hung it up on a washing line in the compound. Ibrahim noticed immediately, however, and charged across, ripped the dress down and threw it at me, shouting, then ushered me back into the room. Instead I hung it on one of the hook-like branches that poked through the walls.

My walking routine, my precious structure, was waiting for me to get up and conform to it. And I wanted to, badly. But I was lethargic; my limbs ached. I knew it was no longer possible for me to walk as regularly as I had been doing. I lacked the muscle for it. I was aware, too, that my pace was slowing – my feet dragging, the soles burning. A light-headedness came over me whenever I pushed my level of exertion. So to retain my structure I was going to have to reduce the load, figure out what could be my maximum effort without wearing myself out. I cut the schedule in half. Starting at 7 a.m. I would walk every other hour: at 9 a.m., then 11 a.m., and so on. Between 1 p.m. and 3 p.m. would remain a break.

*

Once again it was the Old Man and Kaalim who brought in the supplies – food, flasks of water and *khat* – two, sometimes three times daily. The pirates set themselves a useful task and made a shelter from branches and sacks on the right-hand side. Jamal parked himself there conspicuously from morning to afternoon, tinkering with electrical devices when not talking on his phone or napping. I'd decided he was some sort of engineer or technician when he wasn't being a pirate.

Ibrahim and Bambi were the pirates routinely assigned to share my room at night, and they respected the privacy of my washing time but made sure always to come in at the very instant I was finished. The door was shut and locked, and I resigned myself to the two of them playing with their phones for an hour at least, swapping and showing off whatever little downloads amused them, while I contemplated the darkness behind my eyelids.

In the morning I would lift the inner curtain, open the door and wedge it with a rock, then throw the curtain back over the top of the door so it covered the doorway. But in successive days I began again to venture a little 'draping' of the curtain over the door's top edge, allowing me a little more of a view of the compound. My ruse lasted only a couple of days. Then in the course of the lunchtime delivery errand the Old Man caught a clear sight of me peering out through the doorway, and he alerted Kaalim and Gerwaine, who was busily sweeping. They came over immediately, saying, 'No, no, no', and yanked the curtain down fully to leave me in darkness.

My radio was ever more essential to me here, and I had the hugely significant bonus of decent reception in the evenings too. World news dominated, of course, and the news was routinely unhappy. But I was aghast to hear the early reports of the Italian cruise ship *Costa Concordia* having struck a reef and run aground off the coast of Tuscany, at the cost of many passengers' lives. I followed the updates from bulletin to bulletin, fearing this was one of those bad-news stories that would only get worse, and hoping for as many survivors as possible.

More consoling listening came via a new programme on the World Service called *The Fifth Floor*, which I first discovered one Saturday morning, 14 January. It was a quite light-hearted digest of news and offbeat stories from reporters across the Service's global reach – hence reports from Syria, Tunisia, Nigeria, Indonesia. One studio discussion item struck me as unexpectedly plaintive: the two reporters were a married couple, and they described the difficulties of their respective jobs from studios thousands of miles apart. Before the conversation got going, they exchanged quiet and clearly deeply felt *I miss you*s on air. I couldn't but be touched by this.

As always the radio reminded me of the sorrows, losses and hardships of others, in all sorts of situations. It was a solace, yes, but there was only so much succour one could take. I was fed up of going to bed hungry, waking up hungry, wearied and debilitated all the time. Yes, I would get out, I was sure, but, more and more, I looked at what I could see of myself, my poor ailing body, and I wondered: *When the day comes, what kind of physical state will I be in?*

*

That Sunday I was able to sneak a look at the pirates as they took down their washing line and dismantled their improvised shelter. It seemed to augur another change of location. Did I dare believe it? I kept a lid on my emotions, and in due course my instincts were proved right.

I was woken in the night, and I hurriedly complied with the usual routine, counting my blessings that this Horrible House stint had, incredibly, lasted hardly more than a week. I was guided by the low glow of phone screens into the back of the station wagon, the mattress, buckets, and pirate clobber were thrown into the boot, and we bumped off back in the direction of the village. I was fairly sure we were en route to the Big House – until we drove past it, thus casting me into confusion. In fact we drove just a bit further down the road, and then round a corner, stopping outside another compound.

It had two metal gates, seemingly fashioned out of some sort of oil barrel. Once again Gerwaine, appointed key-master, didn't have the right one to undo the padlocks, and hastily he got onto his phone. I shook my head over one more basic logistical bungle on their parts. At last the right key was delivered, the gates opened up, and Kaalim shepherded me inside.

I was in a place inherently similar to Horrible House, only slightly bigger, and notably less dilapidated, with a larger thatched

African house in the same corner place, and two rooms rather than one in the central accommodation. I could see what looked to be a well, heavily concreted all around. The fencing, though, was even more of the 'rush' variety, with the branches of trees hastily enmeshed together. This was no stronghold: clearly it wouldn't withstand even the most feeble attempt to storm it.

I had to step down a little into the room, which was exactly the same size as my room at Horrible House – nine paces long – with the floor covered by green and gold linoleum laid in strips. It was the very same shape, too, with a little window in the far left-hand corner, shrouded by a heavy curtain. The bed frame was a shade smaller than in the other houses, and my grubby old mattress, once thrown down, was a bit too big for it. The bed also had a curious headboard, painted yellow with dribbles of red that gave a cack-handed 'bloodshed' effect. Against one wall was a low chest of drawers with legs, and on top of it a veritable salon's worth of toiletries: aftershaves, oils, talcum, body lotion, deodorant, hair oil.

Ali, Bambi and Chain-Smoker threw down mattresses with the clear semaphore that they would be my roommates for the night. When the door was shut on us, I felt that familiar, uncomfortable sense of airlessness. Given the tin roof, and the heavy curtain over the window, I knew I would be in for another argument about oppressive heat and ventilation. But in other important respects the place was a small step up on Horrible House.

Come the morning I tried to ask Ali what was the reason for our moving this time. Answering at a tangent, as he did so often, he told me this house actually belonged to Tall Man – a pirate who had always been notably civil towards me. And now I was his house guest.

*

My dreams, still, were often strikingly lucid and coherent, with an unnervingly four-square reality about them. One night I dreamt I was at Kneesworth House, talking to Linda, my manager, in her office, about a patient for whom I wanted to organise a home visit. I was absorbed in this conversation, in trying to advocate for this woman, because she hadn't been home for a long time. Linda, however, felt the visit was a risk, and that we would struggle to take three people off the ward for a day just to act as escorts.

As we talked I could see Linda's bookshelf, all of its volumes on social work and psychiatry, plus the framed photographs of her daughters. Better yet, I could see the view from her window, dominated by a big and beautifully shaped cedar tree.

And then it all began to fade: Linda's voice receded, and seemed bizarrely to vie to be heard with the wail of the *muezzin*. I wanted so badly to hear Linda but the interference was too strong, louder and louder . . . and then I was coming out of sleep and returning to consciousness in my room at Tall Man's House. It was 4 a.m., and outside the faithful were being summoned.

The home visit I'd been pressing for so keenly had already happened, of course. And it had gone off just as well as could have been wished for. But waking from that dream was a tough reminder that the world I'd formerly inhabited was busily going on without me. I did think about work a lot in waking hours, so it was no surprise that it infused my dreams too. I mulled over good, satisfying work that I felt I'd done: getting patients home, or back out into the community, or into their own places or group homes. I needed to remind myself that only four months ago I was a professional woman who got up promptly, got dressed and went to work – work that was stressful but also gratifying. A woman, too, who could return to a home that was a haven, to a husband, to a life that was fundamentally good.

It seemed to me I had spent many years – an active project from childhood, even – trying to carve out an identity for myself, make the most of my potential, build a life. I had accomplished something, both for myself and together with David. And I shuddered anew to think of how violently that identity had been assaulted over the last four months. To be confined to a bare and filthy room, to be shouted at by angry men in an indecipherable language, to be shrouded in an alien set of clothes uncomfortable against one's skin, to be humiliated and ridiculed, made to feel like nothing . . . In spite of it all I believed still I was Jude the social worker, wife, mother. But everything was conspiring to turn me into a woman without an identity, without freedom, without co-ordinates, and no comprehension of what might happen to her. It was a very frightening place to be, a very disturbing present tense. I longed for the recent past – for who I had been.

*

The array of toiletries on the chest of drawers in the room was a monument to Tall Man's considerable male vanity, his obvious interest in all varieties of grooming. (There was boot polish and a horsehair brush in the assortment too, and he was forever cleaning his shoes.) But in fact Tall Man was far from the only pirate with such self-pampering interests. Bambi and his friend Chain-Smoker routinely cadged from Tall Man's kit and would oil each other's hair, plastering little quiffs at the front down flat. I had known David to faff around in the bathroom on occasions but these young men were remarkably invested in their personal appearances. Youth, I thought, was probably the decisive element.

I noticed Amina's daughter, and the tall Beautiful Woman, to be more regular visitors at Tall Man's House, bringing food and supplies. But Daughter was content, too, just to wander into my room, peel off her *khimar* and flop on the floor, with a big teenage 'Phew!' Even if I was walking round she would sit and watch, as if seeking a respite from her busy world. On one occasion she offered me a piece of chewing-gum and mimed how I'd use it, in case I might struggle. She was always churning her jaws on gum herself, often while peering at her phone. Often she carried a handbag. One Sunday she came in dressed all in pink, with matching shoes and nail varnish. Ali entered, had some words with her, and told me the girl was 'going to meet someone'. I smiled at her, and took her hand in mine. She was young and blameless, in a place where it was hard to be alive. I hoped that whoever she met that day would treat her well.

*

I had another reason to look kindly on Amina's daughter: for, like her mother, she brought me very occasional treats – in particular, slices of melon, deliciously juicy and sweet. The pirates always got melon too, of course, and they would toss the rinds carelessly into the dust of the compound yard. Invariably little birds, the size of starlings, would hop down from nowhere, feed on the scraps of rind and pick the pulpy fruit utterly clean. Despite my fears around birds originating from that childhood trauma at the aviary, I felt no threat from the 'starlings', and was always pleased to see them and the agreeable distraction they made as they tussled over scraps.

So pleased, indeed, that I started to place my melon rinds outside my door to see if I could lure some of the passing trade. One such afternoon I was lying on the filthy mattress, my head propped up on my hand, peering out from under the curtain to see what I could see. Abruptly a bird hopped into view, tentatively, larger than the 'starlings' I'd seen previously, and beautiful, its head an azure blue, its breast yellow. I held my breath, so keen was I not to frighten the bird away. It pecked hither and thither for a bit, then took off and flew out of my field of vision. I dearly wanted to see more, and so I got up and flipped the curtain over the top of the door, ready to be reprimanded by the nearest pirate, but no one was in sight and nothing happened. So I sat up on the mattress, with my back to the wall, and caught sight of the bird, which had alighted on a branch of the tree in the yard, and was looking about it with quick darting movements of the head. Then it took wing again and flew down to the rind of melon it had abandoned. When it opened its wings the effect was briefly dazzling, rainbow-like.

I was so delighted by this spectacle that on the rare occasions when I had melon I made sure to save the rind for inducement purposes, and I was usually successful in luring the blue bird down to my door. A few other times I experimented by sacrificing a bit of my morning potato and leaving it outside my door. Sadly, it transpired that the staple of my diet wasn't fit for the birds, as there were never any takers.

This innocent little enjoyment was brought to an end by a familiar culprit. I had set out the melon rind and the blue bird had flown down to peck at it. As I watched, Kaalim came out of the African House, saw the bird and then me, barked 'No' and stomped over. The bird flew off, and Kaalim picked up the rind and tossed it away over the wall.

*

On the afternoon of Wednesday, 25 January, I listened loyally to the *Strand* arts show on the World Service, and the focus of the day's programme was a grand and remarkable-sounding exhibition about to open at the British Museum, entitled *Hajj: Journey to the Heart of Islam*. The presenter, wandering around the exhibits and talking to the curator about the themes, spoke of a global upsurge of interest in Islamic art, old and new, in New York and Paris just as in London. The centrepiece of the exhibition concerned the famous pilgrimage to Mecca, which, I learned, every able-bodied Muslim is expected to make at least once in a lifetime. The curator spoke intriguingly of how the exhibition tried to offer some insight into the collective spiritual experience of the great crowds at Mecca by using moving images right along the walls of the corridor through which visitors entered the Museum, enhanced by ambient sound: the desired effect being to make people feel they were moving together in the throng, sharing in the quest.

Increasingly fascinated, I listened to further descriptions of the content of the exhibition: rare and beautiful artefacts from holy Islamic sites around the world, but also contemporary artworks, intended to point up both the cultural specificities of Islam but also its interactions with different cultures, and certain subtle transformations that occurred in these meetings.

What gripped me above all, I think, was the notion of a world of art and cultural richness emanating from and informed by Islam. And I was keen to acquaint myself with it. I was perfectly familiar with the psychological phenomenon of 'Stockholm Syndrome' – whereby prisoners slowly come to identify with and share the values of their captors – and I knew very well that nothing of that sort was motivating me now. What I wanted, rather, was to discover something about Islam beyond the simple rote of prayer and strict ritual that I had witnessed daily out here in the Somali desert. Hankering after the exhibition was one more inner expression of my desire to roam free, regain my old life, break out of the shackles that sat so heavily on me in captivity.

So I said to myself that, yes, I would love to pay a visit to *Hajj: Journey to the Heart of Islam* – and according to *The Strand* I had until mid-April to try to get myself there. That was one more prospective date to mark in the diary, one more aspiration.

*

The following afternoon the radio brought dramatic news, and the moment I heard it I knew it was going to impact on my own predicament. The World Service bulletin reported that two foreign-aid workers kidnapped by Somali pirates three months earlier – an American woman, Jessica Buchanan, and a Danish man by the name of Poul Hagen Thisted – had now been sprung from captivity following a raid by US Navy SEALs dropped into Somalia by parachute under cover of darkness. These special-forces soldiers had entered the kidnappers' camp on foot, apparently intended to take prisoners, but a gunfight ensued in which nine Somali pirates had been killed. I was stunned by the violence of it, but hugely glad to hear the hostages had made it out unscathed; and it emerged from the news that Jessica Buchanan had been in ailing health and worsening, a factor that hastened the US decision to attempt an armed rescue.

As I listened, my memory stirred. In the midst of Ali's occasional reports on all the nations of the world who had citizens held hostage somewhere in Somalia, I was sure he had mentioned at least one American ... And I could only imagine that Jessica Buchanan and her family – and also the American government and people – were elated that this high-stakes operation had been a success. As for the group of pirates who had taken her and Mr Thisted for money, they had been made to pay the highest price.

*

That night I awoke to familiar commotion around me, Ali by the bed with the black bag ... and I couldn't say I was surprised. Ali, Bambi and Ibrahim had settled down to sleep in the room with me but now it was 'action stations' and we were packing up to go.

I decided to ask Ali direct, since I was sure there could be only one answer. 'You know what is this all about?'

He nodded. 'You hear BBC yesterday?'

'I did. So it's about the two people who were rescued?'

'Yes,' he said. 'Big Man not want people in the village to know where you are.'

I wondered then if I was about to be removed some distance from the village, somewhere new, and perhaps more daunting. I was driven past the Big House and out of the village but very quickly, and glumly, I knew we were headed back to Horrible House.

*

It was clear to me that something about the rescue of Jessica Buchanan, not least the swift and startling manner of its execution, had rattled the pirates. Their communal addiction to their phones had been so pronounced that I couldn't fail to notice, the following day, that they were all now deprived of handsets. When I questioned him on this Ali confirmed there had been a mass confiscation by the leadership: I assumed it had to be a security issue, to do with data and the risk of being traced.

'What happens if anything goes wrong here?' I asked. 'Surely you need one phone to be able to contact somebody?'

He shrugged. I felt sure there had to be a phone stashed some-where, even if it was turned off and its sim card removed.

'This doesn't make sense to me,' I pressed Ali. 'At the Big House there were twenty guards, high walls, iron gates – if anyone were to try to rescue me there it would be a tall order. Here it's so much more vulnerable ...'

'Big Man fed up,' said Ali, quite shortly. 'He fed up of paying for you to be here. Ollie must get money ...'

That was disconcerting. I had been on the sparsest rations for so long, I was slowly wasting away. The idea that some austerity drive was about to be applied to the costs of 'looking after me' gave me a queasy feeling. It also seemed to me that the pirates, too, had good reason to be anxious.

'How would you feel, do you think, if soldiers came in here, with guns, and rescued me? Some of you might be killed, if that happened. Does that not worry you?'

Ali only shrugged his bony shoulders and smiled. 'No happen.'

You're all too comfortable, I thought, *and too cocky*. Still, I wasn't allowing myself any daydreams of the SAS parachuting into Horrible House armed to the teeth. In fact the very thought rather chilled me. If I could have sent out a message to the authorities it would have been, 'Don't rescue me. Leave me here and I'll stay the course. I can cope.'

It wasn't that I had such fervent hopes of an imminent release for myself. I remained utterly certain Ollie would do it, but in terms of timings, things had gone worryingly quiet again. I hadn't seen the Negotiator for some time.

Moreover, I was unreservedly pleased for Jessica Buchanan and Poul Hagen Thisted, especially since the American woman's medical situation had sounded quite dire. This rescue had worked, after clearly immense efforts, with great credit to the doubtless crack team of Navy SEALs who had put their lives on the line. But the risks still seemed to me enormous, and clearly an element of luck was needed too. Surely things could always go horribly wrong: sending armed men into a bolt-hole of more armed men made me think how easily people could die – the kidnappers, their victims, the rescuers, innocent bystanders, all.

And I didn't want my kidnappers dead. Some of them were just young boys – foolish and corrupted, for sure, but boys none the less. David had been killed: that terrible act had wrecked my life and my son's life. But if these criminals were killed in turn, it wouldn't affect only them – their families too, their children, if children they had. I was well aware, sitting in my squalid cell of a room, that perhaps I was 'too soft'. I was certainly clear that for these pirates there had to be consequences for their actions. I wanted them caught, made to face trial and punishment – but not capital punishment. I didn't want an eye for an eye. I couldn't stomach any more death.

*

My fears of a new austerity were very quickly borne out. In every respect this new phase of captivity was a bare-bones operation. Only four pirates were guarding me, and just one of them armed with the big tripod-mounted gun. Provisions, too, were shrunk. Rather than the routine of deliveries into the compound, at 5 p.m. each night Gerwaine would wash, put on a jacket and an Arab headdress over his shoulder, splash cologne on his cheeks – clearly an effort to appear 'presentable' – and would head out of the compound in the direction of the village. He usually returned around 7 p.m. I was served one meal a day, an evening meal, of which I immediately learned to save a little for the following morning. But these were starvation measures.

My guards' diet, as far as I could see, had changed too. All they appeared to eat now was unleavened bread and tins of an unappetising-looking cheese.

I was tired, weak and hungry more or less constantly. I wondered if my walking structure would be at all feasible. But before I arrived at a firm decision it was taken out of my hands.

On my second evening of this stint in Horrible House I felt cramps in my stomach, so painful that I had to take to my bed. But I couldn't sleep for the stabbing pains, and I tossed and turned in misery. In the morning Ali saw my pallor clearly, and knew very well how much I had suffered through the night. But he and the other guards simply retreated to the little African round house, and I was left alone again, forlornly listening to the radio from a prone position on the mattress. The pains were going nowhere, and their gnawing consistency reduced me to tears. I was still weeping, curled in a foetal position, vainly seeking some relief, when Ali entered with Gerwaine behind him.

'What the matter? Bad stomach ...?'

He tried to convince me to lie out flat but I simply couldn't. I had a headache and a temperature, sweat was running off me. After tutting a little they left me again and the dark slowly came down, with me unable to turn off my tears. But when they returned they had a tablet for me, a white capsule.

'Make you better,' Ali said. I swallowed it, in hope. But it had no immediate effect – and no gradual one, either.

For the next day and the next I was gripped with pain, my stomach rock hard, periodically reduced to retching. I was so weak that in the toilet I had no choice but to use the protruding branch to pull myself up, knowing I'd come away with bugs on my hand. Nor could I wash myself, as I hadn't the strength to carry the bucket. I was wretchedly ill, and in possibly the worst imaginable place to be so utterly debilitated.

On the third day I told Ali I had to be taken to a hospital. I really feared for how bad I was and how much worse I might get. Hospital was, as I guessed, not an option. But this time I received two sets of tablets, white and red/black, with pharmacy-written instructions scrawled on a piece of paper. Ali explained I was to take the whites every three hours, the red and black at night. I actually believed these pills would work: there was something about the touch of extra care in the prescription. And they did.

*

The gradual improvement in my health was of much less interest to my guards, though, than the restoration of their beloved mobile phones, an occasion for joy followed by hours of adolescent-like absorption in those small screens. For me, the hopes I had of a little more restful sleep now that my pains were receding were dashed: once again I had to lie awake past 1 a.m. as Ali, Gerwaine and Jamal continued to download and trade pictures, phones aglow in the dark.

In the daytime pirates would occasionally try to show me what they had been enjoying on their devices, imagining perhaps that I felt I was missing out on the fun and might be cheered up. Abdullah treated me to one video of an undulating belly dancer – evidence, maybe, of a bit of a roving eye on his part. Ali shared with me a short film of a horrendous multi-car motorway pile-up, shot from behind the wheel of one vehicle, which I dearly hoped was some sort of staged stunt. 'You're weird,' I told him plainly. 'That's really horrible. I don't want to see it.' My reaction seemed quite amusing to him.

I was glad of any distraction or novelty, yes, but it struck me as somehow ironic that this austere-looking, pious Somali's tastes in entertainment ran to much the same kind of sex-and-violence mix as the average Westerner's.

One day I did, out of the blue, see something that rather delighted me. As I sat disconsolately gazing out into the yard I heard what sounded very much like a donkey's distinctive, mournful bray. I decided to investigate. I stuck my head right out of the curtain and shouted '*Musqusha!*' until I attracted attention and permission. As soon as I stepped out I was met by the sight of a great big camel's head above the side of the thatched fence. Chair Man was trying to shoo the beast away by shouts and claps of his hands. But the camel only munched slowly on the leaves of the branches, its eyes ponderous and unmoved under its big dark lashes. I looked at Chair Man, he looked at me, and we both smiled. For both of us, perhaps, the visitor made for a nice distraction from monotony.

*

This stint in Horrible House had lasted six exceptionally miserable days, into the new month of February 2012, when I was awakened in the night and once more got the silent order to pack up and get moving. Processing this mentally, I wondered if 'the heat' of the Jessica Buchanan rescue was felt to have receded, or whether the austerity drive was about to enter another and more excruciating phase. But could anything be more miserly and deprived than Horrible House?

We drove, in fact, to Tall Man's House – a strange sort of déjà vu, enhanced when, once again, the pirates struggled at the gate to get it open, since it was locked from the inside. A hurried phone call was made to wake the sleeper within. Tall Man came out, unlocked, and admitted us. Again I raised my eyebrows at the slipshodness of it all. *What a bunch*, I thought. And yet they had succeeded in holding me for one hundred and forty-five days now. How many more?

16

The one sight I genuinely looked forward to seeing within Tall
Man's compound was the tree where the blue bird had perched.
Bizarrely – and yet with a kind of inevitability – the tree had
gone: evidently uprooted and carted away. I didn't want to believe
this had been done to spite me, somehow. But when I asked Ali
about it, he looked as if the very idea of a tree in that spot was
news to him. Whether he was playing dumb, or really hadn't
noticed, it wasn't worth pursuing.

Like the last time I had made the same move from Horrible
House to Tall Man's House, I felt a small but important benefit.
The Leader came into my room on the first morning and made
a gesture of rubbing his stomach.

'Better now?'

I nodded. This man's version of solicitude was, as ever, very
strange to me. I was 'better' than I had been a week ago, but my
relative decline over the space of a month remained deeply
worrying to me. I now decided I had the energy and strength only
to walk in the mornings, and a little in the evening: I would rest
from 1 p.m. until 6 p.m., then walk again at 6 p.m. and at 8 p.m.
My intention was to start my evening washing routine a shade
sooner, and perhaps to be in bed under the sheet a bit earlier too.

I was in a place where I could cope. The precious goal of freedom still lay ahead. I believed I was walking towards it still – to
home, to Ollie, to my family. But gauging the distance to go was
becoming a dangerously opaque business. I needed structure,
needed to close up the pores of each day with occupations,
because too many gaps in my mind left room for detour to dark

places where I didn't want to go. Occasionally that happened anyway. With my usual disciplines I had to drag myself back on track.

*

The radio continued to offer me certain markers, things to aim for. On *The Strand* I heard about a film I liked the sound of, an Iranian work called *A Separation*. Increasing attention was being paid to the London Olympics in the build-up to the July opening, and I kept telling myself that if I was home to see the Games then I would count it a blessing.

And then, irony of ironies, I found myself listening to a World Service report on the state of Somalia, occasioned by the announcement of a special conference to be held in London on 23 February, hosted by David Cameron and the UK Foreign Office, with high-ranking attendees from around the globe.

I heard that Foreign Secretary William Hague had described Somalia, after twenty years of violence and war, as 'the world's worst failed state', an epically bleak and unenviable distinction. And the programme recited the litany of crisis conditions besetting Somalia: people in poverty, swaths of the country controlled by extremists, prospering pockets of criminality and terrorism. The idea behind the conference appeared to be about making a big commitment to encouraging political progress, enhanced security, and proper representative government in Somalia, and by more than just the usual tool of international humanitarian aid. All the wise heads appeared to agree that tackling piracy, a special symptom of Somalia's malaise, was a major issue.

The show rehearsed an explanation, if not a justification, for the upsurge in Somali piracy: how, after the collapse of governance in 1992, its coastline became a plundering zone for big foreign fishing trawlers chasing tuna, lobster, shark and shrimp – a kind of predation that dealt a massive blow to the staple of the local economy. Some angry Somali fishermen took to launching defensive sorties against these trawlers. Soon, they realised that to board a foreign ship and hold its crew hostage could yield a ransom. The idea caught fire, and now the navies of many foreign nations patrolled the coast of Somalia, while their commercial trawlers employed armed guards. It seemed clear that this new vigilance had helped to turn the pirates' focus towards 'softer targets' – foreign tourists, like David and me.

Obviously I wasn't in a position to verify any of this analysis. But I listened avidly. I had learned for sure that Somalia was not a land of opportunity, and that kidnapping had become a disturbingly, corruptively 'normal' form of business.

One contributor, an expert on hostage situations, expressed the view that Somali pirates treated their hostages relatively well, keeping them in reasonable health and not under threat, so they could be exchanged safely. He also volunteered that the 'average' duration of captivity for a hostage in Somalia was roughly eight months – though an exception was the case of Paul and Rachel Chandler, the British couple taken from their sailing boat off the Seychelles in October 2009, who were kept for more than a year.

Hearing these statistics I did some sums in my head. I had survived five months now: another three felt 'do-able'. But any longer than that? Another seven, making a year, felt like agony. How would I get through it? *You get through a year like you get through a day*, I told myself. *You reason it out into manageable chunks, pieces of time. You've done five months. Twice five is ten . . .*

It was a good job that I remained strong in mind. In body I was permanently tired and sluggish, and my shrunken stomach ached constantly from hunger. After months of a calcium-free diet I worried, too, about the state of my teeth, and had taken to a primitive form of flossing using a thorn from one of the shrubs that formed the compound fence – in this I was only emulating what I saw the pirates doing daily. But my efforts at ritual hygiene couldn't gloss over my thoroughly dilapidated state. I could feel the bones under my skin, my pelvis and ribs disturbingly skeletal to me. I wanted to keep walking home, to remember Ollie's exhortations and be energised by them. But I knew my energies had to be conserved too – or else someone would have to carry or drag me on the last of the way.

*

One morning the Beautiful Woman delivered food and water to Tall Man's House. I was surprised to see her, and surprised twice over since she was wearing the same blue-pink-silver *jilbab* as me. I pointed at her, she at me, and I gave her a thumbs-up. Evidently we shared the same brilliant taste. And we laughed – just as if we had turned up at a cocktail reception both wearing the same dress.

But it was a short-lived sort of laughter. Harsh, intense heat had begun to reassert itself in the days of mid-February, and I was made excruciatingly conscious yet again of how unclean and ill-smelling I was, and how rank my clothing. I had been wearing this dress for months and I could hardly bear it. I was suffering from prickly heat, and if I rubbed my fingers at the knuckles the skin just peeled away with a sickening ease. There was another short laugh to be had there: for such a thorough and effective exfoliation, I could imagine Western women spending a hundred pounds a go at some fancy hotel spa.

But I complained to my guards daily, Ali in particular. One afternoon he came to my room with Gerwaine and I vented my woes freely on them both.

'When Somali women go home, do they keep the full *hijab* gear on all of the time, for all seasons?'

'No, no,' Ali said. 'They have other. Cooler.'

'Well, I need "cooler" too. If I'm going to be stuck in this room for March, April, the really hot months . . . it's not possible, there's no air.'

Gerwaine shook his head most adamantly. 'No, no. You *go* March. March you not here.'

I wondered how he'd arrived at that particular view on my prospects for freedom. But going by past experience I certainly couldn't take it at face value – only as an excuse not to lift a finger in my direction. Some relief arrived, though, that very afternoon. Amina's daughter came to me bearing a carefully folded garment, and when I shook it out I saw that it was a summer dress, sleeveless with straps, low at the back and the neck – but torn and pocked with holes, in spite of how beautifully it had been presented. Still, by god, I was glad of it. My dignity was long gone out of the window, so I had no qualms about donning such a ragged article of clothing. I had to cover my hair just as always, but wearing this threadbare dress did bring palpable respite from the worst heat of the day.

*

Nights in Tall Man's House threw up oddly disconcerting moments, even after all the time I'd spent getting habituated. Increasingly in the daytime I was allowed to have the door open, and the curtain draped over the top, so I didn't need to resort to my torch. But once darkness fell . . . It was something to do with the evening breeze, which stirred the curtain over the doorway as I hobbled around the space, and with the gloom, unleavened by any kind of natural light, and also the muted quality of my hearing, shorn of my usual aids. But somehow it always seemed to me that as the curtain was blown lightly into the room, then a pirate would emerge from behind it, shoeless and silent, like an apparition – and quite often directly in front of me. I felt myself acquiring a new and deeply unwelcome nervous tic: even if I was just sitting on the bed, reading, I looked up with a start whenever the wind blew.

One day the Leader was an unexpected visitor to Tall Man's House. I had the curtain hitched up and was peering out of the doorway when I saw him be admitted through the gate, whereupon he hastened from view and into the African House. Although I wondered what had occasioned this house call, I saw no more of him in the daylight hours.

Later that evening I was sitting on my bed in the darkness, writing in my book by the light of my torch, when I sensed that the curtain had stirred. I looked up sharply, to see the Leader framed in the doorway. Startled, I got up and off the bed at once. He stood and stared at me, unnervingly. In breach of my usual practice of meeting his eye I felt myself backing away from him, wary. He was empty-handed. So what on earth was on his mind? What had he come for?

He came towards me, cupped both my hands between his big plate-like palms, and shook them gently. As he did so, he bowed his head. The moment endured – then he turned away and left me alone again.

In the aftermath of this encounter I nearly had to ask myself if I had dreamt it, so strange and perplexing was the effect it left behind. But the touch of his hands had been real, whatever the meaning. My hunch – it was nothing more – was that he knew I knew what he had done in the early hours of 11 September, and, in that light, his gesture towards me had a look of contrition about it.

*

The operation of guarding me, which still seemed subject to a kind of economy drive, began to seem as casual as it was parsimonious. There were never more than four men in the compound, the personnel rotating every five days or so. But as February wore on I started to sense a slightly lackadaisical air among them. Ali had seemed at first to be very reliant on visits from Abdullah, and they would sit and chat and twiddle their phones before Abdullah slouched off, back, I assumed, in the direction of the Big House. But then, steadily, Ali seemed to become more integrated with the other pirates, and would sit and play dominoes with them as he'd never done before.

Ali busied into my room one evening holding his phone aloft, all smiles, and for a moment I wondered if there was a call for me, until he declared, 'My son! My son on the phone!'

'That's nice,' I murmured, wishing that *my* son was on the phone. But he pressed the handset on me, and I heard his little three-year-old boy chirruping away.

I was shown a touch more friendliness from unexpected quarters. One evening around 7.30 p.m. I was returning from a toilet visit, past the stoop where the pirates played their dominoes and smoked their tobacco, when Kaalim beckoned me to sit down with them. I couldn't guess why he had abruptly decided to 'play nice' but I accepted the offer, and savoured the cool breeze while I could. I didn't stick around, not wanting to miss my 8 p.m. walk. This smallest of gestures, though, got me wondering whether something wasn't afoot, something to improve the mood even of the cranky, quick-tempered Kaalim.

It was no accident, I knew, that I arrived at a new resolution about how to spend my writing time alone with my book and pen. I had known in myself for some time that, once I got out of this place, I wanted to be interviewed, debriefed, about the whole ordeal. And I wanted to give as accurate an account as possible of the pirates and their safe houses: an account that could be of use, a dependable record, in a court of law, if these men were ever brought to justice. For months I had been applying my near-enough photographic memory to my surroundings and circumstances; even so, I was frightened I might forget. And I didn't want to miss one thing. So I began to write detailed physical descriptions of the houses where I had been held, and of the pirates. It was certainly a project, something to occupy me, conducted under whatever veil of secrecy I could maintain.

*

My senses were acute, however much the rest of me had been systematically degraded. And so I smelled the Negotiator before I saw him, when he paid his first visit to me beyond the walls of the Big House – the first, at least to my knowledge. He entered my room with the full reduced cohort of pirates at his back, took one look at me, pointed seemingly at what I was wearing and then said something to the men.

'You very thin,' he finally addressed me. I realised he had been gesturing towards my bony arms.

'I know,' I replied. 'That's because I'm not eating properly.'

The point seemed to be clear to him, as if it had been below his radar until now. He swept out again before I had the chance to question him, however much in vain, about the current state of negotiations.

That evening I thought I could make out a double table-spoon's worth of rice in my dish. In the morning, likewise, I seemed to have been served twice as much greyish potato. I wondered if they hadn't made the decision to 'feed me up' a bit, albeit by the most meagre measure imaginable. But did I dare to think that wheels were turning, for all that I remained in the dark?

*

The Friday of that week, 16 March, the Negotiator called on me once again, becoming, by his own standards, a regular visitor. Again he was flanked by all of my guards plus a couple of new arrivals: the Leader, Kaalim, Chair Man, Tall Man, Bambi, Chain-Smoker. They all appeared outwardly cheerful.

'I need to take another video of you,' the Negotiator said, as if the previous video of six months ago, added to this one, made videos too seem a frequent occurrence.

'What for?' I asked warily.

'For the people who gonna take you to airport.'

'OK ...' I said. 'Are *you* going to be coming to the airport?'

'Yes.'

'Well, why the video then? If you're there, you could tell whoever they are that I am who I am.'

But he was set in his own logic, for better or worse. So I took my headscarf off, and he wrote down what I was to say on a piece of paper and gave it to me. I noticed that his spelling was poor. There were eight questions that he wanted me to answer.

'When you speak,' he instructed, 'you do not say that I have told you these questions. They must not know.'

I nodded. As before, I was filmed against the wall, with its lime-green-banded curtains patterned with tulips. The atmosphere was nearly jovial. *Maybe this is it*, I thought. *Maybe I am going?*

I recited the set text: 'I am Jude Tebbutt. I have been well looked after, I have been fed. I've not been tortured. I have had medical treatment. I have slept well. I have not been harmed. I've had water.'

Satisfied, the Negotiator pocketed his camera phone and left. Ali, who had been sitting down on the mattress where he usually slept, got to his feet and lingered.

'You go soon,' he said.

'I hope so,' I replied, suddenly a little light-headed.

Kaalim and the Leader were left in the room with me. They said something I couldn't understand, then they both did a little jig of delight. I copied them. We all seemed to find that funny. Their spirits were notably elevated. *Could it be*, I wondered, *that you all think you've got your big pay day coming?*

I vowed to myself to stay wary, wait for what would be to be. I'd been told several times before about my imminent release, only for it to have turned out as nothing but a tactic for keeping me under control. But over that weekend, through Saturday, 17 March, and then Sunday, the atmosphere in the compound changed utterly.

*

A couple of days before I had watched Jamal and Gerwaine clean out the African House, fastidiously. In the morning they swept it out, then sprinkled water to keep the dust down. Then they got down to some work on the interior. From under my curtain I glimpsed their activity. The contents of the house were shifted out into the yard, bits of matting and a couple of oil drums. Then they appeared to be working with a lot of empty, white, woven rice sacks, cut open around the seams and stretched taut, which they were fixing around the house's inner walls. It was beyond me why they had turned so house proud.

But on Saturday, around 1 p.m., just after consumption of the lunch-hour delivery of *khat*, Ali came in to me, smiling.

'You come now.'

'I'm not going anywhere until you tell me where I'm going.'

'The men want you come into house? Cool. Too hot for you here.'

I didn't waste another moment disputing that. I grabbed my water bottle, my book, pen, radio and fag-packet game, and stuffed them all in a black bag. Ali took up my mattress and led me across the compound.

Inside the African House the first thing I noticed was the light – my eyes needed some moments to adjust – and the cool breeze at my neck, so different to my gloomy sauna-like pit.

Jamal, Kaalim, Chain-Smoker and Bambi were sitting around, as was Scary Man, a less inviting presence. The big tripod gun was on the floor at his side, part covered by his jacket, but seeing me he pulled his jacket away – simply, I assumed, to unnerve me.

Undeterred, I lay down on my mattress with my water and radio, staring up at the ceiling, admiring the remarkable engineering of the thatching work, noting the proliferation of all those split rice sacks, stamped in places with the words SORGHUM, US AID, and NOT TO BE EXCHANGED.

Here and there black plastic bags hung heavily from the natural 'hooks' of branches – my old trick, and I knew, too, that there were clothes inside the bags. I had seen Bambi and Chain-Smoker take delivery of their laundry, fold the clothing carefully and then stuff it into binbags. Seeing the bags drooping pendulously, I found myself thinking of the habits of the weaver bird, which makes its nest by hanging upside-down and entwining very fine grasses and twigs into a nest suspended from a branch, bulbous and teardrop-like. These bags looked like the handiwork of some monstrous weaver bird. Chuckling inwardly, I felt a rare, and not quite explicable, sense of peace.

The pirates were playing a game, like draughts without a board, a sort of grid in the sand formed with black and white stones, the winner being whoever captured most stones. They seemed largely oblivious to me, lulled into torpor by their *khat*.

So I got out my fag-packet game and, kneeling on my mattress, started playing that. Afghanistan–Kabul, Albania–Tirana . . . Shortly, though, Gerwaine, a non-partaker of *khat*, came in and sat himself down by my mattress watching me. Abruptly he picked up a ticket and asked me, 'What?'

'London,' I said, and he parroted 'London' at me.

'Yes, very good,' I said. He began to pick up more tickets and make the same enquiry, one by one. I wasn't hugely in the mood to accommodate him: I wanted to play my game, not his. But there seemed no escape, and so we went round the bloody world from the floor of the African House. It didn't escape my notice, as Gerwaine was handling my tickets, that I had a good reason to make sure my game came with me to freedom, impregnated as it now was with pirate fingerprints.

The others went on chewing, laughing, chatting, agreeably enough. Then I realised Ali was looking at me.

'What is it?' I asked.

'My friend here' – Ali jerked a thumb at Scary Man – 'his grandmother was English, and he wants English wife.'

'Oh, does he? Where's he going to get one of them from?'

'He looking for wife, he look at you.'

I looked Scary Man straight in the eye. '*Maya* [No].' But it was as if my skin had started crawling.

I made a request to Ali that I be allowed to go back, despite this oasis of cool in the boiling heat. 'Don't like being here,' I said.

Ali said something to Scary Man who laughed, but clambered to his feet and left, staring at me all the way out. The others followed him outside, evidently to smoke and brew up some tea. I left them to it. But after a while I kneeled up and peered into the yard: no one was in sight. I stood, at the side of the door, and looked again: still no one. I assumed they had gone into the room next to mine. Experimentally I stepped out and walked around the perimeter of the yard, savouring the breeze. There was little to the fencing of this place that could have prevented me from slinking away there and then, though I would have had to pass within sight of the pirates' doorway. But the fencing was not the prison, of course. The village was the prison. Somalia was a prison. I had nowhere to go. But what I did have was a newly rising hope.

*

On Sunday morning the Negotiator turned up in my room once again, albeit fleetingly, but with a triumphant look in his eye.

'Twenty-one, twenty-one!' he shouted.

I couldn't be sure what to make of this but I had a good idea. Today was 18 March. Could release be just seventy-two hours away? The optimistic feeling was enhanced, somehow, when Amina's daughter then appeared, bringing with her a bottle of perfume that she proffered to me as a gift. It did seem rather more like a kind of going-away present than a token towards making my prison (and my person) a touch more fragrant.

Then, around 1 p.m., I was once more invited by Ali into the African House. *They're so kind* . . . I thought for a fleeting moment, and then had to catch myself.

Before he escorted me across the yard Ali asked for my book and pen, and I watched as he carefully inscribed a phone number and email address on the page.

'When you go home?' he said. 'Please, ring me, text me: "Blue room hotel".' Then I know you're home.' I nodded, having no such intention, struck more by Ali's seeming conviction that I would soon be on my way.

In the African House spirits remained high among my guards: they were smiley and thumbs-up, even those ordinarily as sour-faced as Kaalim and Chair Man. 'You go, sleep at home soon,' said Ali, making swooping aeroplane gestures as Amina had when semaphoring her wish to pair off her daughter with Ollie.

'I go and you go?' I asked Ali. 'You see your wife, your son?'

He nodded keenly.

'Have you planned how you're going to get back home?'

'Big Man give me money,' he said, casually. 'Everyone get.'

'Everyone gets paid for their part in keeping me here?'

He nodded. I wasn't surprised.

'And what do you think you'll do when you get home?'

'I fish. My wife cook me good food. Not like this food.'

I was with him on that score. But there was something else I was curious about.

'What if these pirates came and got you again? If they wanted you to help them again, with another hostage?'

'No, no,' he said resolutely. 'They kill me, they *kill* me.'

He wasn't making himself wholly clear but what I sensed he meant was that he would rather die than be conscripted into service again. It was another profession of his aversion to their cause, and of some kind of solidarity with me. Even now, after six months of tenuous rapport and so many conversations with this man, I wasn't sure what to make of him. And yet, still, I preferred to believe that he really wasn't 'one of them'.

'When you see Ollie?' he said, smiling. 'You say hello from Ali.'

I decided to let that one pass with diplomatic silence. And yet he persisted.

'I like to see London. If I come to London, you take me out?'

'I don't think so' was the reply I settled on, after a moment of careful consideration.

And yet, whether it was demob happiness or a genuine belief on their parts that they had things to look forward to, things with which I could help them – they carried on pressing this line. When I was back in my room Ali entered with Gerwaine, who looked a little sheepish.

'This man,' said Ali, 'he ask, do you think he is bad person?'

Again I had to ponder: *Should I be honest here?*

'I don't know him, as a person. But what he's done is very bad. It's ruined my life, ruined my son's life.'

Ali relayed this and there seemed to be a little reconsideration between the two, before he said, 'If Gerwaine come to London, would you say hello?'

'No,' I said, feeling my patience stretched. 'I would ignore him. You understand "ignore"?'

'So you no say hello . . . ?'

'That's right. No hello. When I leave here, I leave. I try to forget you all, forget this – yes?'

I didn't think I could be clearer, or wish for anything more devoutly. That I was expected to mind their feelings, much less think well of them, was bizarre to the point of surreal, and I might have been angrier were it not such patent foolishness on their part.

*

For the first time since my ordeal had begun, events seemed to be moving apace with my hopes, indeed my mounting anticipation. On Monday morning the Negotiator came and told me I would talk to Ollie today. I had endured three months without a call. This one seemed to promise more than ever before.

The moment I heard Ollie's voice I detected a tension there, a clenched quality that was new and distinct.

'Mum, we've been told you're going to be released tomorrow, Tuesday. What have they told you?'

'All I've heard so far is "Twenty-one", which is Wednesday.'

'OK, right. But listen, Mum, if it doesn't happen, we're still working to get you out. Stay focused. It's just a matter of time ...'

'Don't worry,' I found myself wanting to reassure Ollie. 'We'll get through it together.'

That night I was sitting on the mattress doing word games by torchlight when Ali rushed into the room, in a panic, frantic – most uncharacteristically.

'Telephone number, email I give you? Gerwaine going to look at your books. He take them away!'

My first thought was of concern for all that I'd written in my books, whether I would be exposed, and the material confiscated. But I could see Ali's urgency, and it had to be dealt with. I found what he had written, ripped out the offending page and gave it to him, whereupon he calmed down. But the state he'd got himself into was further proof to me that things were afoot.

When he was gone I knew I had to take care of my own business. The physical descriptions I'd written of the pirates, the sketches I'd made of the various compounds where I'd been held – I couldn't let Gerwaine or anyone else see them, couldn't risk maybe jeopardising my release. So I carefully tore the pages in question, and also their equivalent pages, so as to leave no suspiciously frayed edges. But I didn't intend to lose this material down the privy. I was determined to spirit it out with me somehow: I would have to secrete it somewhere. A great notion occurred: the pirates would surely have no interest in the cellophane-wrapped packet of tissues they issued me with. So I opened the tissues, wrapped the folded pages within a single tissue, and tucked my prize carefully back inside the packet.

*

The morning brought another call with Ollie.

'Mum, we've been told you'll be released tomorrow. Now I need you to write something down ...'

I hastened to get my book and pen.

'OK, now, tomorrow you're going to be taken to an airport, and a plane is coming to get you there – a small plane, and on it is a man who will tell you his name is Jack. You can trust this man, Mum. Get in the plane with him, and he will bring you to me in Nairobi.'

That Ollie was in Nairobi made my deliverance seem stunningly close at hand. The details he gave were so precise, so long wished for, that I almost had to catch my breath.

'Now did you write that name, Mum? Tell me what I just said ...?'

I read everything back to him as I was told, and he was satisfied.

'One more thing, Mum. At the airport, or when you're taken there, if anyone says they want to interview you, don't say anything, don't answer any questions.'

'OK, I understand.'

'Right. So with a bit of luck I will see you tomorrow, we'll be together.'

Those simple, familiar words, 'see you tomorrow', had never been so full of promise.

'OK. I love you very much. And, Mum, don't forget, if it doesn't happen tomorrow, for whatever reason, don't worry, we're still going to get you out.'

'I understand, Ollie. I trust you, I know you'll do it.'

The line went dead, the phone was taken from me and I was left alone. But part of me just wanted to skip around, laugh, jump in the air and shout 'Hallelujah'. I restrained myself, I listened to a logical inner voice that said: *Remember, it all hinges on the pirates honouring whatever deal's been made. So keep it calm, don't get excited, and maybe – maybe – this time tomorrow you'll be homeward bound . . .*

Ali came back in, grinning, both thumbs aloft. 'You go tomorrow, me go, we go together!'

'You're sure that's true?'

'Yeah, yeah! You go.'

The Negotiator joined us, looking smug. 'You see?' he said. 'I told you: Twenty-one. You go tomorrow.'

'But am I going home tomorrow?' I felt that I needed to hear the word from the horse's mouth, as it were.

'Yeah,' he shrugged. 'Different pirates. But you go . . .'

That sent a shiver up my spine. Did he mean I was going to be taken out only to be handed over to a different pirate group? That old threat of the Fat Controller's, to sell me on, cut his losses?

'What do you mean? You're not making yourself clear.'

'I tell you, you go home, find yourself another husband.'

'No,' I said quietly. 'No more husband for me.'

'Sure you get husband. You go home, you have big story to tell . . .'

And with that he strutted off, unassailable in his arrogant delusion. I felt a bit deflated. Was I being over-cautious, looking to pick holes in the apparent good news? Maybe so. But I knew for sure that as of now I just had to give myself up to the unfolding of events. And so I started another walk, not letting myself think that it might be the last, that home was in sight on the horizon . . .

I was soon conscious that outside in the compound there was a lot of activity, things being tidied up, the usual augury of a move. Amina's daughter came in with a piece of melon for me. She smiled, gave me a big hug, and waved as she went out, as if in farewell. Shortly thereafter the Beautiful Woman paid me a visit too, taking my hand in both of hers, shaking it gently and bowing her head. Then she touched my face, with a smile, and walked out. Together these felt an awful lot like last goodbyes.

Then Ali came back. 'We go, we all go. We all leave tonight,' he said. 'To town. But first you sleep. I wake you up, like before. You get your things ready.'

I didn't need telling twice. Into my black binliner I packed my exercise books and pens, my tissues with concealed descriptions, my fag-packet game. Into the cardboard box that normally housed my water bottles I placed various things – my torch, the clothes pegs from the Big House, a thorn toothpick wrapped in tissue, my tube of toothpaste (utterly flattened) and toothbrush (bristles ragged). Pride of place, though, was my 'going-away outfit', folded up in its very own binbag. All the signs were telling me that its moment had finally come. I put the black binliner on top of the box, ready for the off. I walked, washed my hair, and was under the sheet as usual by nine o'clock.

*

My bed rattled beneath me. I woke straight away. *God, it's going to happen*, I thought. The usual hushed flurry of activity went on about me, Ali and Kaalim taking charge of clearing the room. I checked my watch. It was 11 p.m. Impulsively I asked Ali if it might be possible for me to say goodbye to Amina. He hastened out.

I saw that my black binbag was no longer sitting on top of my box but had been shifted back to the floor – clearly it had been interfered with while I slept. My heart sank. I checked inside, and knew straight away that something was amiss. My writing books were gone: someone had rummaged in the bag and removed them. The fag-packet game was gone, too – after all my labours in its making. I was certain Gerwaine had helped himself to that: certainly he had coveted it. And the English–Somali school workbook Jamal had given me had also been reclaimed, though I wasn't surprised, for I'd noticed it had phone numbers written on the back cover. But my books were a bitter loss. They represented such a vital part of my life over six months: so much had gone into them, and they held a great deal of meaning for me. I didn't query the loss, not wanting to draw attention to my feelings on the matter. But as the pirates' clearing went on around me I made a token search, even using the torch to peer under the bed. It was hopeless, however. I was a bit crushed, but I told myself: *They're only books, Jude. So you'll just have to rely on your memory. Get your head on straight – you're leaving.* What I still had, vitally to me, was my set of written descriptions of the pirates and compounds, safely secreted in a packet of tissues. I

[267]

resolved now to keep that packet held tightly in my hand: there was no way I would allow them to get it from me.

Then, to my delight, Amina came in. I hadn't seen her pleasant face for months, and she looked fantastic in a bright red *jilbab*. She laughed and hugged me tightly, big as ever on human contact, the simple thing that I'd appreciated above all in her. She patted my head and my shoulder, said, 'You go, you go', beaming at me. I tried to let her know I had been grateful for the kindness she'd shown me. And then she was gone.

Ali tapped my shoulder. 'My watch? I need from you.'

I unstrapped the black plastic Casio he'd loaned me all those months ago – a little ruefully, as it was one more item of evidence I had hoped to smuggle out, and had been playing dumb about in hope. But now I had to return what was his.

I put my black bag inside my box, lifted it in my arms – and then I realised, for a moment at least, that I had been left alone. All the pirates were now outside, busily and hastily dismantling things. The curtain had been detached from over the doorway and I could see flashes of illumination from phone screens flitting about the darkened yard as the pirates lit their way in the usual improvised manner. I felt a cool breeze about me, as I turned and surveyed the room: the mosquito net and mattress were gone, as indeed was any trace that I had been the tenant in this place. I looked about, and felt myself briefly suffused by the strangest sense of leave-taking that I had ever experienced.

Was I really leaving, though? It still felt to me, rather, that I was awaiting an uncertain fate.

Ali came in, smiling broadly. 'We go now,' he said.

'But where?'

He simply took the box from my hands. I saw now that Kaalim was outside, beckoning me through the door. Even he looked to be in cheery spirits. We passed out through the narrow gate of Tall Man's compound. The moon shone above and I realised that there were a lot of bodies milling around: all the pirates were in attendance, including some faces I hadn't seen for months. I remembered Ali's words: 'We all go. We all leave tonight.'

Three cars were parked in close formation and I was directed into the middle vehicle. To my surprise the Leader was at the wheel, Chair Man riding shotgun. I climbed into the middle of the back seat, clutching my black bag. And I sat there, unattended, in silence, while all the cars were loaded up with goods and chattels. I craned my head round and saw that my box was stacked in the trunk of this car. It was nestled amid full boxes of water, black binbags stuffed with clothing, assorted pieces of weaponry, and my green bowl and water containers.

A sudden terror overtook me: *I shouldn't need that bowl any more – unless I'm not going, unless they're taking me to new pirates, trading me in, so I have to start all over again, in a strange place with strangers . . .* I could feel my hand slipping from the tiller of composure, and I struggled in myself to wrest back control. *Come on, think positive, they've just emptied the place so as to leave no evidence . . .* Of course, everything pointed to this being my best chance of deliverance yet. It was only that I had been taken to the edge before, could not bear to be let down – had grown frightened of hoping.

Ali, Jamal and Mohammed joined me in the back of the vehicle, and I saw Gerwaine locking up the gate of Tall Man's House. Then we pulled away, taking a route out of the village that was new to me. I saw a pharmacy, with a light on, and someone sitting in its doorway. A donkey was tied up at the right-hand side. But the car's headlights were turned off, as ever, and through the windows the darkness of the night was profound. Yet I had the strangest sense that I was emerging at last from the depths of a dungeon, stepping into the light.

17

We travelled in convoy formation, with 'my' car in the middle. Once we passed into desert, we quickly picked up speed. The car in front zoomed off into the distance. Chair Man muttered something to the Leader, who stepped on the accelerator and starting gaining ground. The lead changed hands several times as we travelled over hard sand and defined tracks, but rocky areas slowed us down, requiring the Leader to make some sharp swerves. The surrounding countryside was treeless, but with lots of low thorny shrubs. We drove through the night, with occasional stops for someone to relieve himself. In the back I had to twist and use my elbows to make space. Even so, Jamal's AK47 poked into my arm, and then my ribs, for some hours.

As we sped onward – the mood in the car tense, restrained and silent, the vehicle's headlights revealing precious little of the pitch black all around us – I couldn't help starting to feel that, rather than being ferried towards light, I was being taken down a dark and endless tunnel, towards a perilous unknown.

And then from out of the relentlessly arid landscape came a surrealistic wonder. We approached an old bus at the side of the track with three men standing by it as if it had broken down. It was painted in the brightest, near-psychedelic, colours – red, yellow, turquoise, like something one might see in Bangalore – and was further festooned with plastic flowers. Our convoy pulled in behind it, the Leader climbed out, and I had a sickening feeling that we had reached a spot where I was to be traded to some new pirate group. I sat in the back, clenched inside, awaiting my summons. The Leader returned, evidently from one more 'rest-room break', and we were off again, leaving that magic bus behind us in the Somali scrubland.

*

The sun was creeping up as I felt the car slow down, and through the windshield I seemed to see a man lying supine under a blanket by the side of a desert track, as if he'd made his bed there the night before. The Leader parked up beside him. I wasn't permitted to get out, but the others all did, and they greeted the desert pilgrim in friendly fashion, shaking hands, chatting. We dallied there for twenty minutes or so, until the car behind joined us, at which point the pirates all set about their prayers. I sat and watched, nearly boiling over with impatience, with nothing else to look at but the flat countryside all around beneath the rising sun. I knew I would have no peace today until I was sitting on that plane.

Pieties completed, the pirates all piled back into the cars and we pushed off again. The Leader produced his phone and tried to make a call, unsuccessfully, seeming to struggle for a signal. He barked at Chair Man and Jamal and they both made similar efforts, to no greater effect. At last the Leader got through and had a short, sharp conversation. For me this was a kind of déjà vu, reminding of all the tortuous calling required to get me onto dry land after I was taken up the Somali coastline in the skiff.

It was around 7 a.m. when we pulled into a sparsely wooded area, and there we waited. In the silence Ali nudged me. 'They wait for the men from the town to come and get you,' he said helpfully. But nothing was putting me entirely at ease yet.

The Leader took another phone call, and as soon as it was done we drove on just a little further, into a clearing marked out by four big mature trees set out almost in a square, hemmed by lots of tall shrubbery. Here, the pirate convoy had gathered. We seemed to have reached our destination. The pirates got out and mingled. From my back-seat berth I counted bodies and nearly all of them seemed to be in attendance: Kaalim, Gerwaine, Abdullah, Tall Man, Money, Bambi, Chair Man, Limping Man, Scary Man, Ibrahim – the whole contingent, the rogues' gallery in full.

Then came a new arrival: a cream-beige car pulled into view, announced by a cloud of dust. A well-dressed man got out, sporting reflective aviator sunglasses, attended by a mini-entourage of two more smartly dressed men. 'Aviator' greeted and hugged Gerwaine, then strode past 'my' car and conferred with Chair Man, whose big muscular swagger seemed to evaporate before this new man's notable self-assurance. Chair Man instantly turned gofer, and went round to lift open the boot of my car. As of now my panicked thought was: these are the new pirates, I'm about to be exchanged. But to my surprise Chair Man pulled out my box and brought it to Aviator, who issued a fresh instruction, whereupon Chair Man upended the box and tipped the contents out onto the sand.

'What are you doing?' I shouted from my sedentary position. 'Leave my stuff alone!' It was a moment of madness, I think. They ignored me, Aviator impassive with his arms folded while Chair Man took my torch apart then shook out my black bin-liner so my carefully folded going-away outfit joined the other items in the dirt. Ali and Abdullah were looking on, they too in seeming deference to the new authority. And then it was over. Chair Man shoved everything back into the box and returned it to the car boot.

This no longer felt like an exchange to me. What was perturbing was the demeanour of some of 'my' pirates. They

appeared newly nervous and edgy, and bristling with guns. I saw
Kaalim, ribbons of bullets criss-crossing his body, run off with a
big machine-gun and assume a position at a distance. Limping
Man took up a mirroring position, while Scary Man got set up
with his tripod-mounted weapon. Other pirates dotted themselves about, guns at the ready, visibly in anticipation of something big being about to happen. Gerwaine and Jamal, usually
smiling, appeared fraught. I was unutterably tense. When Ali
then climbed back in beside me, I leapt at him for information.

'Why did he just do that with my box? What's going on?'

'He just check,' Ali shrugged.

'For what?'

'Don't worry, everything OK.'

'So what happens now?

'You stay here, we wait. I wait with you. Men come, then you
get in other car. We go . . .'

As I logged this information I was conscious of the extreme
peculiarity of my situation: here I sat, in conference with the
modest kidnapper who was first to show me a morsel of consideration on the night I was taken. It felt like a full circle, and a
surpassingly strange sort of private moment we were sharing.
Beyond my window there was palpable tension: newcomers on
new turf had taken charge, seemed to be calling the shots. But
Ali and I, ensconced in the back of the car, carried on in the
manner we had established, running down the clock on our
forced association.

'I not see you again after today,' he said finally.

'No,' I said. 'That's a good thing. Will you be happy to see
your wife and son?'

'Very happy,' he smiled. 'I give him big hug.'

'Right. What about your wife, though?'

'She will make me good food,' he said, his priorities clear. 'And you?'

'I'm looking forward to seeing my son,' I murmured.

'Yes. Say hello to Oliver for me.'

Not on your nelly, I thought. But by now I was peering through the window fixedly. Another beige Toyota Land Cruiser had pulled into the clearing, and from the back of this vehicle stepped the Fat Controller and the Negotiator. The Leader hastened forwards to greet them, and the Fat Controller, visibly agitated, took his *kufiya* headscarf and fastened it under his chin, in the manner of a northern English housewife, looking as disgruntled as ever and yet more ridiculous. The Leader, inexplicably, did likewise. Then the Fat Controller got onto his phone and began a heated conversation, with lots of gesticulations and wandering about in small circles. The Negotiator, near by, was wearing his little blue spectacles and a patterned silk shirt. At intervals the Fat Controller would confer with him and he would make an agitated call of his own, pacing up and down the sand. Ali slipped out of the car and left me to my thoughts.

And then, all of a sudden, we had more company. A sleek black vehicle with mirrored windows pulled up, and some more well-dressed men climbed out. I was seized by anxiety: they looked very much to me like some new pirate clan, albeit a much more upscale operation. Again I feared I was about to be bartered, passed on, a new and higher price put on my life. The principal figure in the new party was a man in a blue linen suit who strode up to the Fat Controller with every sign of expecting a respectful reception – which was what he was given.

Meanwhile another vehicle came into view: a big truck with an open back packed full of soldiers – on closer inspection all very young men in camouflage uniforms, led by one older, bearded man, all of them with rifles. As it parked up, I could see some of 'my' pirates welcoming the previous newcomers with hugs and pats on the back. Yet there was a visible distinction between the two groups, like that between city slickers and country folk, the authority evident in the clothes of the new men. They were spick and span, well groomed, their clothes newly bought, their shoes Western. By comparison the Fat Controller's men had a jumbled, ill-fitting, rag-tag charity-shop demeanour about them.

There were more huddles and conversations punctuated by gestures and pacing. I had begun to fear that they were throwing dice for me, after a fashion. Then, in an instant, something had changed. Suddenly everyone was happy, shaking hands and hugging again, tramping off towards their respective vehicles. I couldn't understand what I was seeing: I hadn't noticed any sort of exchange of money – to my mind the crux of the matter, if I was really to go free.

The Negotiator came over to the car I was in and indicated that I should wind down the window. For some deep-seated personal reason I chose not to, leaving him to make himself understood through the glass.

'Ten thirty,' he shouted.

'What does that mean?'

'Airport ten thirty. Your flight ten thirty.'

'So I *am* going today?'

'You released today,' he said coolly. 'You released . . .'

A flush went through me. My heart pounded. Now Ali was coming back. He opened the car door and leaned in.

'I say goodbye to you now. We go.'

'So everything is fine? Has the money been exchanged?'

He shrugged. 'I don't know, but we go now, into bush. You go town. You get out of car.'

[276]

'I don't want to,' I heard myself say. For whatever reason, the thought of exiting the car filled me with a profound dread of the unknown.

'You must,' Ali insisted, surprised. 'You go with good people, they take you to town, then you go airport. You see *Oliver* today.'

He beckoned me out and at last I complied. He handed me my box from the boot, and I found myself standing in a pool of shade beside a bush, feeling strange to be outside, with the wind on my face, weary of mind and body. I still felt fearful and confused: whatever the good news, I had an obstinate feeling that this final stretch of my journey home might be the most precarious.

A young man in a red T-shirt sidled up to me. He was clean-shaven, short, quite handsome. He was flanked by another young guy whose T-shirt was blue, and who took my box from my hands.

'Where are you taking that?' I snapped. It was just a tatty old cardboard container of rubbish, and yet it was mine.

'I'm just going to put it in the car,' he replied in calm, mellifluous English. 'Then we'll go to town.' Still, I watched him all the way to see he did as he said.

Mr Red told me he was a freelance journalist, and could I talk to him? But I remembered Ollie's directive on this matter.

'I don't want to say anything,' I said.

'Can I take your photograph?'

'I can't stop you but I'm not saying anything.'

And so Mr Red trained a little video camera on me. He even asked me to walk around a little. I flat refused to play the circus act for him, and stood there, looking away from his lens, but for an occasional glare.

Mr Blue then stepped forward. 'We'll go in this car now,' he said.

And I realised that everybody was doing just that all around the clearing – making as to depart en masse. 'My' pirates were getting back into the fleet of three vehicles, an uncomfortable squash of five or six bodies per car.

'Where am I going?'

'Just up the road, to town. You'll have something to eat. You can rest before you get on the plane. Now would you like to come this way . . . ?'

The courtesy was pronounced: no more tugging on my sleeve or prodding at me with a gun barrel. And yet, crazily, some part of me still found assurance in the devil I knew rather than the one I didn't. These young men might have had unarguably better manners, but I wasn't fully persuaded of their intentions for me.

But I walked – rather, hobbled – and allowed myself to be guided into the back of their four-wheel-drive. A third young man had joined us, wearing a white polo shirt; he was mixed race, with rather European features. As everyone buckled in, Mr Red, at my side, introduced himself properly as Ahmed. Then we were approached by one of the soldiers from the truck – turbaned, with a full beard, and conspicuously older than the others. 'Don't worry,' he said to me, then turned tail back to his truck, managing to seem not so much reassuring as enigmatic, even a little scary.

This car inched forward, and then stopped, as if to observe formally the passing out from the square of 'my' pirates. The car in which I'd been driven here was wheeling around and away. Ali and Limping Man were in the vehicle behind, and they rolled down their window and waved at me. I found myself raising a hand in response – since it was the familiar, strangely enough, that I was leaving behind. I could see the Fat Controller waddling off too, followed by the Negotiator, who also saw me and waved. To him, though, I didn't respond in kind. Now ahead of us the black vehicle with mirrored windows was heading off in the direction opposite to the pirates. The truck of soldiers moved off behind it, and our car followed. I didn't look back.

*

We crossed flat barren desert, while, despite my earlier refusal, Ahmed hadn't given up his efforts to question me, and I continued to disappoint him. Abruptly we hit a tarmac road – pockmarked by huge potholes, but indisputably tarmac. I thought, *My god, civilisation!* We turned right and didn't drive far until we passed a sign: WELCOME TO ADADO.

The car stopped in front of an impressive building hemmed by white walls. Gates opened inwards to admit us. I noticed guards stepping aside as we drove in. The truck of soldiers was already parked up, as was the car belonging to Linen-Suited Man, who beckoned me out of the car.

'This way,' he said. I followed him into the building, which was smartly appointed, clean, and impressively cool, and he showed me into what appeared to be a boardroom, dominated by a big long oval wooden table. I was joined by the three young men who had brought me, and a newcomer, a bespectacled fellow.

'Hello, you must be really tired, please sit down,' he said in beautiful English. I noticed, though, that he was holding an audio recorder and a microphone.

'You're a journalist, I assume?'

'Yes, I am with the BBC World Service.'

I readily took that for bona fides. 'Oh, the World Service really kept me going while I was there.'

I asked him if he had a press card and he indicated that he hadn't got round to that. And then he expressed some condolences for David's death and asked me for my feelings. I was thrown, to say the least. But I talked to him. I broke Ollie's rule. As I began to speak of David I felt the emotions well, and knew there was no way to convey them adequately. Freedom felt close now, and yet undeniably David wasn't there . . . For two weeks back in September I had fantasised about the fullest possible reunion. But I knew Ollie was waiting. When I spoke of Ollie's loss and what he must have suffered, I felt pride rise in me at what he had achieved, and my anticipation of seeing him. And I felt that was sufficient. There were, to my mind, a few too many people in the room.

'Do you think I could go somewhere to maybe freshen up?'

Ahmed led me down a long corridor and showed me into a room with two made-up single beds, and an en suite with a toilet and a shower, but, I discovered, no running water. I saw that someone, unbeknownst to me, had conveyed my box to this room. I was left for a little while, marvelling to be in a bright, clean room that smelled of detergent and polish. But I'd hardly collected my thoughts before my three car companions rejoined me. I asked for some water, hoping to wash, but they brought me a small bottle to drink.

Ahmed said, 'The women of Adado are very sorry for what happened to your husband.'

'How did the women of Adado know him?'

'This is a small town, news gets around. You must be hungry. Can we get you something to eat?'

'Pancakes?' I said.

It was the first thing I thought of. To my surprise my order was taken. Then the bespectacled young man who had presented himself as a correspondent for the World Service entered the room, holding a mobile phone.

'I have a call for you,' he said. 'It's your son.'

I was taken aback, but I took the phone gratefully. The voice at the end of the line was Ollie's.

'Hi, Mum. Is there a Mr Ahmed there with you?'

'Yes, there is.'

'Good. OK, soon you're going to be taken to an airstrip, you'll get on a plane to Nairobi, people will meet you there and they'll bring you to me. We'll see each other very soon, Mum.'

I said nothing, just listened to his voice intently, detecting a definite excitement there.

'Do you understand what I said, Mum?'

'Yeah, OK, honeybun . . .' No sooner had that term of endearment from Ollie's childhood escaped my lips than it sounded quite absurd to me. 'Oh! I'm sorry.'

'It's all right, Mum . . .'

We exchanged goodbyes, and then he was gone. After I returned the phone to the bespectacled man I was left alone for a while, in which time I relished the Western-style amenities of the bathroom. Then my pancakes were brought to me, and the room filled up with people once again. I ate keenly, though soon I was less thrilled to realise that I was being videoed in the act.

'Is this really necessary?' I asked, and Ahmed ushered everybody out. Alone again, my breakfast eaten, I took my 'going-away outfit' from my box and changed. Then I lay down on a single bed and rested. The Negotiator's 'Ten thirty' was on my mind. I'd lost track of time again without Ali's watch, but that appointed hour had been seared into my memory.

Linen-Suited Man appeared in the doorway and beckoned me again with a finger. *Strange*, I thought, *since he can speak*

English. A woman appeared and asked if I wanted to take my box with me; but I had decided already that this was where the box and I parted ways.

I followed Linen-Suited Man out to the driveway, passing three women who waved at me amiably. We got into his car with another man, and we rolled out through the gates and onto the road, again behind the truck of soldiers.

'Are we going to the airport?'

'Airport, yes.'

Still I had butterflies in my stomach. And then as we were going down the road I could see to my left a windsock, a small white light aircraft, a dusty landing strip . . . The truck of soldiers veered and with all my heart I urged, *Please turn left* . . . We parked, Linen-Suited Man got out, as did I – and then I just stood there, feeling the breeze, conscious of a small throng of people to my right snapping photos. I tried to shield my face.

The door of the plane opened and a set of steps came down. Out came a big guy in a bush hat. *Crocodile Dundee*, I thought. *It's got to be 'Jack'*. Almost by instinct my feet started moving me towards him. He was certainly making a beeline for me. At the last he detoured and made a hasty handshake with Linen-Suited Man, who was right at my back. Then he turned to me and took my arm, firmly.

'I'm Jack. C'mon, we're going home.'

He started to pull me along with him swiftly. The urgency put me in mind of the night I was snatched from the *banda* on Kiwayu – a curious full circle. And then I was inside the plane, the door was wrenched shut, Jack called out, 'Go, go, go . . . !'

And I felt myself very suddenly inside a cocoon – safe, shielded, among faces smiling at me. The plane shuddered down the strip at speed and lifted off into the air. I felt utterly drained – and at the same time, stunningly light, relieved of an onerous weight. I saw a digital clock reading 12.03 p.m. I was free.

18

My cabin stewards – my saviours – on this unscheduled service were Jack and two colleagues, one who looked to be Somali but spoke with an American accent.

'I come from Somalia, and I'm so sorry for what happened to you. We're not all like they are.'

'Of course you're not', I said.

The other, who introduced himself as James, brought me a cup of tea, and I smiled to recognise its distinctive fragrance.

'I believe you like green tea?' Jack asked.

'How did you know?'

'Your wonderful son told me. Speaking of which . . .'

He passed me a letter, folded, and I opened it to see Ollie's unmistakable handwriting: 'Dear Mum, if you are reading this I know you are safe . . .'

And safe was how I felt – safe and comforted, understood, and free at last from threat. It was as if I had entered a womb, liberated from the world of menace into which I'd been plunged.

I was quiet awhile. Jack spoke up. 'I've rescued a lot of people, and I know, sometimes they feel like talking, sometimes not. It's entirely up to you, you can tell me anything.'

I began to talk, and found I couldn't stop.

I told Jack about how I had concealed my wedding rings from the pirates, how I had smuggled out my descriptions and diagrams.

It was a way of reasserting myself.

Suddenly the pilot shouted from the cockpit.

'We've done it, Jack!'

Jack leaned forward to me and said, 'We have now left Somalia airspace.'

I felt unalloyed euphoria. I think I cried, 'Yay!'

For his part Jack told me they had all felt some nerves while sitting waiting on the airstrip behind a locked door for 45 minutes: it seemed that there had been a need for some eleventh-hour discussion with the Mayor of Adado – Linen-Suited Man – before I could board the plane and get away. That was the meaning of the handshake I observed between him and Jack.

Jack told me they were carrying a change of clothes for me, which came as another tremendous blessing. Having made the escape from Somalia I was desperate to strip off my prison uniform, the forced and denuded hostage identity. I was given a bag and I went to change. Inside the bag were cargo pants and a top. I drowned in them, had to hold the trousers up by the band – not because the sizes were so wrong but rather because of my emaciated state. But these clothes were an important step back to normality. Most precious of all to me was the act of taking my wedding rings out of hiding in the packet of tissues and reinstating them on my fingers – a moment charged with significance for me, a vital gesture in the direction of reasserting my selfhood.

The flight to Nairobi seemed short, perhaps because relief and exhilaration were coursing through me. Jack had time to explain exactly what would happen 'on the ground': we would be landing 'military side', where officials would meet me and take me to Ollie. My need to see him was all-consuming. I couldn't begin to imagine anything beyond that – other than seizing the first opportunity to take a long soak in a hot bath.

*

We touched down at Nairobi. Jack opened the door and said, 'This is where you and I part. I go back to rescuing people. You go live your life.' He helped me down the steps, and with a smile and a squeeze of my arm he disappeared back into the plane.

I was met by a two smart, smiling people: a woman introducing herself as Kelly from the UK High Commission; and Matt, the Foreign Office's man in Nairobi with responsibility for Somalia (who reminded me strongly of a psychiatrist I used to work with). 'We're going to take you to Ollie,' said Matt. 'He's waiting for you at the residency.'

I was shown to a big blacked-out saloon car, and I got in the back with Kelly, Matt opposite me. I began to shiver, and wondered about nerves or shock, until I appreciated that the air-conditioning was on full and the car as chilly as a fridge. Matt took his jacket off and draped it round my shoulders. We chit-chatted for the short duration of the drive, Kelly reading my mind when she told me that there was a care package of 'nice girly toiletries' awaiting me at the residency. I shared a few tales from captivity. It was all a shade unreal. I hadn't had a real conversation for six months. Now I was drawn just to stare out of the window, watching people going about their daily business, walking the streets, some with goats, women with baskets on their heads. I couldn't be sure it wasn't another dream.

I turned to Kelly and had to blurt out exactly what was on my mind: 'Are you real?'

She smiled warmly. 'Yes, I'm real. All of this is real.'

I was reassured, and glad she understood. I was only beginning to 'warm up', to feel human again, to believe I was among people concerned for my well-being, who intended to look after me.

The car turned and drove up a wide street of rather grand residences, replete with CCTV cameras. 'This is posh,' I said, still giving my thoughts free expression. Cameramen were milling about in front of double metal gates, but Kelly said, 'Don't worry, they can't see you.' Security men opened doors, and we drove up to a beautiful colonial building – and for an instant I felt as if I had returned to Zambia – hibiscus and frangipani, thick-leafed grass on the lawns, that air of well-tended opulence.

I was looking for Ollie, but he wasn't among the welcoming party, which comprised the ambassador, the affable Jim Collins and Catherine Bray from the Foreign Office, and Rob Jeffrey of the Metropolitan Police. Then I was brought inside this palatial house, all light and fragrance, beautiful fresh flowers arranged on polished walnut tables, staff in stiff-starched white jackets. I was so glad of these surroundings. But really there was only one thing I wanted done on my behalf.

And then Jim Collins beamed at me, gesturing at the grand central stairway, lush-carpeted, to the upper floor. 'I've got someone waiting for you upstairs.'

*

For six months I had been walking home, telling myself it was only a matter of time. In my heart this now felt like the final leg of the odyssey. The staircase seemed to stretch out for ever. I had to take one step at a time, because I was so weak, and yet I wanted to leap up them in twos and threes. With Jim at my side I made it to the top and he led me to a doorway into a bedroom.

'This is where you'll be staying. Just take your time now. We'll be downstairs whenever you're ready.'

I stepped inside. My son was standing, arms folded, leaning against a wardrobe. Our eyes met. And tears welled in my eyes.

He came towards me: without rushing, he opened his arms and we embraced, for a long time.

He kept touching my head. 'I can't believe you're here.'

'I didn't mean to cry,' I said, wiping my wet cheeks. 'I meant to be strong.'

But Ollie was being strong for both of us. He held me very tightly, and I knew it was going to be OK. We stood there for as long as I could stand, but finally I needed to sit. He led me into an adjacent sitting room, pulled two chairs together so we could sit facing one another, then we sat and he held my hand. For a while neither of us spoke. There was so much I wanted to ask him. But the emotions between us, the commingled joy, relief and sadness I knew were eloquent on each other's faces. Words could wait.

Finally I said what I wanted to tell him. 'You did it. I don't know how you managed, but I knew you would, always. And I'm so proud of you. Thank god I'm here, because of you.'

'No,' he said softly. '*You* did it.'

His modesty made me smile. 'Well, then, we both did it. You did your bit and I did mine.'

He shook his head gently. 'I don't know how you got through it. It's me who's proud of you – you were amazing.'

'Ollie, as far as I'm concerned, all I had to do was just get through each day. That's all I concentrated on. But you gave me the strength – your phone calls, they inspired me, so I knew it would happen. But even then . . . you still had all the hard work to do.'

'It wasn't just me, Mum. I had a whole army of amazing people helping me. I couldn't have done it without them.'

There was a gentle knock on the adjoining door and a maid entered. She came up to me and laid her hand on my head. 'He's at peace now,' she said. 'God will look after him.'

For all that neither David nor I ever set any store by religion, the fact that she wished to tell me this felt like a sincere and compassionate gesture. I looked in her eyes and I saw genuine warmth and sympathy there, nothing pious, only one woman reaching out to console another. And I was moved.

She then asked me if I would like anything to eat. I was taken aback by this act of kindness and courtesy, virtues of which I had seen scant sign for more than six months. I couldn't think what to reply but Ollie suggested fruit – something else I'd hardly seen for the term of my captivity. The maid slipped out quietly, and returned shortly after with an amazing and colourful array of fruit plus tea and cakes.

Left alone again Ollie and I poured our tea. And then even Ollie's stunning composure gave way, and his tears flowed. He sobbed, in a way I hadn't seen since he was a child. His emotions had the effect of drying my own eyes – because I knew it was now my turn to be here for him. I went over and knelt down by him.

'I haven't cried until now,' he said. 'I didn't cry for Dad, didn't cry for you – just because getting you out of there was my only focus.'

'Ollie, it's good, it's natural, look what you've been through.'

'Saz has been there for me, she's helped.'

We were lost in our thoughts awhile.

'What do we do now?' he said.

'Actually the thing you've got to do', I murmured, 'is give me a hand, because I don't think I can get up . . .'

He laughed, and I laughed too. It was good to share laughter, however ruefully it came, because there had been no laughter for six months, and everything we could share now was precious. On both of our minds, though, was the sorrow that David wasn't sharing it with us.

*

Ollie wanted to give me some private time to clean myself up and so he headed to his own room only a couple of doors down. I went in the bathroom, and for some time I simply stood there, in the quiet and the light, surrounded by comfort and immaculate hygiene, as if I were a trespasser in some extraordinary realm of luxury. I ran an admiring hand round the marble-topped sink before I thought to turn on the tap. I stroked a thick white towel on a rail.

My hair, uncovered, was wild, a mess, like the sweaty entangled head of a child, just one massive knot of sparse hair. But then I spotted a wealth of pricey toiletries in a huge bag. Kelly was as good as her word. Soon I was uncapping and sniffing and spraying the air with fragrance.

I undressed, stepped into the shower stall, turned the knob – and immediately it was as if needles were being dropped from a height onto my bare skin. I managed to stand my ground long enough to lather and rinse my hair, but the pain brought tears to my eyes. I got out and reached for a towel to dry myself, only to find it so heavy that, absurdly, I couldn't hold it long enough to dry myself properly.

The bathroom had a full-length mirror. And in the glass I saw a person I didn't recognise. I had to look really hard, because everything in my head was saying, 'Who is that?'

She looked emaciated, beyond question. There was no flesh on her arms. You could count her ribs. Her hip bones protruded, her kneecaps seemed huge. I thought: *If that's me, then if I move my arm the reflection will move the same way . . .* I did so, and this woman moved her arm in concert. It was me, with my feet planted on a cool marble floor, staring at this weeping emaciated figure. It was another moment where I was grateful David wasn't there to see me. This frightening reflection would have upset him so much, this tiny, birdlike creature, fragile enough to break. The evidence that I had been starved for six months could not have been more stark.

And even as I recovered from the unnerving failure to recognise myself, I had to tell myself, in all honesty, that I really wasn't sure who the woman in the mirror was. Who she *used* to be, yes, I was highly familiar with that. But not this apparition before me. Too much had happened, and it was still much too soon to process the changes.

I felt like half the person I had been. Physically, I had shrunk. It was clear to me I had lost as much as 50 pounds in weight. (Later I would discover that I weighed a mere five stone.) But mentally, too, I felt I had used up a lot of capacity in captivity, never switched off, never sleeping properly. That too had taken a toll.

I was accustomed to that traveller's feeling of wonder: *Just think where you woke up this morning, and where you are now.* But I'd never known a more shocking disparity than this: from a dark, dirty hole of a cell to this place of privilege and luxury. And though my physical circumstances had changed, the effects of my ordeal were inscribed all over my body. My mind was going to need some careful shepherding even to begin to come to terms with the aftermath.

*

The air of unreality persisted, and carried on through dinner that evening. The ambassador's table was huge, circular, beautifully laid with the best silver and crystal glasses. The menu was presented on a crest-embossed card, describing a gourmet interpretation of fish and chips. Ollie and I sat with the ambassador and his wife, Jim and Catherine, Matt and Kelly. The company was altogether pleasant, but it couldn't be intimate or cosy. There was an air of formality, and small talk, almost inevitably, strained to be about everything except what had happened to bring us all here.

My hosts could not have been kinder: it was hospitality of a rare order that I wouldn't and couldn't refuse. None the less, I knew in my heart that my ideal way to spend the evening would have been with my son. For six months I had been under the pirates' orders. They had decreed what I could do, what (little) I could eat, and at what hour. Now I was free and in luxury, but it was a diplomatic version of a decompression chamber, where I was still allotted times – to see my son, to sit for dinner – and my presence was required.

I decided to have an early night, and made my way back upstairs. I was helpfully advised that every night the top floor of the residency was security-sealed by a thick alarmed metal door, so no intruder could reach the bedroom quarters.

It was my first night restored to freedom, and I was sure I would sleep soundly. In fact I didn't sleep at all. Even as I undressed I had the strangest sensation that the bed was some uncanny replica of the one on which David and I had lain down to sleep in Kiwayu: huge, with white linen, shrouded by mosquito nets. A sash window had been left slightly ajar for fresh air: the mosquito net rippled in the breeze. And I began to be plagued by the recurrent feeling that someone else was in the room. I couldn't reach the window to push it closed. And I didn't want to wake anyone up. But I was afraid of triggering the alarm if I stepped out. I tried to make myself drop off, but I stirred repeatedly, looking about me, thinking frantically, *Is someone there?*

By the time the sun rose, I saw no use in lying around in the bed. Once I was sure the house had stirred I crept downstairs. The front door was open, maids were scurrying about, a man was sorting post on the sideboard and started at the sight of me. I assured him that I didn't need any help, that all I wanted was to take a walk outside.

The sun was warm but a light and pleasant breeze was blowing. I was barefoot. I walked down the concrete steps onto the grass, damp with dew. The sensations were all welcome and pleasant. As strong as my sense of disorientation remained, I was starting to find my feet, alone and unobserved. I touched the hibiscus, watched a hummingbird, sat down on a low-cut tree stump, pulled my knees up to my chin and hugged them. *You're out*, I told myself. And then, crazily, a thought bubbled up: *I wonder what the pirates are doing now? What's Amina up to, not having them to cook for any more . . . ?*

It was a momentary drift, and I got hold of myself and diverted my mind as I'd become accustomed to doing. I went back to the front door, where one of the staff offered me tea. I asked if I could have it outside and he said, 'Of course.' It was served on best china, naturally.

*

Later in the morning a doctor called on me to give me a medical examination. I was surprised she hadn't brought so much as a stethoscope. She asked if there was 'anything I was worried about', and I wasn't sure where to start, or indeed finish. I spoke of my poor diet for six months and extreme emaciation, my sleeping on flea-infested mattresses, the bites all around my body, the debilitating illnesses I'd suffered in captivity . . . She considered this, and determined that, basically, I sounded all right.

'You've been through a traumatic experience, and you are underweight. But my advice is to go home, see your doctor, and a nutritionist if you can. It's going to take time.'

Ollie had stepped out of the room when the doctor arrived, but when he returned I told him he hadn't missed much.

In the afternoon I received a phone call from the Prime Minister. Jim Collins had told me that my case had been discussed at meetings of the Government's COBRA crisis committee, chaired by David Cameron himself and attended by William Hague, Secretary of Defence Philip Hammond, and the heads of MI6 and MI5. And now Mr Cameron was on the line, asking for 'Mrs Tebbutt'. I asked him to call me 'Jude'. In our short conversation he sounded concerned and genuine. I told him I had heard news in captivity of the big London conference on Somalia. I wished him well in any concerted endeavours to combat piracy, and told him I was sure it was clear to him as it had become to me that the issue called for a great deal more action than the simple allocation of aid monies.

Mr Cameron mentioned, too, that he was on his way to Ulverston for the announcement of a new investment by Glaxo-SmithKline. This was no word of a lie, for when I spoke to my mother on the phone later that day she told me the Prime Minister had told local people that he 'had never spoken to someone more courageous or brave'. My mum thought he was lovely, such a nice young man . . . For my part I couldn't resist the feeling that I had stepped onto something of a political bandwagon. To the pirates I had been one sort of commodity. Now, my life seemed to be tending towards a kind of public-relations narrative. I felt 'on show', and I didn't want to be.

My second night in the residency was more relaxed and easily enjoyable. The meal was a little more private, the setting just as opulent, the food just as good. But I was more than ready for home. The following morning Ollie and I were driven to Kenyatta Airport in a car with bulletproof windows, ambassadorial flags flapping. In the back we linked hands, looking at each other now and again with smiles, glad to be on our way out of Africa.

The nine-hour flight home to England was happily uneventful, save for one disconcerting moment. I dropped off to sleep, but I awoke in great consternation, absolutely sure that my creaky bed frame was being kicked in order to rouse me for one more move, to another pirate compound ... In fact the Virgin Atlantic airbus had simply run into a spot of turbulence: hence the bump in the night. But I was shaken, feeling that I had been served an unsettling notice of how the mental vestiges of captivity might dog my life for a while to come.

*

After our plane landed at Heathrow the captain announced over the tannoy: 'We will have a short delay before everyone can disembark the aircraft, just because there is a passenger onboard who requires a police escort to the terminal ...'

I wondered if my fellow travellers were imagining there was a serious criminal among them. But I made my way to the exit with Ollie's assistance and at the top of the steps I saw a police cordon waiting on the tarmac. It was dark, the night air was cool, the airport lit up, and I was so happy to be back in England. I fought back a momentary urge to mimic the old papal routine of falling to my knees and kissing the ground.

At the foot of the steps a policewoman greeted me.

'Welcome home, Mrs Tebbutt. It's nice to see you. Would you please come this way?'

She set off rather faster than I could keep up with, but we entered the terminal by an exclusive side route, and went down and around various corridors, until we were met by a woman in a red Virgin Airlines uniform who showed us into a posh hospitality lounge, with food and tea and cut flowers set out on a table. I had a cup of tea and was joined by three gentlemen who politely introduced themselves as John Lee, Sam Abangma, and Neil Hibberd from the Counter Terrorism Command at New Scotland Yard. Their manners were considerate and respectful. They also had something to ask of me. It was essential, they said, that I be debriefed by police and experts about my experience, in a carefully selected safe house, so that the maximum information could be gleaned. 'Obviously we'd be really grateful to you for this,' said John Lee. 'We can do it at your pace, whenever you feel able, in a few weeks or a month . . .' I told them the sooner we did it the better: I wanted to do it, but I also wanted to conclude that chapter promptly, the quicker to start trying to pick up the threads of my life.

The room was throwing up a lot of human faces and information for me to process. After six months in a barren and near-solitary confinement, stimuli of any sort felt overwhelming. I kept looking to Ollie for reassurance, still not certain that I wasn't about to wake up once again to the *muezzin*'s calls and the walls of Horrible House. Ollie was being protective, trying to orchestrate things, asking me, 'Have you had enough, Mum?'

The policemen left, and Jim Collins approached. 'You can stay here as long as you want, but just so you know, your family are waiting for you at the house we've prepared near here. Cars are ready to take you any time.' In Nairobi Jim had asked me who he should make arrangements for, and I had asked for Paul and Maxine, my sister Carol, my nephews Cameron and Callum and my niece Isobel. I knew my mum just couldn't make the journey south at her age. These were the people I was closest to, most wanted to see, and yet I felt nervous, wondering if I could keep it together.

It was a short drive through countryside to the safe house. Then we were rolling up a long gravel drive to a huge mansion set in manicured lawns, housekeepers waiting by an open door to show us into an entrance hall in reds and golds and dark wood, portraits in oils pointing the way up the stairs. I could hear my family, chatting, laughing, before I saw them – and then Jim showed me into a sumptuous drawing room, and there they were, all squeezed onto two generous sofas, before a blazing fire in the hearth. They looked up and saw me, and suddenly there was hushed silence.

My sister Carol was first to rise and come to me. 'Oh my god,' she said, and I broke down in tears. She hugged me, stroked the back of my head, told me how sorry she was, for me, and about David. 'You're home now. Thank god you're safe. We're going to get through it.' And then I greeted them one by one: my sister-in-law Maxine, a lovely big bear hug from my nephew Cameron that nearly winded me, and my niece Isobel, who wept.

The last person was Paul – taller and broader than his brother but otherwise so very much like David, in his looks, his mannerisms, his laughter and his character.

'I'm so sorry for what happened to David,' he said.

He enveloped me in a hug, and we stood there awhile, my face pressed to his T-shirt as the tears kept coming. Paul, too, was coping with the loss of a beloved brother. Like David, he had a gift for leavening a situation, lightly and gently. When at length he murmured to me, 'My chest's getting soaked, Jude', we were both able to laugh.

I sat down on a deep wide velvet sofa, feeling as small as Alice in Wonderland. Carol sat next to me and held my hand. A gin and tonic was brought for me, but I just couldn't hold the heavy crystal tumbler in my hand. I was conscious of being looked at, by Carol especially.

'You're so small,' she said, her voice full of concern.

Conversation didn't come easily, for lots of good reasons. For one, Carol hastened to explain to me that they had all been briefed by an FCO psychologist, whose line was: 'Don't ask her any questions, but if she wants to talk that's fine.'

In truth I was feeling like an empty vessel with nothing to say. It felt strange even to hear my own voice aloud, after the relentlessly interior mental experience of captivity. What I could feel, though, and what gratified me, was the renewed freedom I had to construct proper sentences, relieved of hidden agendas, not designed to extract information from anyone without their realising it. Here, after six months among incorrigible and unscrupulous liars, I was with honest people, in kind and loving company. I could relax.

And so we muddled along. I made an easy quip about the posh room, and asked Isobel how she was getting on with her studies. She told me she hadn't been able to concentrate at college, had been Googling me constantly for any news. I soon understood, though, that for security reasons the circle of confidentiality around the negotiations for my release had been kept ultra-tight: Ollie had been in charge, with Paul as the designated back-up just in case at any time it had all become too much for Ollie.

There was no denying the painfulness of feeling that lay behind our being gathered in this way. But we were glad of any chance to laugh, to share in something that relieved the sombre mood. My sister was brilliant in this respect, describing the fraught experience of having watched me in live BBC *News* pictures of the handover at Adado airport, as Jack coaxed me toward the small aircraft. 'I was watching you stood here, Jude,' she said, 'and I wanted to shout at the screen, "Take them bloody flip-flops off and *run!*"'

The housekeeper entered discreetly to tell us that dinner was served, and we were shown into a majestic dining room, set with all of the splendour – bone china, crystal, silver, pressed napkins – to which I was becoming weirdly accustomed. We ate delicious lamb – Callum with particular relish, his keen appetite giving us something else to be fondly amused by. But I didn't say much, only listened. There was an obvious joy in reunion, but it was also, inevitably, an evening of nervousness and overpowering emotions. I didn't want my family to have to attend on me like mourners, but nor could I be really at ease and conversational. It was, to say the least, still too soon.

I went to bed early; Ollie and his girlfriend Saz and Paul and Maxine stayed up a while longer. In my bedroom I found a bag with toiletries and night clothes, and also two parcels sitting on the king-sized bed, wrapped up in pink tissue paper. These were gifts from Carol: she had bought me a kimono and knitted me a cushion. The gesture touched me to the heart.

*

I woke up early, in the common state of having forgotten momentarily where I was, waiting for reality gently to reassert itself. In my opulent surroundings, though, the process took a shade longer than usual. I spent some time staring out through the window at immaculate lawns and glorious oak trees in the pale light of early spring. *What just happened?* was the irresistible thought in my head. And the question seemed reasonable. How many people, after all, set off on a two-week holiday, only to be locked up by armed hoodlums for six months?

This is where it starts, I told myself. *My life begins again from here because I have got to make a new life for myself, to get over what's happened to me and to David.*

I dressed and crept downstairs. The hall was silent, no one around. But in the hallway the daily paper lay face up on a console table. And there was I, on the front page: HOSTAGE FREED, FULL STORY PAGE 5. I picked up the paper and paddled through it, stunned to see all that I had just been through turned into a series of splashy paragraphs, illustrated by news-agency snapshots. And then a detail jumped out that shocked me.

I learned that a former groundsman at Kiwayu by the name of Ali Babitu Kololo had appeared in court in Kenya the day before, charged with having led my kidnappers to the *banda* where David and I were staying on the night of 10 September. Mr Kololo was pleading his innocence, claiming to have been coerced, and his trial would begin in a month – at which time, according to the reporter, 'Mrs Tebbutt' would have to return to Kenya to give evidence.

I heard myself scream, 'No, no!' Charlotte, one of the housekeepers, came running to me and must have seen that I was shaking uncontrollably.

'It can't happen,' I cried out. 'I can't do this. They can't make me do this.'

Charlotte shouted to her colleague to 'Get Ollie, now!' But the disturbance I had caused in the house had already woken Maxine, who was first down the stairs, where she found me in a chair, rocking myself, desperate for reassurance. The thought that I was still powerless, still hostage to some unbreakable sequence of events, was terrifying to me. I showed Maxine the paper. She cursed them in language she would never use ordinarily. 'Why won't they just leave you alone? Of course you're not going back.'

Ollie came in and immediately put his arm round me.

'Mum, you're not going.'

'Really?'

Ollie tore the newspaper up and stuffed it into the rubbish bin. Soon everybody was up, and apprised of the situation, and of the same mind. Paul found another copy of the paper, and he disposed smartly of that one. When Jim Collins arrived, having stayed the night near by, he appreciated my distress straight away and made a telephone call. I had forgotten I could say 'No.' It was so important to have that vital right restored to me.

*

After breakfast Ollie and I walked in the grounds. It was sunny out, and we sat together on the bench. I was just so happy to share this closeness, and to have been reminded again of how hard he had worked and how strong and resolute he had stayed in the teeth of dreadful circumstances, from the moment he got the news on the morning of 11 September.

'You're amazing,' I kept telling him, though he steadfastly batted away the compliment. 'How did you do it?'

'I can't tell you too much, Mum,' he said quietly. 'And what I do tell you, you can't repeat.'

'Don't worry,' I shot back. 'I'll forget anyway.'

But he smiled, and as we sat there in the sun he explained to me just a little of what he'd had to do.

19

The reader will understand that Ollie had co-ordinated my release with the assistance of a private security firm, through whom arrangements were made for the delivery of a sum in ransom to the pirates, and for my safe passage out of Somalia. Because of the multiple sensitivities involved in a process of this kind I can't disclose within these pages too much of the information I learned subsequently about my rescue – and some of it has had to remain secret even from me. Details about sums of money and methods of negotiation, for instance, are bound by professional confidentiality agreements. Yet more crucially – for reasons I know will be well understood and appreciated – some parts of the tale cannot be told until such time as the men who were responsible for David's death and my kidnap have been brought before a court of law.

*

The security guards (*askaris*) at Kiwayu Safari Village were accustomed to having a cup of tea at midnight. Therefore they were off duty for a narrow window of time. Any intruders to the facilities had to be forearmed with knowledge of when that lookout was down. They also had to know how to steer a path through sand dunes in darkness, and, if they were planning to leave the island by boat within that same narrow window, they had to have a precise understanding of the local tides and the challenging coral reefs around the shore that could otherwise make navigation highly hazardous. By whatever means, the pirates who broke into our *banda* after midnight on 11 September came armed with all of that information.

Shoeprints later discovered in the sand suggested that the pirates did not head directly to Banda Zero, where David and I were sleeping; rather, that they first inspected Banda Seven, which is where George Moorhead had been staying with his wife, until that night, at which point he had moved next door to Banda Eight. The pirates, however, headed off in the opposite direction, down the row to Banda Zero.

Quite possibly they were getting desperate as their window of opportunity ticked away. Entering our *banda*, they must have disturbed David, leading to the struggle that I witnessed as I was woken and dragged outside. There were high seas around Kiwayu that night, and a strong wind, which meant that only one of the *askaris* heard the gunshot shortly after midnight. But when they hastened to Banda Zero they found David's body, and realised that I was gone. My footprints, and those of my kidnappers, were visible in the sand for more than a kilometre up the shore to a cove. A search commenced immediately, but they were too far behind the pace to stop me being spirited away in the skiff.

George Moorhead immediately called the police, and navy and air searches were instigated, while he himself was tasked to secure the crime scene. In the early hours Ali Babitu Kololo was found by *askaris* in the vicinity, and they held him until police arrived, whereupon he was taken south to Lamu. (A week later he would appear in court there, where he pleaded not guilty to charges of robbery with violence and kidnapping. He did confess that he led the gang to Kiwayu, but claimed to have been under duress, at gunpoint, having been accosted by them in Boni Forest, forty miles north of Kiwayu, earlier on Saturday, 10 September.)

By 13:00 GMT on Sunday UK law enforcement had been informed of events through their Nairobi liaison officer. They deployed swiftly to the crime scene in support of the Kenyan investigation, and were able to send out their very best people in the fields of counter-terrorism and murder-scene analysis, armed with an array of tools for meticulous forensic and ballistic analysis and interpretation. What followed was ten days of extremely close work, from dawn until dusk. But when I learned subsequently of the high calibre of police personnel involved I was gratified and comforted: this was an honourable effort, and no less than David deserved. (When his body was then flown back to the UK these senior Metropolitan Police officers made a point of travelling on the same plane and seeing that he was taken into safe hands on the ground in London: a gesture of respect that I also appreciated very much.)

What had happened to David seemed very clear, based on the physical evidence. There were rubbing marks, 'defensive marks', on his arm, confirming that he had wrestled with a gunman, and that the barrel of the gun had rubbed up against his skin. The police believed he had tried to wrest the gun from his attacker. I know as sure as I know anything that he would not have surrendered or gone willingly. He would have done anything to prevent them taking me. But the gun was fired, a deliberate act, and the bullet entered his chest, struck a rib and was deflected into his heart, killing him instantly. The fatal bullet was later found some distance out of doors, in the sand dunes.

*

Ollie was in Glasgow for his work, staying in a hotel, when police contacted him bearing the terrible news from Kenya. His boss drove him all the way from Glasgow to Watford, a incredibly kind act. He was then taken to the Foreign and Commonwealth Office in Whitehall and briefed by dedicated FCO personnel on the state of affairs as they saw it. Their initial suspicion was that the kidnappers belonged to the militant Islamist group al-Shabaab – which, if true, made for a special predicament, since the policy of the British government is to have no dealings or negotiations with terrorist organisations, and al-Shabaab is considered to be a group who will take hostages not for ransom but as bargaining chips. Ollie was advised that if this were the case then I could be held for a matter of years, with very little that he or anyone else could do about it.

One thing the Foreign Office could do for us was to manage the media side of things, and from that day they did a brilliant job of ensuring that press and broadcasters observed a virtual silence on my captivity, thus giving the pirates nothing extra to work with.

For Ollie, the sum of what he had been told was that his father was dead, and that he would have to prepare himself for the same bad news about his mother, or at best an agonising, possibly interminable wait. And for ten days that was as much as anyone could hazard. What changed was the first communication from the pirates to the British High Commission in Nairobi, whose representatives asked the pirates for proof of life and of capture, leading to my phone call of 21 September with an employee of the High Commission. (Curiously, the video that the pirates took of me in the Big House was never seen by anybody externally – and nor was the one recorded days before my release.) However, from there, communications between Ollie and the pirates were opened quite quickly; likewise it was clear that my captors were not Islamic militants but common-or-garden extortionists whose sole interest was money.

Ollie's point of contact was, of course, the man I knew as 'the Negotiator', who introduced himself to Ollie as Daoud. I can only guess how excruciating it must have been for my son to enter into these business talks with the people responsible for his father's murder and his mother's incarceration. Daoud tried to insist to Ollie that David's death 'shouldn't have happened' and was so craven as to ask him not to break the news to me once he and I were permitted to speak on the phone. The pirates worried, as well they might, about what would be the effect on my morale to know the truth of what they had done. Clearly, too, they shrank from the realisation of how the serious violent crime that they had planned had become immeasurably more grave in the execution.

In the midst of this, it fell to Ollie, working in tandem with David's family, to arrange for the funeral of his father. Ollie and Saz together made a heroic job of consulting assorted old address books to put together a list of invitations. And two months after his death David was cremated, per his express wishes, at Parndon Wood in Harlow. The service was humanist, in accordance with David's atheist convictions. Ollie made a speech and selected the music – the exact same music, as it happened, that I would have chosen myself.

Once ransom negotiations were under way the phone calls between Ollie and Daoud were many, but the progress painfully slow. There was a great amount that had to be done administratively before Ollie could begin to address the pirates' demands, which in any case were, at the outset, quite impossible. After the freeing of Jessica Buchanan and Poul Hagen Thisted by US Navy SEALs on 25 January, Daoud went silent for a full four weeks, rattled, but perhaps also hoping to apply pressure.

I marvelled all the more at how Ollie had managed to hold himself together through this terrible trial – his life becoming tied to this vulnerable process, making daily calls to Daoud, waiting for a call in return, rarely being allowed contact with me.

What Ollie told me, in his inimitably self-effacing way, was that in his mind he was largely 'doing nothing', in the sense that so much was simply out of his hands. There was everything to worry about and yet, in a special twist of fate, there was nothing – because his degree of control over events was so limited. He found it impossible to gauge the truth of what Daoud told him over the phone – a judgement I knew to be well founded from my face-to-face experience with the man. But he was able to accept the pragmatic advice of experts that Somalia was by no means the worst place in the world to be kidnapped, since the record showed that hostages were rarely hurt or killed there. Meanwhile he had people he trusted and loved who gave him the emotional succour he needed to keep going: his girlfriend, his own friends, his uncle Paul and the rest of the family.

But Ollie approached the negotiations in a businesslike manner, conscious that whenever he was speaking to Daoud he couldn't afford to betray any true emotions – nothing that my captors could seize on for bargaining purposes. And with me, too, he had to uphold a strict inner discipline and reserve, affection kept at an absolute minimum: he had to hold all that at bay within himself, and not encourage it in me, until the bitter end of all the bargaining. Even on the morning of my release the professional security people were still cautioning him: 'Don't rely on your mum coming back. We can't know for sure what's going to happen. It could still go wrong.' I know that he listened, and followed their advice; but I know too that in himself he always kept the faith.

*

A curious footnote to the events around my release on 21 March was the behaviour of 'the man in the blue linen suit'. Although

I visited his house in Adado, and he drove the car that took me to the airstrip, and evidently spoke English with ease, he never introduced himself. His name, I learned later, is Mohammed Aden, and his story is interesting.

He fled Somalia as a young man in 1992, when the country descended into chaos, and made his way to the US where he got himself a college degree and ran a small healthcare company among the Somali diaspora in Minneapolis. In 2007 he returned to Somalia with aid for his clan – the Selaban – in the midst of a terrible drought. He stayed, and in 2009 became President of the Himan & Heeb Authority, a small start-up local adminis-tration, which prospered under his energetic leadership.

Mohammed Aden has a hand in everything that happens in Adado, from law and order to local enterprise and development – things of which, without doubt, all of Somalia stands in sore need. The airstrip at Adado, where the plane carrying Jack and his colleagues landed, was developed under Aden's aegis and is a significant source of revenue for his administration. The pirates, too, were clearly respectful of this rare form of local authority – hence the distinct deference that I observed them showing towards Mohammed Aden as I waited in the back of the car in the clearing early that Wednesday morning.

20

I stayed at our resplendent safe house for a few days, as I had been invited to and made welcome. But a couple of tasks loomed before me that felt like hurdles I had to surmount.

Already I was focused on the formal debriefing by the police to which I had consented, and was keen to get down to. I was determined to recall as much as I possibly could of what I'd stored away, wanting very much in my own way to improve the chances of bringing the pirates to justice. *They're not going to get away with this*, I thought, *not if I can do anything about it*. I was aware that this commitment to the debrief meant more time spent under observation, in a safe location, my movements circumscribed – in other words, I would be 'captive' again, subject to a system. But the nature of the task, the discharging of my duties, was vital to me. I wanted to be done with it, and to resume my real life. I also had a sense the process might offer me some valuable catharsis. And while the police at first stipulated that for the duration of the debrief I couldn't contact anyone, I prevailed on them to be allowed to see Ollie.

The other challenge I faced – ostensibly simpler, and yet far more daunting – was to return home to our house in Bishop's Stortford. I wanted this, badly, and yet at the same time I simply didn't know how I was going to feel about it. I was well aware that Ollie would have stayed with me, but my overriding feeling was that I needed to start to learn to live on my own.

I knew I would be driven there and escorted to my front door, that the inevitable media interest on my doorstep would be deftly handled and a way cleared for me. But after that, I would be on my own. I had never feared change before, had always faced up to challenges, not wanting to postpone them. But to return to the home David and I had worked so hard to have, the home we'd made together – it was intensely difficult to imagine crossing that threshold and David not being there.

*

The house was strangely quiet and cold. The thought did cross my mind: *That was a bloody long holiday . . .* The cats came to greet me, and straight away I fell into the routine of feeding them – a funny kind of back-to-normal.

Then I went into each of the rooms, one by one – a natural thing to do, perhaps, but, in the back of my mind, I was conscious that it was as if I were looking for somebody. There was a low sound in my head, asking me: *Did it really happen? Have I just had a horrible dream and woken up in my house? Where is David?*

I reached the spare room and it was there that I realised it wasn't all just some nightmare imagining – there, I knew for sure that David wasn't going to come home from work tonight. Because sitting on the bed were the holdalls we had taken away on holiday with us – bags we had bought expressly for the trip, because they were so capacious and lightweight. They had been flown back to the UK together with David's body. The zips were undone. I could see the Masai blankets we were given on our last morning, lying neatly folded at the top of my bag. And I could see David's walking shoes poking out of his. Tears welled up and out of me, and I didn't fight them back.

I took his shirts from the bag, held them against my cheek. And then I noticed a sealed plastic bag, and recognised what was inside instantly – it was the postcard I had written to Ollie from Serian Camp, telling him what a great holiday we were having, all the animals we had seen. I remembered sitting at the desk in our tent, writing, David lying on the bed behind me, my asking him, 'What else did we see . . .?' It told the story of that wonderful first week of a precious holiday. And we never did get to post it.

I looked at the card more closely: it had been stamped NOT TO BE DISPOSED OF, and the ink was smudged here and there, by swabbing for DNA. Thus a gift-shop keepsake had been turned into a *memento mori*, forensic evidence of how a catastrophe befell us. I came upon another exhibit from the investigation, a police inventory citing all the items they had examined and tested, notes of David's DNA records obtained from his dentist, references to which articles were bloodstained. It was all set down in black and white, the facts of the case, altogether certifying how David's life had ended.

I knelt on the floor and I hugged my husband's belongings – the vestiges of him. Inside I had a burning urge to carry these bags back to Serian Camp, so that we'd be there as we were then, and we wouldn't go to Kiwayu Island; we'd change the fates, go somewhere, anywhere, else instead . . . But there was no escape from the desolation in the room. I stayed there for some time.

At length I came around, my mind drew me back to the present. It was grief, I knew, that was working on me. For six months I had waited to begin my grieving: out there in the stony, unfeeling pit of my captivity, any such remembrance had been quite impossible. Now it had begun, and it was right and proper – but it wasn't doing me any good. I had to turn my back on the room, literally close the door on it, go and sit down elsewhere, seek some sort of purposeful distraction.

That night I switched on the radio and the television, and I watched through a blur of tears. I poured myself a small glass of whisky – not my thing normally, but David had taken a glass on occasion, and I thought it might help me sleep. Finally a moment of clarity came. I had been weeping for hours, my eyes were stinging, my nose was sore. And in my head I felt I could change the gears. *You've done enough of this for one night. This is when you stop.*

And I did. I switched the television off. I knew that in the morning a police car would come to take me away to the debriefing. I knew I had to sleep, that tomorrow I had an important job to do, for which I needed a clear head. I didn't know where we'd go or what the police questioning would entail, but I had no fear of it. I was going voluntarily – indeed I was looking forward to doing something constructive. Every morning I awoke in Somalia I had a clear goal, to make it to the end of another day. With the gift of freedom I needed new goals, and the debrief was the first one in front of me. This re-entry into my 'old' life, now so transformed by circumstances, was going to have to be gradual. But home would be waiting for me when I was done with the police; and now I looked forward to it.

In the morning I said goodbye to the cats, wrote a note for Ollie, packed a few things in a bag and closed the door behind me for another week.

21

When I returned home in early April I found that my house had become the focus of a deeply unwelcome media scrum. Newspaper reporters, I learned, had been trudging up and down my street, knocking on doors, trawling for information. I was anxious about how far journalistic persistence was going to be pushed – whether anyone would take no for an answer, or whether intrusion into my life would be a daily occurrence unless I relented.

The Metropolitan Police graciously arranged for a rapid-summons security system to be installed at the house, with a box-set in my bedroom and even a handheld call-button alarm for me to carry about, so that if I was pestered face to face by the press the local police could be alerted immediately. For some weeks officers patrolled my street as a special service, though reporters were still knocking and ringing at my door, and every morning I could observe them from my window, however hard they endeavoured to look 'inconspicuous'.

Quite apart from this unnerving sense of being under siege, I found it difficult getting accustomed again to the four walls of the house. But of course there was so much to be grateful for. This place had been David's and my haven, our sanctuary from the stresses of work, for twenty years – and I was glad of its comforts now.

I couldn't wait to restock my fridge and larder at Waitrose, back among the aisles that I'd mapped precisely in my head and mentally revisited while I was starving in captivity. I realised very quickly that I would never again look at the sheer groaning plenitude of supermarket shelves without a sense of awe.

My eyes, though, were rather bigger than my stomach, as the saying goes.

I wanted to get back onto a normal diet and regain weight as soon as I could. Ollie was very keen that I do so too. He confessed to me how worried he'd been by our first embrace in Nairobi, his feeling that I was all skin and bone, 'not like my mum'. And indeed my health concerned no one more acutely than me. My spine was giving me considerable pain, and when I sat I struggled to get comfortable, fearing sometimes that my bones might crack. I couldn't sit down on my rear for very long in any case: it felt as though there were no padding, no muscle or fat there. Ever since my excruciating shower in Nairobi I had shrunk from revisiting that sensation, but bathing made for its own share of discomforts: even lowering myself into the water was a chore, owing to the sheer lack of strength in my arms; and any hard surface underneath me was agonising.

It took me a little longer than I had hoped to secure an appointment at my local doctor's surgery, but once I got there I was treated very thoroughly: my blood was tested and I was sent for a bone scan, which revealed that all those jarring impacts on the skiff that bore me away from Kiwayu had managed to twist my coccyx, creating a scoliosis at the base of my spine. I was also diagnosed with osteoporosis, which came, sadly, as no great surprise. The doctor prescribed tablets for this but warned me of nausea. Indeed the pills began very quickly to make me feel awful, and so I stopped taking them, resolving instead to eat more cheese and to resume my Pilates classes.

The deleterious mental effects of my ordeal, naturally, also kept making themselves apparent. For days, into weeks, I kept pinching myself, banging and thumping on walls – not hard, but just to make totally sure of the physical reality of my surroundings. I could be standing at the sink washing up when the dread thought might crawl into my head: *Oh god, this is not a dream, is it . . . ?* Whereupon I would turn the water to scalding hot and hold my hand under it, until a red mark rose up on the skin. I had no surety unless I saw that. These odd habits persisted: I wanted them gone but, at the same time, I was truly terrified by the thought that I might wake up and find myself back in that room again.

The Victim Support charity, whose work I generally admired, had contacted and offered support to my family during my captivity. Through that channel, they extended an offer to me also, if I wished to get in touch. And yet I didn't feel I was in need of their services. In spite of some lingering vulnerabilities, I genuinely felt that I had a perception of what had happened to me that was properly sorted in my head, not least after a week's intensive debriefing with the Met. And I didn't particularly want to discuss all of this with anyone else – certainly not another stranger. What could they say or do? I had the good fortune to number among my friends people who are trained counsellors and psychotherapists: speaking occasionally with them, and with Ollie, felt like therapy enough for me. I had a strong instinct, too, that writing my story down would be the most truly beneficial process I could undergo, and that intention was firming up in my mind.

*

As I began to feel a little stronger in myself, I decided to review the inventory of David's personal effects which the police had deposited at our house along with our Kenyan travel bags. Almost immediately I realised that David's items of jewellery were not listed.

On his left ring finger David had always worn his Turkish three-band wedding ring as well as his grandfather's old wedding band; and always on his right hand was a signet ring that his mother and father gave him when he turned eighteen. He was wearing these rings when we went to bed that last night in Kiwayu, and also a gold necklace that I had bought for him (paid off in instalments) when we first moved to Andover. Because of an arthritic complaint in his knuckles David could not have removed his rings even if he'd cared to. And yet I was now to understand that they were not on his person by the time his body was conveyed from Kenya back to the UK.

Immediately I contacted my police family-liaison officer, who told me he would check up for me on this deeply disturbing omission. It then took a few weeks to establish the facts, but I wanted to know, and I would accept nothing less. It emerged without doubt that at some point between the transfer of David's body from Kiwayu and arrival at a funeral home in Nairobi, his jewellery must have been stolen. The implications of this were utterly outrageous to me. I insisted that inquiries be vigorously pursued into how this had happened; and they were, albeit with continual frustrations and intimations that we were 'not to know'. It became clear to me quite quickly that David's jewellery would not be returned to me, which was deeply upsetting in itself. But I was not prepared to let the matter rest. I felt I was entitled to a formal acknowledgement of the theft and an apology from the party on whose watch it had occurred. And I am waiting still.

*

Kneesworth House had made contact with Ollie while I was still in Somalia, and now they wrote to me confirming that my job would remain open for me until September if I wanted it. This was a dilemma for me, one that I discussed with Ollie. My job had felt hugely worthwhile to me, but also incredibly stressful. I had to ask myself if I had the energy, the focus, and the strong nerves to resume it. The honest answer, I knew, was that if I went back then I probably wouldn't last a day.

The challenge was about far more than just my condition, mentally, emotionally, physically. The women there, some of them with psychopathic personality disorders, knew everything about me – and, whether they meant to or not, they would end up using that information in a way that would be a barrier to any prospect of my working with them successfully again. I could foresee their efforts to engage me about Somalia – to console me, or taunt me, or otherwise pussyfoot around the business we were there to accomplish.

My manager Linda came to visit me at home, and she was just as thoughtful and candid as I knew her to be. 'I don't really know how you *can* come back,' she told me ruefully. She was only echoing my own thoughts.

I advised her verbally of my decision to resign without delay and wrote and sent my resignation letter, so that we could all move on. But in my heart I felt it to be a great shame. I had acquired such a lot of experience and knowledge in the job over the years. But owing to circumstances beyond my control, and to the demands of 'best practice', I was going to have to file all that professional expertise away for the foreseeable future.

*

Our Kenyan travel bags stayed on the spare bed for weeks and weeks. Finally I emptied my bag, put away my things, folded the bag and stashed it in the loft. But David's bag stayed there for longer, and I would go in and look at it. I didn't want to touch it, knowing how I would feel. In myself I knew that eventually I would have to get rid of both bags, because of the memories that they embodied.

Once a little more dust had settled on my homecoming, I decided that I wanted to do one or two things for myself – things I had enjoyed in my 'old' life, the enjoyment of which I hoped had not receded for me in the interim. I took a short holiday to Cyprus with Ollie and Saz, where we spent our days picking our way through Roman ruins, eating together in the evenings.

On Monday, 25 June, I gave testimony under oath to the trial of Ali Babitu Kololo in Lamu, Kenya. Ollie was very aware of my fear of travelling to Lamu and so, following much negotiation between him and the Metropolitan Police, a video link was set up from London and my evidence was relayed to the court on a screen, while Senior Investigating Officer Neil Hibberd was present in person for the proceedings. It took me all of two hours to read out my prepared statement about the events in Kiwayu on 10 and 11 September, and everything I said was translated simultaneously into Swahili for the court.

In terms of Mr Kololo's fate, the nub of my testimony was plain: having seen pictures of the man in custody, it was clear to me that I had never seen him before, though I could not say for sure that he had not been in our *banda* that night. However, I also advised the court of what Ali had told me in the Big House, about 'the sixth man' whom the pirates had left behind them on Kiwayu. I found the whole experience taxing – and I was so grateful to Ollie and Saz for accompanying me, sitting off camera and giving me looks of quiet support and encouragement whenever I faltered. But I was relieved to have discharged my responsibilities in difficult circumstances. (Neil Hibberd subsequently told me that he had encountered unprecedented problems of his own out there in Lamu: at one stage as he stood outside the shed-like courthouse waiting to give his evidence, he had been forced to break up a fight between a pair of fractious donkeys, to avoid proceedings within being disturbed.)

With Mr Kololo having already spent nine months in custody, I hoped that the deliberations of the court would not be unduly tardy. However, there did seem to be an inherently stately pace to Kenyan court business, with hearings of only one or two days at a time routinely punctuated by breaks of four days or more. I knew I would have to summon all of my patience.

*

David's funeral service had taken place early in my captivity, as was right and appropriate, and I was glad it had been arranged and conducted so well. But for me, having been unable to attend owing to circumstances far beyond my control, the need in me to pay my own respects to my husband was acute. Even during my captivity the thought had occurred to me that I would find something very precious in the organising of a proper celebration of his life. Having begun at last my true mourning for him, this need to rejoice in his life and the life we had shared was more powerful than ever before.

In fact Stephen Page, Faber and Faber's Chief Executive and David's close colleague and friend, had suggested to Ollie that it would be a fine and fitting thing to hold some form of memorial service for David. When I was advised as much, I signalled my wholehearted support and immediately we set down to planning it. In this I was especially glad of the help of Rachel Alexander, Faber's Director of Communications, not only a hugely sympathetic and patient person to work with but also someone with the gift of making perfect suggestions. One such was the proposal of the Wigmore Hall as a venue for the service: its main hall was beautifully decorated and generously sized, yet also somehow intimate. With Faber I drew up a considerable list of invitees: I approached David's closest friends and colleagues, asking them in turn to pass on any suggestions to Rachel who collated the final list.

It all came to pass on Tuesday, 3 July, and it wasn't long into proceedings that I felt sure things would go off just as I had hoped. If there was solemnity and deep feeling in the room, there were also the good, lively spirits that David's memory naturally inspired. The Benyounes Quartet, four gifted young female musicians, gave exquisite performances of pieces by Mozart, Elgar and Puccini. Since David loved many and diverse forms of music, we also heard the Kinks' 'Waterloo Sunset'. Ollie gave a terrific speech, assuredly and from the heart. There were warm and deeply felt addresses, too, from Stephen Page and from Phil Tanswell, David's oldest friend since grammar school, who had shared so much history with him. Faber Poetry Editor Matthew Hollis also spoke, on behalf of all of David's colleagues at the firm, and gave a superb reading of Louis MacNeice's 'Apple Blossom', a favourite of David's and mine:

> For the last blossom is the first blossom
> And the first blossom is the last blossom
> And when from Eden we take our way
> The morning after is the first day.

When my turn came to speak I felt very comfortable, gratified, and aware that, for all the emotions of the occasion, I was in control of my own. I was drawn in particular to hymn David's great appetite for life, because it was also so often a source of humour for us both – and his avid love of music was a very useful example in that way. I told the gathering about how keenly David had gone about purchasing new music that he'd discovered (quite where, I often knew not), and how excited he would get once the Amazon packets finally dropped through the letterbox – he would routinely resort to tearing and stabbing at those stiffly glued box-wrappers in frustration, with a paper knife or sharp scissors or whatever pointed implement was to hand. And after all these wrangles, what would drop out onto the floor would be a CD of Mongolian throat music – the bafflement on my face reversed exactly by the rapturous look on David's.

He took his music seriously, but there was some music he found seriously funny. To wit, the piece that I'd heard him specifically cite as 'the one he'd want to have played at his funeral' was 'Big Shot' by the Bonzo Dog Doo-Dah Band, and so this was the tune on which we played out the memorial: a very English pastiche of discordant modern jazz and spoken 'tough guy' vocals in the style of American pulp fiction. Vivian Stanshall's ridiculous tale of a man named 'Johnny Cool' who meets a girl with 'the hottest lips since Hiroshima' ends on lines that always made David giggle:

A punk stopped me on the street, he said, 'You got a light, mac?'
I said, 'No, but I've got a dark brown overcoat . . .'

The Bonzo music seemed to me the right note on which to close proceedings and allow the guests to thread their way out into the Wigmore Hall foyer. There they mingled, smiles on their faces: I heard laughter, and that was important to me. Laughter always came easily around David.

*

In July I took another holiday, with my sister Carol, to Australia for three and a half weeks. She and I had never holidayed together before, and now seemed to be the right time to share that experience. Australia was a place David and I had never thought of visiting together, and as such it was an ideal spot for me and my sister to discover.

The travel, the sights, the company were all good for me. It wasn't that I was trying to 'put things behind me' by putting more miles between me and home. Reminders of my condition and the marks of my experience were, in any case, unavoidable. I had regained a little weight but less than I had hoped: I remained awfully thin to my eyes, and I didn't feel that my old appetite had truly returned. Sitting down remained an awkward negotiation. Even in Australia, four months after my release, I couldn't take a bath with any comfort. I had learned to tolerate showers, but the excruciating sensation of having a crate-load of pins emptied on top of me took a long time to recede.

Just as distressing to me, in a way, was the lingering effect of captivity on my sleeping habits, the shadow that still hung over my nights and mornings. At home I felt I had to keep the windows closed at all times. It was ridiculous and illogical to me, and yet I had been left with that trace of fear. In the night I needed to have the curtains open as I slept, for light and for transparency. But sleep didn't come easily, and at times I had an unnerving sense of someone else in the room, slipping in silently through the door. It was a chilling sensation, and it made me catch my breath. To this day I sometimes think I feel my bed beneath me is being shaken by some intruder, and my heart lurches as I scan the room to make sure no one is there.

*

As the first anniversary of my kidnapping loomed, I could feel a certain desire mounting inside me, a wish to articulate my views on piracy – to contribute to the debate, and perhaps help to make a difference. These feelings crystallised when I received an invitation to travel to the Seychelles for a government-convened conference on piracy, to be attended by delegates from most of those small nations looking out to the Indian Ocean and having to confront this ongoing problem. It was no surprise that the Seychelles had placed itself at the forefront of counter-piracy efforts, given the damage wrought on its tourism industry and wider economy by Somali pirates in particular. (It wasn't lost on me that Paul and Rachel Chandler had been taken from their boat in waters ninety miles off the Seychelles archipelago in October 2009.)

I discussed the invitation with Ollie: he was understandably wary of my revisiting the Indian Ocean. But I consulted with Jim Collins (who would be attending with me) about safety concerns, and he offered reassurance. It was what I needed to hear – because I had a strong instinct about the potential benefits in my being able to convey my story to an audience of people committed to combating piracy. And so I went. The experience was indeed enlightening and inspiring, and a useful test of my new resolve.

Preparing to give my talk, I was nervous, very worried that I might break down in tears. For I was desperately keen to be seen not as a fragile, quivering figure but, rather, as a credible and serious witness, a speaker to whom the conference could give a hearing, who would not become visibly upset and oblige the delegates to lower their eyes in sympathy. I did hold myself together and said my piece, and it seemed to be appreciated. I felt the risk had been worth it, for me to put a human face to my story, to give the gathering a deeper appreciation of the toll taken by piracy.

On a personal level I was often ill at ease during my four-day stay, despite the unfailing courtesy of my hosts. I never left my hotel room unescorted, and Jim and Catherine Bray always saw me back there in the evenings. My windows were always firmly shut, my curtains open. And although the hotel was right on the beach with an ocean view, I never once set foot on the sand – not even in daylight, and no matter who accompanied me.

This instinctive wariness aside, everybody I met and every place I visited was impressive. I talked with Joel Morgan, government transport minister and chairman of a high-level committee on piracy, who was also acting as head of negotiation in efforts to free two Seychellois fishermen, Rolly Tambara and Marc Songoir, held in Somalia since November 2011. I visited the operations centre of the Seychelles Coastguard, and also their training base for drilling staff and new recruits in techniques of counter-piracy. And I met Will Thurbin, English governor of the Montagne Posse prison where a hundred or so Somali pirates were serving time. His attitude towards the inmates in his charge impressed me: he treated them as human beings, understood that they came from nothing, and that their punishment needed to include efforts at constructive rehabilitation in order to break the cycle of offending. In short I was full of admiration for the concerted efforts of the Seychelles, a small country sending out a clear message that it wouldn't stand for this criminality in its waters.

*

In October 2012 I took up a second invitation, this to Seville, to speak at the annual international conference of the Serious

Organised Crime Agency (SOCA), which took kidnap and abduction as its main topics of discussion. Jim Collins and Neil Hibberd accompanied me and we gave a joint presentation to an audience of 150 delegates, a lot of them top law-enforcement officers dealing with serious crime. I told my story; Neil outlined the police's role and procedures, and Jim talked about the FCO's general approach to hostage crises.

One thing that I was keen to impart to delegates was that I understand entirely just how life threatening a kidnap can be, but that I am also acutely conscious of the high risk of any effort to free hostages from captivity by force. I was truly grateful to be standing before this audience, alive and well, a full year on from my capture. But that had been possible only because of the paying of a ransom. There is, of course, often an emotive argument over whether criminals ought to profit by ill-gotten gains, whether crime flourishes if we permit it to 'pay'. My challenge to the delegates was, essentially, this. Try for a moment to put yourselves in the shoes of people and their families who have suffered this ordeal, and ask yourself, honestly: what would you do?

Possibly as rewarding an experience for me as any other part of the conference was sharing a table in the hall with a fellow ex-hostage, Patrick Noonan, who had been taken in Sudan on 6 March while on his way to work at the offices of the World Food Programme. (In the twelve months prior to his kidnap he had helped to distribute tents and cooking equipment to a quarter of a million Sudanese.) He was held for eighty days in a tent of a family with whom he became 'friendly', in the effort to make himself appear human to them – an effort I well understood. Patrick's release had been secured finally on 30 May.

There is something powerful in meeting a stranger with whom you share such a remarkable and harrowing experience.

After Patrick had delivered his own talk he came over to me, and I wasn't sure quite what was 'appropriate', since we had only just met – but, really, I wanted to give him a hug, in consolation for his ordeal. However, being momentarily unsure whether this was 'the thing to do', I simply touched his shoulder and told him how well he had spoken, and how sorry I was that he had been through such an awful lot. 'So have you,' he said quietly. After that we talked a little more during intervals in the schedule.

It was clear to me that we shared concerns about the effects of being robbed of our liberty and held in isolation: how you lived with that afterwards, how you recovered your definition of self, the identity you know is rightfully yours. Neither of us wanted our respective ordeals to claim any more from us than they had already, so unjustly, managed to steal.

The other interesting lessons of Seville for me were low key but intensely personal, and arose from the time that I spent by myself. For one thing, having spent pretty much my entire adulthood as a married woman, this was the first time in my life that I had travelled somewhere carrying my own passport and bearing responsibility for all the logistics of getting from place to place. I accept that not to have managed this feat before might sound like oddly 'dependent' behaviour, not least from a professional woman in her fifties. It might have had something to do with the class and generation from which I come, and old habits never broken. But now, for the first time in my life, I went sightseeing around a city on my own. The mixture of emotions was often sharp and poignant. I missed David every second. And yet at the same time I told myself, *You're managing this. You're learning something else about how to cope.* So the sadness was twinned at least with some small but valuable sense of self-reliance.

One or two experiences during the trip were a little more dis-concerting. Stepping inside a restaurant where I thought I might have lunch one afternoon, I found myself waiting to be seated in front of an older couple who were chatting away to one another keenly. Surveying the other diners I noticed quite a few couples, and began to mentally calculate their ages. A thought came unbidden: *Why couldn't that be me and David?* Whereupon the maître d' busied over, looked past me, and escorted the couple behind me to their table first. I was made to feel invisible; and it made me cross. I called the maître d' back, asked him pointedly for a table for one, and he seemed at last to get the picture. Then I sat and had a salad, watching the couples, think-ing: *That was once me,* us – *we used to do that. Is this how life is going to be from now on?* I realised I had to accept I had joined the ranks of single people, one among millions, and I would have to get used to it, learn how to function in that way.

I endured a rather more visceral shock to my system on our last evening in Seville when a number of us went out to a tapas bar intending a convivial end to the visit. It seemed a nice enough place, and as we stood by the bar with drinks I saw some people ordering food. Then, however, I noticed that an Irish police offi-cer in our party was staring quite fixedly away from the group.

'Would you look at that . . . ?' he said in some wonderment.

And, though in the blink of an eye Neil Hibberd had moved himself smartly so as to shield my view, I did indeed catch sight of a notably large cockroach scuttling along the top of the bar. Instantly I could feel myself shake with revulsion at this creepy reminder of the company I had been forced to keep in the squalid rooms of my captivity. By now Neil had heard my accounts of those places, and so he knew exactly what was required.

'Barman?' he called out. 'Large wine, please.'

The other setback to my spirits in Seville came upon me unawares at first. When I tried to make a purchase by bank card in a shop, my card was refused – and, little did I know, back home my bank's fraud detectors went off, since they weren't aware I was travelling abroad. David would have remembered to inform the bank before departure, without doubt. But when I went to settle my hotel bill I discovered a 'stop' had been placed on my card. I was on my own, and couldn't reach anyone back home on the phone, and so I was thrown into a panic of illogical fear. Was this something I could be arrested or detained for? How could this have happened? Only yesterday I had been chatting on first-name terms with Seville's Chief Police Commissioner . . .

Eventually the matter was sorted amicably, without my having to scrub pots and pans in the hotel kitchen to pay for my keep. But it was a stiff reminder that I would have to learn to sort things out by myself from now on; also that, however 'well' I was doing, there remained circumstances in which I was desperately fragile.

*

In Seville I was asked more than once a certain set of questions that, I knew, would keep on recurring: namely, what were my feelings now towards my captors? And what sort of punishment would I want for them, in the event that they are apprehended some day? There was no rote answer to give on that. My feelings were and are a little more complicated than people appeared to expect.

There is, of course, a hierarchy in the organisation of any group of Somali pirates, and I observed as much in the men who kidnapped me and killed my husband. The sum paid in ransom for me had to be divided many ways: it's quite likely that the first cut went to settle a loan with interest that the pirates took out to finance the operation in the first place. Keeping me captive was a pricey business: if I was cheaply fed I was expensively guarded, and those guards had to be kept in cooked food and *khat* and wages. Once those bills were all accounted for, the rest of the proceeds will have been divvied up from the top down, with the smallest shares no doubt going to the teenage 'run-arounds' whose sole function was to guard me against escape or capture by a rival gang.

The men who conceived this operation, those who funded it and profited by it, those who took David's life and those who were in charge of my imprisonment – I am sure these people had not a scintilla of regard for me or for David. Our lives were held cheap. And so I believe those men should be made accountable: there ought to be consequences for their iniquitous actions. I can imagine I would derive some satisfaction from their being tried and convicted and sentenced to serve serious prison terms.

Nothing can undo what was done to David, Ollie and me, but it does seem to me that others could be spared similar tragedies if some of the key players within Somalia were brought to justice. To speak only of Daoud, the Negotiator: as an English speaker his services are much sought after and dearly bought, and I am sure he was engaged in other 'negotiations' simultaneously with mine. If he were put behind bars that would constitute a significant blow to piracy in Somalia, and would send an important message to the higher-ups that they are not untouchable – as they may currently believe they are.

Ali Babitu Kololo was not among the five men who took me off Kiwayu in a skiff. But if he is found guilty of the crime for which he stands accused then he is deeply complicit – things would not have happened as they did had the pirates not been guided around the island as they evidently were.

What of Ali, my ostensibly sympathetic ear, the fisherman navigator who told me his hands were tied just as surely as mine? Again, the pirates could not have achieved their objective without him. In this, was he really an innocent party, under duress, as he insisted to me? All I can say is that through my captivity I gave him the benefit of the doubt. Then again, since my release, it has been put to me by experts in the field that the pirate gangs always retain one member who speaks English well and 'befriends' the captive, simply in the hope of keeping them more pliant and biddable.

This brings me to the 'runarounds' – the teenagers like Bambi and Chain-Smoker, often silly and giggling in their manners, who were nonetheless paid to train guns on me and might even have been authorised to fire them. I looked at these youths during my captivity and thought, *Do I hate them?* I wasn't sure, although I was certain I didn't harbour for them the same visceral abhorrence I had for the likes of the Fat Controller and Daoud. I hated what they had done, their part in it. But I found myself trying to see through that. It was the social worker in me, perhaps, that felt they were products of their environment, doing probably the only real work available in the vicinity.

Am I too lenient? Some may think so. Wise heads have advised me, 'You shouldn't feel the slightest sympathy for any of them. They all know exactly what they're doing. They're all as ruthless as each other . . .' But I can't help seeing a division of labour in Somali piracy, in which the younger hired hands – while certainly culpable – cannot be considered as utterly reprehensible as their older paymasters, who could do something different and better with their lives instead of being criminals and exploiters. Piracy is corrupt, and its corruption spreads and pollutes the ecology so easily – especially when it is a seeming cornerstone of the local economy. For this reason I have to assume that the local people of Amara had no significant quarrel with the notion of me, a captive white woman, marooned in their midst. But in a society, a country, so deprived in terms of regulative norms, it seems all too easy for deeply abnormal, even immoral behaviours to become routine and reinforced.

All I can say is that when in October 2012 a new Somali government was sworn in, I sincerely wished it well: Somalia needs proper governance, directed towards the common good, beginning, perhaps, with the question of how to make the best possible use of its social and economic resources. Any improvements in that regard will surely decrease the likelihood of young Somalis taking up guns, or having guns pressed into their hands in exchange for money and *khat*.

Quite apart from these material considerations, I don't dwell unduly on thoughts of retribution for my captors. Yes, for all the reasons discussed above, I want to see justice served. But equally I have to accept there might never be any sort of reckoning for those pirates whatsoever, and so I don't intend to live my life in bitterness, over things I cannot influence. That was not the person I was when I was taken, and it is not who I am today.

I admit, in certain other respects, I wait still for the 'me' I was on 10 September 2011 to come back, because I miss that person, and I wonder how long it will take for me to feel 'like myself again'. Inwardly I accept that I can't fully recover who I was. Nevertheless I want to know myself and be known by others not as 'an ex-hostage' but as Jude – woman, mum, professional, etc. If I allow my ordeal to define me ad infinitum then it becomes, in effect, a double captivity. And that is a predicament against which I must continue to fight. The pirates ended my life with David, the only man I have ever loved, and with that they took enough from me. I will not allow them to take any more.

CODA

One night in November 2012 I dreamed that I was assisting British police in the construction of a three-dimensional model of the room in which I was held at the Big House compound. It was one more aspect of the investigation into my kidnap, and of the larger project of intelligence-gathering into Somali piracy, and I was happy to help, and found the police solicitous and meticulous as always.

But the mood shifted suddenly, as in dreams it is wont to do, and I found myself surrounded by strangers, all telling me that they felt it would be additionally useful if I were to spend some time inside this life-sized replica of my Somali prison – just to authenticate the feeling of my having been there. And so they swung open that familiar right-side metal door, and I looked through, and before my eyes was 'my' room, as true as a photograph. I could feel dry desert heat, see the rockery-like pile of stones I'd collected in a corner, the cream-gold curtains, the green plastic chair, the coral-pink lino ... *No, I won't*, I screamed – loud enough to force myself awake in the real world. The bedside clock read 3 a.m. I was clammy and shaken, so glad to be released from my nightmare, so unnerved by the sensations it revived in me.

I suppose I could be described as a 'survivor' type. My captivity showed me that I could come through a deeply adverse experience, a true test of resilience. But it's clear to me now that an essential element in this was the *not-knowing*, the manner in which the ordeal was thrust upon me. Now, the idea of having to face up to any sort of term of captivity is something I couldn't contemplate under any circumstances.

No one will be surprised to hear that I am desperately keen to put my ordeal behind me. But it's more easily said than done, when so many things serve to remind me, not just the memories that have been stored up in my own mind and body, but odd external stimuli that can stir the embers of memory unexpectedly. Some of these are aspects of trauma bearing directly on my experience in Somalia. (For instance, I find it difficult now to travel in a car at night, after the nerve-straining drives I was subjected to in captivity.) But some of the other thoughts that assail me are more fleeting and perplexing.

One morning I was travelling from Bishop's Stortford by train when through the window I glimpsed a woman in a black *jilbab*, seeming almost to float down a street that was separated from the tracks by a wall – and suddenly thoughts of Amina rushed into my head. *It's 9 a.m. here, midday in Amara – I wonder, is she cooking?* I had to catch myself: *Stop, don't go there, you don't want to know.*

Again, some people might hear this and be put in mind of Stockholm Syndrome – of the hostage who ends up identifying with her captors. I don't believe I've ever had a shred of such feeling. And every day I am so grateful I am here and not there. But as long as the shadow of captivity is over me, until a greater stretch of time has interposed itself between my present and those terrible days, then I am still forced to compare and contrast 'here' and 'there'. It is part of my mental furniture.

For instance, at home I have found it far more difficult to get out of the bed in the morning and start the day than I did in Amara. The emphasis is different, let's say. Now I see the day stretching out ahead of me, a daunting expanse. What am I to do with it? In Somalia every day gave me a consuming focus, proposed a particular challenge – the challenge to get to the end of it, to figuratively put one more black cross on the calendar, marking off days towards the deliverance that I felt sure was coming. My only real activities, as I noted in my diary, were 'walking, waiting and writing'. Now it's very different. I have my freedom, so what am I going to do with it? What am I going to do without David? Where do I go from here?

Had I come home from captivity to David, the challenge would have been immeasurably lessened. Instead, having to contemplate a life without David is something I still don't do very well. His murder is something I will never 'get over', and I miss him acutely every day. Sometimes I find myself looking for him, or abstractly expecting him to come through the door. I walk round the house, and I know he's not there, yet still I walk, thinking somehow I will come upon him in some familiar pose – standing before the bathroom mirror, say, razor in hand. I find myself cooking enough for two, and it depresses me – but then I find few things as dismaying as 'cooking for one'.

We all know that death is terminal. Yet the heart does persist in wanting to restore the loss. Fundamentally I feel robbed, cheated. This wasn't meant to be. It wasn't supposed to happen this way. David and I were meant to work hard all our lives, then enjoy a lovely retirement together – and we were on schedule for that. We could entertain idle thoughts of grandparenting, a role in which David would have been fantastic, a natural, with so much to share and impart. There is so much still I want to say to him, experiences and trips and travels I want to enjoy with him, books and exhibitions. We never did go to Hampton Court as we planned, never rode on the London Eye. But most of all I miss him as my husband, my best friend, my partner through life.

I have periods of feeling strong and on top of things, a sense that I am coping pretty well, all things considered. I see friends, socially I am 'out and about' more than ever before. But I am making myself do it now, where once my default preference was really to be holed up at home with David. I don't enjoy being a single person. But nor do I wish to be part of another partnership.

I do a fair bit of voluntary work and I'm happy to do it. I haven't got my old job, but I just couldn't possibly have returned to it. Perhaps a different kind of job lies in store for me somewhere? The logical part of me says I will find it – not necessarily paid but something self-realising, which might require retraining. I want to do that, and I believe I will.

But it's what to do on a personal level. I'm not a wife any more, not one half of an amazing partnership that flourished over thirty-three years. Every time I get on a train at Stortford I want David to be there with me. One battles those memories. Every day I am reminded of what's happened, by David's absence, his not being in the same bed, the radio silent where once it was his daily accompaniment to the morning shave. These days I can hear David's laugh, giggly and schoolboyish, in my head, but somehow I can't seem to hear his speaking voice. One lives with these things. One cannot purposefully forget, and so many things serve only to remind me of what's been lost.

There are nights when I can't stop crying and I know I'm simply a wreck. On another level, in the domestic sphere, I find myself struggling with the most mundane of decisions. I keep forgetting to put the recycling and rubbish bins out, and in the correct sequence – black one week, blue, green, brown the next. David took care of that: he would have the timetable taped up and marked in colour. I can't record programmes on the television. A hunt round the house for a simple screwdriver can reduce me to tears of frustration. I know in the grand scheme, considering what has happened to me, these things may seem unimportant. But the little things, the seemingly inconsequential minutiae of life, have so much meaning packed inside them and maybe especially when that life has been made by two people together.

Why can't I find the old photos I'm looking for? I know they're here somewhere ... David would know where they were. His memory was phenomenal – for days and dates, phone numbers, passport numbers, National Insurance numbers. Sometimes I can barely remember my home address. He was 'household manager' whereas I was cook and cleaner and gardener. David was happy to mow the lawn or pull up an occasional shrub, but his main interest in the garden was as a place to sit and read the paper. His fastidiousness was something else. I was so used to him, with the cheque book in his hand, finding me and wanting to cross-reference the stubs against the bank statement. 'What did you buy at Jones' on this date? For sixty-four pounds?' It used to drive me spare at times but, my god, I miss it now so much. And his meticulous nature proved a godsend, for if our legal affairs had not been in such good order then it's possible I might still be staring at a wall somewhere in Somalia. My captors would likely have kept me for as long as it took.

I think back on the portentous conversation David and I had only a couple of weeks before we left the UK for Kenya: 'If I died now I'd be happy, because I know you are going to be looked after, and I know you wouldn't be frightened.' He was right, as he so often was. I don't feel frightened of the future. I'm just very angry and saddened that David won't be there to share it with me. And so I cannot let go of the past just yet.

*

Of all the interested questions put to me after my release, the one I found most bizarre was when I was asked, more than once, whether at any point in my captivity I had felt like committing suicide. As low as my spirits sank on occasions, that thought never occurred. For one thing, I wasn't going to let my captors see me so reduced. I needed them to know I was made of sterner stuff, just as I still am determined that what's happened will not define the rest of my life or ruin anything else in it. I won't let it. There is too much to live for.

The other reason why I never even considered self-harm is that I had my son to think of. He had been robbed of one parent, and I would not bereave him twice over. For my part I knew I had a life to come back to, for all that it was life without David. And I was going to come back to it, so I needed to do all I could. Above all I had my son. I have one person in this world whom I trust entirely, rely on, and would give my life for, and that person is Ollie. Every telephone call I received from him in captivity was pure inspiration: Ollie was my rock, my reason to press on out of darkness into light.

I am immeasurably proud of him for what he achieved in bringing me home – for remaining so calm, assured and stalwart throughout my captivity. Indeed the way that Ollie comported himself impressed some very seasoned people in the highly difficult and dangerous profession of security. David and I left for our Kenyan holiday with Ollie still 'my boy' in some regards, but in the course of the nightmare that unfolded he became a man, without question. He may never realise just how much he means to me, or how much of David is in him: he is, in certain precious and vital respects, his father's son. But above all Ollie is his own person and he will carve out his own way through life. I have been forced, unexpectedly, tragically – to take a very different path from the one I expected. But I believe a time will come for me when I can begin to enjoy my life again.

*

These days, though, I feel myself drifting on the ocean of life, cast adrift by circumstances beyond my control. I'm not grounded – my anchor is gone – no more David. I wait for other boats to pass by, in the shape of friends and family, who offer precious comfort and support and fellow feeling. But when they have sailed off once more, as they must, and I am left alone again, I feel the drift, and I wonder how long I will be at sea.

I try to bring myself back the best way I know how, which is briskly, self-chiding: *You and a million others are thinking the exact same thing. And in fact you are probably a good deal better off than most of them are. So stop feeling so sorry for yourself and get on with it.*

I have noticed a tendency in other people, naturally and under-standably, to want for me to be happy, achieve some 'closure', get over it. Often I am asked, solicitously, 'How are you feeling?', and I hear myself say, 'I'm OK.' But I'm not. And nothing anyone can say can make it any better. I also have the understandable tendency in me not to want to make people uncomfortable, but then for my own good I also need to be able to speak frankly. I find this easiest, perhaps, with people who have known the same loss as me. After my release I remade the acquaintance of a woman I used to know who subsequently lost her husband to illness, and I have found her views and advice very instructive. 'For two years,' she told me, 'you are just getting through the days, just getting used to the fact you're on your own. After that? You never forget it. You're not the same person. But you get through it. You will get through it, Jude.'

I know what she means. It's nothing but time: only time can possibly make a difference.

Just as I felt that I could hear David's voice in captivity, only days after I learned of his death – I feel right now that he wants me to carry on. I think he would have been proud of me, of the way I got through my ordeal. I don't believe he would have been happy with the thought that one of us lived on but somehow 'gave up', succumbed to self-pity, resigned on life. I was privileged to enjoy the life I had with David. It was a truly good life; it could not have been better. We enjoyed everything and every part of our being together. I have to treasure David's memory and not be haunted by it – not while so much of life remains. I'm reminded of this feeling whenever I look out at the copper beech tree in my garden – in the sunlight, scarlet and orange, colours I never saw in Somalia. My life won't be the same, but it is life itself, and its value is clear: it is all that we have and all we ever can have, and it must be cherished, respected, never ever taken for granted.

ACKNOWLEDGEMENTS

Thanks to my amazing son Ollie, who gave me hope, inspiration and motivation to keep walking towards my release.

To Saz, who supported Ollie throughout.

To my family – thank you for being there.

Richard T. Kelly, who used his skill and patience to help me turn my words and thoughts into the book I had hoped for. You are a kind and sensitive man.

Neil Hibberd, Senior Investigating Officer, for demonstrating thoroughness, professionalism and tenacity in seeking justice.

To all my friends who have played their part in helping me return. A special thanks to my very best friend Annie, who has witnessed many tears and much laughter, and has provided me with a precious escape. Also to Sandra and Janet, for their joy in life which is so infectious.

Shelley, my Pilates coach, whose teaching was (unbeknownst to her) vital to me even in captivity, helping to keep my body and mind as healthy as they could be.

Virgin Atlantic and Virgin Trains, who were exceptionally generous – both to me and to my family – in their offer of travel arrangements subsequent to my release.

A big thank you to Stephen Page for his support and encouragement throughout the writing of this book and also his support to Ollie during my captivity.

To all at Faber for their encouragement and kindness, but especially to: Julian Loose, who was the first person at Faber to hear my story and who gave me the courage to write the book; Rachel Alexander, for her guidance and patience; Donna Payne, who took my suggestions and created a powerful jacket cover; Anne Owen for her work as desk editor; Eleanor Crow for her artwork; and also Jill Burrows for her copy-editing of the manuscript.

Jude Tebbutt
May 2013